VISUAL JOURNALISM

A Guide for New Media Professionals

VISUAL JOURNALISM

A Guide for New Media Professionals

Kishore Sharma

CENTRUM PRESS
NEW DELHI-110002 (INDIA)

CENTRUM PRESS
H.O.: 4360/4, Ansari Road, Daryaganj,
New Delhi-110002 (India)
Tel: 23278000, 23261597, 23255577, 23286875
B.O.: No. 1015, Ist Main Road, BSK IIIrd Stage,
IIIrd Phase, IIIrd Block, Bangalore-560085 (INDIA)
Tel: 080-41723429
Email: centrumpress@gmail.com
Visit us at: www.centrumpress.com

Visual Journalism: A Guide for New Media Professionals

First Edition, 2010

ISBN 978-93-80540-66-5

PRINTED IN INDIA

Printed at Mehra Offset Press, Delhi

Contents

Preface

Visual journalism is the practice of strategically combining words and images to convey information. At a time of accelerating change, often words cannot keep pace with concepts. Visual journalism incorporates ancient symbols that resonate with humans across cultures and across time and convey meaning instantaneously at a deep level.

Public journalism practitioners and theoreticians argue that the content of stories generated through public journalism methods is significantly different from the content generated by traditional reporting methods. News designers are taught that the form of their designs must reflect the content of the stories rather than artistic preference or trends.

Visual journalism is an outgrowth of the practice of graphic facilitation and recording that began entering corporate board rooms, conferences, and think tank meetings in the 1970s with the leadership of David Sibbet, founder of The Grove Consultants International.

But its roots date back to ancient cave paintings and carry forward in the work of designers, architects, and engineers. Only recently has interactive visualization of this sort moved out into common use in all kinds of group engagements. The scholarly father of this visual form of communication is Robert Horn, Ph.D., a fellow at Stanford University who wrote the book Visual Language.

Chapter 1

Visual Communication in Public Journalism

A comparison of the design and photography of public journalism projects with non-public journalism shows there is a difference, but not a radical one. Between 1990 and 1996, more than 400 media outlets had undertaken public journalism projects. Much has been written about the philosophy behind public journalism, its goals, and techniques. Individual public journalism projects have been analysed and compared against these goals and philosophies, and also compared to traditional journalism to see what, if any, difference exists. However, no study has yet focused on the visual communication of public journalism in newspapers.

Public journalism practitioners and theoreticians argue that the content of stories generated through public journalism methods is significantly different from the content generated by traditional reporting methods. News designers are taught that the form of their designs must reflect the content of the stories rather than artistic preference or trends.

This prompts the question: If the content of stories generated through public journalism methods is different, and design is driven by content, doesn't it follow that design for public journalism will be different than design for non-public journalism? This is a key question that visual communicators and public journalists must address if the final product is to truly integrate verbal and visual meaning.

The purpose of this research, the first of a two-phase study, is to explore how public journalism projects have been visually communicated in newspapers practicing this approach, and how they differ from the visual communication of non-public journalism.

Through content analysis, textual analysis and telephone interviews, this exploratory study examined the design and photography of projects at six newspapers; four practicing public journalism and two practicing non-public journalism to explore how public journalism projects were visually communicated in newspapers that practiced the genre, and whether the visual communication of public journalism differed from the visual communication of nonpublic journalism.

Public journalism is a product of the 1990s — its first well-documented experiment was in late 1989 in Columbus, Georgia. Even a decade later, there are as many operational definitions of public journalism as there are media outlets that practice it. For a conceptual definition that speaks to the developing theory of public journalism Jay Rosen has said: "Journalism can and should play a part in strengthening citizenship, improving public debate and reviving public life."

Public or civic journalism is widely understood as an approach designed to address issues that readers say are important, rather than only those issues identified by experts. It seeks to promote a public conversation about those issues that will result in a collective working through of the problem to resolution. Among its goals are strengthening citizenship, improving the quality of public debate, and reviving public life. It proposes a more active role for the press than has traditionally been adopted.

Public journalism derives many of its philosophical foundations from the social responsibility theory of the press and agenda-setting theory. While some scholars of public journalism trace its roots as far back as Thomas Jefferson, John Locke and John Stuart Mill, it seems unarguable that the development of the ideas that infuse public journalism were an outgrowth of the debates between John Dewey and Walter Lippmann over the proper role for the press in a democracy. Dewey and other scholars helped lay the foundation for a gradual shift toward the emerging social responsibility theory of the press, which was akin to Dewey's proposal of the role of the press in helping build a more pluralist and tolerant society. The evolution of the social responsibility theory culminated in the Commission on Freedom of the Press' report in 1947.

The Hutchins Commission's work can be seen as a forerunner of public journalism in that it called for the press to offer "a method of presenting and clarifying the goals and values of the society" and for reporting to project "the opinions and attitudes of the groups in society to one another."

Although social responsibility theory has been challenged as a product of its time, the developing concept of public journalism has drawn heavily from the Hutchins Commission and expanded on the role of the press by incorporating ideas from Dewey; philosophers Jurgen Habermas and Hannah Arendt, and political scientist Michael Sandel. Arendt, Habermas and Sandel all acknowledge the important role media play in society — without communication there is no public sphere. Contemporaries whose thoughts have added fuel to the public journalism fire include Daniel Yankelovich in Coming to Public Judgment, Russell Neuman, Marian Just and Ann Crigler with Common Knowledge, Clifford Christians, John Ferre and Mark Fackler's Good News, James Carey, Jay Rosen, and Davis Merritt.

Public journalism also incorporates aspects of agenda-setting theory, which says that one of the effects of mass communication is to direct the audience's attention to certain problems or issues. By conducting focus groups and taking polls of what the audience considers important before reporting on issues, public journalists make a self-conscious effort to avoid agenda-setting by the media or others, including government and special interests.

While there is no consensus on what public journalism is, or even on what to call it, the premise that all agree on is that it is the duty of the press is to improve the quality of public life by fostering public participation and debate. Some of the methods and techniques public journalists are best known to have used toward these goals include focus groups and citizen advisory boards to discover issues of importance to people; avoiding conflict framing of stories; using ordinary citizens as sources as well as officials and experts; seeking to clarify the core values behind opinions and underlying causes of problems; focusing on solutions and success stories; and taking an active role in promoting discussion among citizens with public forums and town hall meetings.

While public journalists are still focused on inventing their craft, they are understandably concerned with fine-tuning the proper reporting and writing techniques. As is historically typical in journalism, the visual aspects of journalistic storytelling — photography and design — are postponed for attention after the verbal aspects have been worked out. While they may momentarily forget this essential element, journalists have come to realise that visual communication can be just as important, if not more so, as verbal communication.

Inherent in all definitions of design is the idea that it is not simply decoration or dressing up a page, but that form carries a content of its own. The literature laments the use of designs that overemphasize form to the detriment of communication. Originally, design developed in response to the mechanical needs of page make-up. With the advent of photocomposition, mechanical concerns were eliminated as well as the design conventions they necessitated. Today, the story content and needs of the reader drive design.

It is the consensus in design theory that form is inextricably linked to message meaning. The form, or design, of news changes the perception of its content. If newspaper page design is truly to be used to communicate meaning derived from the story's content, and if public journalism has changed that content, then design must change to reflect that. Design must now communicate the public agenda. If public journalism is an attempt to better address the goals laid out by the Hutchins Commission, how can design and photography encourage this? Perhaps public journalism photographs should reflect citizens more often than candidates.

Photojournalists might also refuse to participate in photo opportunities organized by public relations people in the interest of letting the public set the agenda, rather than PR professionals. Public journalism design could also make use of design elements which help communicate its goals, such as summary boxes describing the values in conflict over a certain issue, or graphics telling readers how to get involved, express their opinions, or get more information on an issue. These and other topics must be addressed by public journalism's visual communicators if the final product is to truly integrate verbal and visual meaning.

There is some indication in the public journalism literature that design is beginning to be considered. Most are references made in passing with little follow-up as to how the goals of public journalism might be achieved with visuals. Others offer some specifics. For example, in a speech to the Regional Reporters Association, Jan Schaffer of the Pew Centre for Civic Journalism suggested building in "graphic devices that invite and encourage readers and viewers to contact the news organization and react to an issue, a controversy, a public problem."

Jay Rosen made the connection between public journalism's goals and design when he commented that, "If the pages of the newspaper are thought of as a public space designed by journalists, then what the (Wichita) Eagle did is arrange this space so that the proper concerns of politics ('issues in depth') shone through." He then described how the Eagle accomplished this with visual elements.

For each of the major issues, the Eagle published a list called Places to Start, with the names, addresses and phone numbers of organizations and agencies working on the problem. Repeated invitations were issued to readers to contact the paper with their comments and suggestions. At the Charlotte Observer, the Where They Stand feature was more than a voter's guide. If candidates refused to answer the questions the public posed, then a blank appeared under the candidate's name. This was a powerful use of space, charged with visual meaning. A survey found that one of the most useful features was the Where They Stand box.

The Pew Center's Schaffer also reported that a focus group at one newspaper responded differently to information conveyed graphically than when the same information was reported in a bylined story: "They loved the voter's guide in a grid and asked why we didn't give it to them earlier and repeat it often.... It seemed to them fairer and more factual.

There was no byline and no news peg, just distilled information. Even though it was from bylined stories, the way it was presented seemed to make a difference in how much people believed it."

At the Virginian-Pilot in Norfolk, a new feature was inaugurated on the front page to stimulate more productive dialogue about controversies in the news. The paper also created a new design element that graphically conveyed its new treatment of controversy.

After summarizing the themes of the issue, readers were directed to question themselves. For example: "If you tend to disagree... in what part of (his) argument can you find merit? Even if you tend to agree... what part of (his) argument do you have problems with? Where is the common ground?"

It is much harder to find discussions of photojournalism that promotes the ideals of public journalism. One example that was widely discussed appeared in the Wisconsin State Journal when citizens gathered in the seats of their representatives at the state capitol to question candidates. The result was "a startling visual," according to Rosen, a visual symbol that things had changed.

The value of visual communication to public journalism's goals is even beginning to be addressed tangentially in some scholarly research. Paul Riede concluded that, in the Wichita Eagle's The People Project, the most journalistic depth came in the form of the graphics: "the graphic goes beneath the surface, personality-based coverage of politics typical of traditional journalism." This same study called the "innovative use of the `core values' graphics'... the project's most promising attempt at depth in coverage." In order discover how public journalism projects have been visually communicated and whether they differ from that of non-public journalism, one research question and six hypotheses regarding visual communication were developed based on public journalism characteristics derived from the literature.

They are:

*H*1: Public journalism will visually convey more mobilizing Information to help citizens participate in their communities than non-public journalism.

*H*2: Public journalism will visually convey more interactivity, i.e.: ways to contact the media.

*H*3: Public journalism photographs will use fewer managed photo opportunities than non-public journalism.

*H*4: Public journalism will use more photographs of citizens and "real people" versus candidates or experts than nonpublic journalism.

*H*5: Public journalism will use more visual devices to convey views of citizens and "real people" than non-public journalism.

*H*6: Public journalism will use more visual devices to convey common ground and solutions than non-public journalism.

*RQ*1: Does the visual communication of public journalism differ with circulation size?

The unit of analysis was all the stories on the public journalism topic in one day's issue of the newspaper. Forty-one newspaper issues were sampled. The 41 issues were drawn from six newspapers in two circulation sizes using one week from each paper. For this study, large newspapers were defined as greater than 200,000 daily circulation. Small newspapers were defined as less than 100,000 daily circulation. Medium newspapers, 100,000 to 200,000 daily circulation, were not included in order to maximize comparisons. It was postulated there would be little difference, for reasons such as resources, between medium and large papers, but the difference would be greater between small and large papers.

One week's issues from two large-circulation non-public journalism newspapers were compared against one week's issues from four public journalism newspapers (both large and small circulation sizes); one week's issues from two small-circulation public journalism newspapers were compared against one week's issues from two large-circulation public journalism newspapers; and one week's issues from two large-circulation public journalism newspapers were compared against one week's issues from two large-circulation nonpublic journalism newspapers. This allowed comparison of the presentation of public journalism against non-public journalism two ways, and also allowed comparison of the presentation within the genre of public journalism.

Sampling time was limited to one week because one newspaper's series ran for only six days. In addition, the large number of variables examined made a larger sample unwieldy.

All elements associated with the stories in each issue, including stories, headlines, photos, illustrations, sidebars, boxes, logos, refers, graphics, charts, maps, tables, schedules, lists, pullquotes, readouts, and jumps, were coded for size and presence of public journalism criteria.

Since the purpose of this exploratory project was to learn as much as possible about a subject which has not previously been studied, examining all relevant appearance variables was deemed to be more important than a large sample. If even small differences were detected, the results of this exploratory study could help point the way toward future research.

The public journalism stories were sampled using the latest public journalism projects at each newspaper; the non-public journalism stories were sampled using the newspapers' latest series that was on a similar topic as the public journalism series in its comparison paper, or, if that was not feasible, a project that ran as a series of similar magnitude was chosen.

This study analysed the content of the appearance variables of all stories dealing with the subject except opinion pieces and letters to the editor. The focus of this study was on differences in photography and design. Editorial pages are highly formatted and generally do not vary in presentation, so they were not deemed suitable for this study.

Purposive sampling with newspapers stratified by circulation size and chosen for their experience with the public journalism approach was used because it is better suited the purpose of comparing the visual presentation of public journalism to see how it varies within the genre, and of comparing the visual presentation of public journalism to non-public journalism.

The four public journalism newspapers were initially chosen for a different study by the Pew Centre for Civic Journalism. The basis for this decision included the level of experience each paper had with public journalism philosophies and techniques, and Pew's director's and assistant director's assessment that these particular papers were doing some of the more interesting work within the public journalism genre.

Because of their early entry into the movement, the philosophies and practices of public journalism at these papers are assumed to be more highly developed than those of papers just beginning to practice public journalism. Therefore, the visual communication of public journalism stories should have achieved a deeper level of consideration in these newsrooms.

Also, by experimenting with the photographiy and presentation of public journalism for a longer period, their practices should be more finely tuned and may represent the direction that other newspapers will take in public journalism.

The two large circulation newspapers not practicing public journalism were chosen by this researcher for their similarities with the public journalism newspapers in circulation size, morning publication, and market demographics, and also to represent specific regions of the country. Their editors have publicly stated their opposition to the public journalism approach.

The differences in design styles across the different newspapers were taken into account in the textual analysis.

The characteristics of each newspaper sampled are:

Public journalism - large circulation:

- San Francisco Chronicle: 489,238 daily circulation. Public journalism project on commuter transportation. Published October-December 1996.
- Charlotte Observer: 239,173 daily circulation. Public journalism project on the 1996 election. Published September and October 1996.

Non-public journalism, large circulation:

- Philadelphia Inquirer: 469,398 daily circulation. Corresponds with San Francisco circulation. Series on changes in a suburban neighborhood in the past 50 years. Published February 1997.
- Omaha World-Herald: 232,360 daily circulation. Corresponds with the Charlotte Observer's circulation. Stories on the 1996 election. Published September and October 1996.

Public journalism - small circulation:

- Wisconsin State Journal, Madison: 86,585 daily circulation. Public journalism project on the 1996 election. Published September-October 1996.
- Binghamton Press & Sun-Bulletin: 68,919 daily circulation. Public journalism project was the community's economic problems. Published September 1996.

Content analysis followed the methods recommended by Klaus Krippendorff and Earl Babbie with two independent coders. Using Scott's Pi, an average reliability estimate was calculated at.98 coder agreement.

Textual analysis followed the methods of Stuart Hall to determine if and how the written content differed from the visual content. Telephone interviews using open-ended questions were conducted with the designers following methods described by Norman Denzin and Y.S. Lincoln, and T.R. Lindlof.

One-way analysis of variance was used on interval data; chi-square was used on categorical data. Since some chi-square cells contained less than five, correlation was also used to determine probability level. Forty-one newspaper issues were analysed. For the purposes of statistical analysis, alpha was set at.05. Because data for this exploratory study were not drawn from a probability sample, the variability of the sample statistics cannot be estimated.

Although the conventional tests of statistical significance have been computed and are reported along with the findings, readers should interpret these with caution. However, in the absence of any research on the visual communication of public journalism, it is hoped these results will add to knowledge and stimulate further study.

When public journalism issues sampled in this study were compared against non-public journalism issues on the six public journalism characteristics, the scores showed a significant difference for two variables, H2: Ways to contact the media, and H6: More visual devices for common ground and solutions. Two other variables, H3: Fewer managed photo ops, and H4: More photos of real people, had means in the direction hypothesized. Two variables showed no significant differences; H1: More mobilizing information, and H5: More visual devices to convey views of real people.

In addition, these same hypotheses were used to compare large public journalism issues against large non-public journalism issues in order to help control for the greater resources of larger circulation newspapers, and to compare the presentation in small public journalism papers to large public journalism papers to see if public journalism is being practiced consistently across circulation sizes. When significant, these results are presented in the discussion section.

COMMON GROUND AND SOLUTIONS

Results showed that the public journalism issues sampled in this study used significantly more visual devices to convey common ground or solutions than non-public journalism issues. None of the non-public journalism issues sampled used visual language to convey common ground or solutions, while 21 per cent of the public journalism issues sampled did so.

Reporting common ground and solutions is fairly unique to public journalism, with non-public journalism traditionally focusing on past events.

Common ground and solutions speaks to Yankelovich's idea that media should facilitate a working through stage that ultimately leads to solutions, rather than stopping at the consciousness-raising stage. That none of the non-public journalism issues sampled visually conveyed common ground or solutions reinforces the belief that non-public journalism limits itself to issue-raising.

Even though there is a significant difference between public and Nonpublic journalism in this sample, fewer than one-quarter of the public journalism newspaper stories sampled (21 per cent) used visual devices to convey common ground and solutions. It is hoped that higher ratios would be achieved as public journalism develops. However, this is a sign there is beginning to be an awareness of the need to visually communicate this information.

This hypothesis also showed a marginally significant difference between small and large papers within public journalism in this sample. Larger papers in this study used visual devices for common ground and solutions in 36 per cent of their issues, while only 7 per cent of issues sampled in small papers did so. Perhaps this speaks to the difference in resources between small and large papers. It may be that common ground and solutions are harder to conceptualize, thus, small papers with smaller design staffs, more inexperienced designers, and less time to design each page, will not have the resources to devote to such complex issues.

The other side of this argument is that a box conveying possible solutions with typography is neither hard to conceptualize nor time-consuming to execute. Alternately, it could mean that reporters and editors at small papers are not including common ground and solutions in stories, thus the designers are not either.

This seems to be the case with one small public journalism paper sampled. In the textual analysis, the Wisconsin State Journal's We the People project on the fall

1996 election showed no common ground or solutions in either the text or visuals. The possibility that the topic may not lend itself to exploring common ground and solutions is unlikely since the other public journalism paper that covered the election, the Charlotte Observer, did visually present common ground and solutions.

On most days, the Observer had a box on the issue of the day (i.e.: crime, school vouchers, etc.) that outlined different sides, gave background, and told where there was agreement or not. The solutions box on school tuition vouchers explained three reasons for supporting vouchers and three for opposing them. Common ground was explained this way: "Critics and supporters agree that school vouchers, if offered on a national scale, have the power to dramatically change the face of public education. Where both sides disagree is whether those changes will improve or ruin public schools."

Table. Small Vs. Large Circulation Public Journalism: Percentages and Fisher's Exact Test of public journalism

Variables (per cent with yes values)	Small PJ stories	Large PJ stories	Exact probabilities
Common ground and solutions	7%	36%	.07
Interactivity with media	79%	71%	.31
Mobilizing information	78%	14%	.001
Views of real people	36%	50%	.26
N=28			

Public journalism election coverage in the Wisconsin State Journal more closely resembled non-public journalism in the Omaha World-Herald. Both focused on differences in the candidates' positions rather than where there was agreement on issues.

The main difference was that the public journalism election treatment included forums for citizens to question candidates, whereas the non-public journalism coverage did not. This difference between the small public journalism issues and the large non-public journalism issues could still be partly due to staff resources. But the possibility that journalists at the small paper did not have as great an understanding of public journalism is another likely explanation. In the informant interviews, two designers at the small public journalism paper indicated they had received no training in the philosophy, goals and techniques of public journalism, while the design director at the large public journalism paper said design staffers had been included in educational sessions with one of the founders of public journalism.

READER-REPORTER INTERACTION

The hypothesis that public journalism designs would visually convey interactivity between readers and the media more than non-public journalism (H2) was also significant. Seventy-five per cent of the public journalism issues in this sample used visual elements to encourage readers to contact the media, while 46 per cent of non-public journalism issues sampled did so.

In addition, the number of different ways public journalism provided for readers to contact them (address, phone, e-mail, web site, fax) was highly significant. Small circulation mean = 2.1, large circulation mean =.5). There were no significant differences between small and large circulation issues on this variable, as would be expected if all size papers were practicing public journalism the same way.

PHOTO OPS AND PHOTOS OF 'REAL PEOPLE'

The two public journalism characteristics that were not significant when public and non-public journalism issues were compared but whose means were in the direction hypothesized both dealt with photographs; whether public journalism relied on managed photo opportunities less often than non-public journalism (H3), and whether public journalism photos featured citizens and real people more often than candidates or experts (H4). The non-significant findings may be due to the low number of cases sampled (N = 41), but it is important that for both hypotheses the mean ratios of non-managed photos and photos of real people to total photos showed that the public journalism issues sampled used fewer photographs from managed photo opportunities and also used more photos of citizens and real people than candidates or experts.

Comparisons within public journalism showed no significant differences between small and large papers' photos in this sample regarding photo opportunities or the use of citizens and real people in photos versus candidates or experts.

Textual analysis revealed both small public journalism papers, Binghamton and Wisconsin, used all photos of real people from non-managed photo sources. In the large public journalism category, San Francisco used all non-managed photos featuring citizens in its series on transportation. Since Binghamton's series was on the local economy and primarily covered the citizen's forums, and San Francisco's series was on commuter woes, it is perhaps not surprising that they were able to find photo subjects that did not involve officials and experts.

It is more unusual for election coverage to avoid photos of candidates, yet that is just what the Wisconsin paper did. It achieved this goal mainly by running only one photo (citizens at a forum) over all seven issues; six issues had no photos at all. In the large non-public journalism genre, Omaha used all photos of candidates, as would be expected for traditional journalism.

The variation is mainly explained by the non-public journalism Philadelphia paper's use of all non-managed photos of real people, and the public journalism Charlotte paper's heavy use of managed photo ops of candidates — findings that are counter to what would be expected in ideal public journalism. The story subjects provide partial explanation.

In its series on a typical suburban neighborhood, Philadelphia used five to eight pictures every day in its non-public journalism series, all were of real people and none were from photo opportunities. In its election coverage, the public journalism Charlotte paper used mug shots or photo collages of candidates on nearly every cover, plus cutout photos of candidates in its full-page graphic of candidates' answers to voters' questions. In addition, Charlotte used four conventional campaign trail photos over the course of the series, in traditional political photojournalism style.

The only real-people photos Charlotte used were approximately three to five photos daily of the citizens who asked questions of the candidates or whose opinions were quoted. The Charlotte design director indicated in a telephone interview that the amount of campaign-trail photographs shot were "not nearly as many as five years ago... An effort was made to take photos of real people, but that makes things harder." The convention of candidate photographs for election coverage apparently remains strong, even at papers that have embraced public journalism principles.

The design director's acknowledgment that finding photos of real people is harder than attending photo opportunities is a candid admission that goes to the root of the difficulty of altering established conventions.

Comments by designers at the public journalism papers in Binghamton, Madison, and San Francisco, all indicated their photographers tried to avoid photo opportunities in favour of real people; however, photo ops could not be entirely eliminated. The former graphics editor at the Madison paper provided some background on the thinking:

The photo staff hates dull pictures, first of all. There is nothing worse than a talking head (politician) or a grip-and-grin. They do try and look for action or images from the issue they are addressing. It is a combination of public journalism and aesthetics.

He also attributed the lack of photos (one photo over seven issues) to aesthetics: With 'We the People,' the premiere events are these town meetings. They don't make particularly good photos. They are often held in the capitol, which has miserable lighting, and it's a sea of people sitting around.

The marching orders are we will shoot that, but we would probably try to limit that to one. Otherwise, we would have photos and stories about journalists from different media getting together to organize 'We the People'."

The idea of using photos of real people that are not the result of photo ops orchestrated by people seeking to manipulate publicity goes to the heart of public journalism philosophy and reflects a conscious effort to avoid agenda-setting effects. The use of this type of photo would be a sign that public journalism's goals are beginning to be translated into practice. Helping citizens participate in civic life

Of the two remaining hypotheses, neither showed any significant differences between public and non-public journalism. One was the hypothesis that public journalism would visually convey more mobilizing information to help citizens participate in their communities than non-public journalism (H1). There were no significant differences between the sampled public and non-public journalism issues' use of mobilizing information.

However, when comparisons were made within public journalism between large and small papers' issues, there was a highly significant difference in the visual communication of mobilizing information, with small papers scoring better. Only 14 per cent of large papers' stories used visual elements to convey mobilizing information, whereas 71 per cent of small papers' stories used one visual element, and 7 per cent used two.

In the public journalism genre, issues from both large papers sampled (Charlotte, San Francisco) used no mobilizing information in visual format. However, both small public journalism papers sampled visually conveyed mobilizing information. The topics—the Charlotte Observer's election coverage — cannot be the reason, however, since the two other papers which carried election coverage, including one non-public journalism paper (Omaha), listed mobilizing information.

The other large public journalism paper, San Francisco, gave almost no mobilizing information on its transportation series. Both small public journalism papers listed mobilizing information frequently; Wisconsin had the most and most regular mobilizing information with its boxes for forum broadcasts, call-in lines and registration information for upcoming town meetings. Wisconsin even developed regular graphic devices its designers called democracy boxes.

Perhaps the convention of having these boxes to fill kept mobilizing information in the forefront for Wisconsin designers. Binghamton usually publicized an upcoming priority setting conference or results of the economic teams' reports.

One reason for these results could be that mobilizing information is not new or unique to public journalism the way other variables can be.

For this study, mobilizing information consisted of news citizens could use to participate in community life. However, the importance of information which allows people to take action has been discussed in scholarly and trade publications since at least the 1970s.

Well before the advent of public journalism, traditional journalism has offered dates of neighborhood watch meetings, names and addresses of redevelopment agencies that offer grant money, etc.

Because of the length of time over which journalists have been aware of the importance of mobilizing information, and the ubiquitous nature of such information, it may not be surprising that there are no significant differences in the amount of mobilizing information conveyed visually in public and non-public journalism.

The greater resources at larger papers cannot help explain why small papers used more visual devices for mobilizing information than large papers. Mobilizing information should be quite familiar and top-of-mind to designers at both small and large papers, public journalism and non-public journalism.

Perhaps another explanation for the highly significant difference between small circulation and large circulation public journalism designs that visually convey mobilizing information can be found in James Lemert and colleague's findings. Because small papers may better reflect their small communities, there is more awareness of readers' desire for visual display of mobilizing information.

If large public journalism papers are not providing mobilizing information, this supports Lemert's theory that mobilizing information is regularly missing when issues are located outside of town, where audiences ordinarily can't look up addresses and phone numbers. This may be the case for large newspapers that cover many different communities.

VIEWS OF REAL PEOPLE

The other hypothesis that was not significant was that public journalism would use more visual devices to convey views of real people (H5).

This non-significant finding between the public and non-public journalism issues sampled is interesting because views of real people rather than experts or politicians are one of the central tenets of public journalism.

Although all designers interviewed said they tried to include views of real people, two said it was a copy desk decision and would be done mainly through pullquotes. However, textual analysis revealed that not all public journalism papers visually displayed views of real people. Both Wisconsin and San Francisco used no graphics or design elements for views of real people, although these views were carried within the text.

A lack of significant difference between public and non-public journalism's use of views of real people may signify that visual journalists do not fully understand or embrace this idea. If a significant difference were found to exist in the written communication of views of real people, but not in the visual communication, this would have implications for the integration of the designers and copy editors with the reporters and editors.

It may indicate that designers have not been included in sessions devoted to explaining the philosophies of public journalism and do not understand its principles fully, or, they are aware of the importance of views of real people but are leaving it to reporters to include in stories rather than employing content-driven design to convey this visually. There was also no difference in the sampled issues between small and large public journalism's use of visual devices to convey views of real people, but this would be expected if all papers practiced public journalism the same way.

THE IMPORTANCE OF UNDERSTANDING

Two final points of interest were revealed in the interviews when designers were asked whether they designed differently for public journalism than for non-public journalism.

Designers at two papers said yes, public journalism design was different from non-public journalism design, and designers at the other two papers replied no, there was no difference.

Interestingly, the no difference responses came from designers whose papers did not have training sessions on the concepts and techniques of public journalism, or who did not include visual journalists in those sessions.

Both affirmative responses came from newspapers whose designers did participate in public journalism education sessions.

Understanding of public journalism principles was one of the explanations offered for some of the findings in this study, and the perception of designers regarding the difference in designing for public journalism reinforces such an explanation.

Visual journalists who did not attend sessions aimed at explaining public journalism's goal and principles may not understand it as well as those who did and, therefore, may not consider ways to visually communicate those goals and principles.

Also, one of the designers interviewed complained that too many journalists at the paper felt like they had been ordered to do public journalism with no opportunity for discussion or input.

This chapter did not offer training sessions in public journalism. "If they're really going to get people on board to do this and do this well, there has to be that discussion," said the designer, who asked to remain anonymous.

"There are numerous ethical challenges in doing this, and they need to at least be explored, as do the possible pitfalls." Both these insights have implications for managing editors contemplating introducing public journalism into their newsrooms.

Table: Large Public Vs. Large Non-Public Journalism: Percentages and Fisher's Exact Test of Public Journalism Characteristics by Size of Paper

Variables (per cent with yes values)	Large PJ stories	Small PJ stories	Exact Probabilities
Common ground and solutions	36%	0%	.025
Interactivity with media	71%	46%	.13
Mobilizing information	25%	63%	.42
Views of real people	50%	39%	.25
N=27			

This study has used the emerging theory of public journalism, which claims a significantly different content than non-public journalism, and the theory of content-driven design, which says that visual meaning must reflect the written content, to examine the question prompted by these theories: If the content of stories generated through public journalism methods is different, and design is driven by content, shouldn't design for public journalism be different than design for non-public journalism?

The results from this study are mixed. Of six hypotheses that speak to the question of whether public journalism is visually different from non-public journalism, two showed significant differences among the newspaper issues sampled. Public journalism stories in this study used more visual devices to convey common ground and solutions, and ways to contact the media than did non-public journalism stories.. Four hypotheses showed no significant differences between public journalism and non-public journalism, but two had means in the direction hypothesized.

The public journalism issues sampled were more likely than non-public journalism to use fewer managed photo opportunities and more photos of real people than candidates or experts, but the differences were not significant These are signs that some of public journalism's goals may be beginning to be translated into practice by visual journalists, but that there are other goals that are not being addressed visually, at least in these newspapers.

The fact that the public journalism issues sampled were not significantly different from the non-public journalism issues in how they visually conveyed views of real people — one of the central tenets of public journalism — should be of concern. That the public journalism issues sampled visually communicated no more mobilizing information than the non-public journalism issues is less cause for worry because mobilizing information is not unique to public journalism the way the other characteristics can be.

This study has also found that, in some cases, public journalism papers that have established new conventions in place of the old have found it easier to adhere consistently to public journalism principles; for instance, the development of standing graphics such as democracy boxes for mobilizing information.

One problem in the consistent communication of public journalism characteristics seems to be with journalists' fundamental understanding of public journalism. Confusion over and even unawareness of public journalism principles seems to be a basic, underlying reason why the practice of public journalism is not significantly different from non-public journalism in terms of visual communication.

In addition, it appears that not all designers are practicing content-driven design. For instance, this research found stories which included views of real people in the text but not in the design.

In conclusion, there appear to be some significant differences in this sample in the way public journalism is visually communicated compared with non-public journalism. However, there is not enough significance to say that it represents a radical departure from non-public journalism, at least in the issues studied here. It appears another researcher's conclusion regarding the content of public journalism may be correct for the visual display as well: "there is no overriding, core philosophy of public journalism at some of the papers practicing it; instead it has become a label used to name a variety of special projects."

The news industry has been undergoing a fundamental paradigm shift since the end of last century. An increasing number of media companies around the United States, such as the Washington Post in Washington, DC, Media General in Virginia, the Tribune Company in Chicago, and New England Cable News, have taken solid steps to merge different media such as newspapers, television stations, radio stations, and online journalism companies to disseminate news content on multiple media platforms.

As a result, in a metropolitan area, one company would own print, TV, and online venues. Media call this industrial trend "media convergence," though the concept means much more than media mergers. Media convergence muddies the lines among broadcast journalism, print journalism, and online journalism, leaving college journalism educators to wonder whether traditional journalism programs have become dinosaurs.

After surveying 200 newspaper publishers worldwide, the World Association of Newspapers (WAN) found, "Despite a somewhat gloomy outlook for wholesale convergence in media companies worldwide in the near term, convergence is already being implemented with varying degrees of enthusiasm and speed among the world's media companies". The Innovation International Media Consulting Group estimates that at least 100 of the world's multiple media companies are planning and implementing integration strategies. South and Nicholson (2002) drew a sketch of a converged media company:

Daily journalists need to embrace the 24-hour news cycle, with continuous deadlines. And the story needs to be reported and produced for a multi-platform audience. That may mean delivering content first to the Web and cell phones, a streaming video broadcast later in the day, a TV talk-back interview still later, and a "second day" interpretive story for the next morning's newspaper.

Dominic Gates (2002) pointed out, "Convergence with broadcast and online media is the shape of things to come for newspapers." The trend remains controversial. Critics complain that such cross-ownership of both a television station and a newspaper in the same market is a threat to democracy because it limits the number of voices.

Delegates of the Communication Workers of America, a 60,000-member guild, passed a resolution in June of 2002 at the group's annual convention in Las Vegas, pledging to increase public awareness about the risks of ongoing media convergence.

The delegates complained that shrinking media markets are a threat to editorial diversity and job security. In 1975, the Federal Communications Commission (FCC) ruled that no new broadcast licenses would be granted to companies that own a major daily newspaper and a local television station in the same city. Fairness & Accuracy In Reporting (FAIR) calls on the FCC to roll back limits on media consolidation.

The Newspaper Association of America (NAA), on the other hand, has asked the FCC to appeal the rule. On June 2, 2003, the FCC voted 3 to 2 to relax or eliminate some ownership restrictions, such as a rule barring media companies from owning television stations in markets where they publish daily newspapers. Although some lawmakers and advocacy groups are still fighting in the courts and on Capitol Hill to overturn the FCC's new media ownership rules, these rules will be likely to encourage cross-media ownership in the years to come.

The mergers have raised questions about whether they are good for the craft of journalism itself. Critics complain that by requiring journalists to be jacks of both trades, print and broadcast, the journalists will be masters of none. Robert J. Haiman, president emeritus of The Poynter Institute, compared the media convergence trend to an Amphicar, a cross between a boat and a car.

The Amphicar, hawked in Florida during the 1950s, flopped. "It flopped because people quickly discovered that while it really was an ingenious combination of a car and a boat, it was a lousy car (because it also had to be a boat), and it was a lousy boat (because it also had to be a car)".

Willingly or unwillingly, many news practitioners' functions are gradually changing or are expected to change as media convergence rolls on. For a reporter in a converged media environment, knowing how to write is probably no longer enough. S/he could be expected to write the same story for different media in a timely manner. Ideally, s/he can readily talk in front of a video camera. As a photographer, knowing how to tell a story both in video and in still images is more and more in demand.

A designer should know how to prepare still graphics for print, moving graphics for television and dynamic graphics for the Web. At the online version of the Chicago Tribune, for instance, staffers are supposed to cover stories, take pictures, operate video cameras, and create digital pages. The editors, too, need a wider variety of skills than the traditional paper editors. Along with infrastructure changes and the attempt to create synergy among the various media outlets, a new breed of journalists-digital or multimedia journalists-is expected.

As media jobs become more demanding, some news practitioners are beginning to team up to complete projects. At the same time, fear, confusion, and frustration from news practitioners are creeping into newsrooms. Carr (2002c) wrote: "Convergence frightens many people who wonder whether their current skill sets have prepared them for-or will even be needed in-that great undiscovered country, the future.

This is probably the primary reason why I still find such great hostility to convergence among certain journalists." Killebrew (2001), a mass communications professor from the University of South Florida, suggested that "journalists must be prepared to either crosstrain themselves or seek training from other sources while management must be prepared to give them the opportunities and time to do so."

The 1999-2000 president of the Association for Schools of Journalism and Mass Communication (ASJMC), Shirley Staples Carter, questioned whether, in the midst of the "Internet revolution," programs are prepared to educate journalists of the future. When specifically talking about writing, Keith Hartenberger, manager of news and programming for Tribune Regional Programming, said that journalism schools should make their students aware of the many ways to present the news. "It's a multimedia world out there," he said. "If you're just being prepared to write newspaper stories, you won't be prepared". "At some point, this [cross-media training] is something we're going to expect from everyone".

Media convergence, as a trend that is gradually shaping the landscape of the media industry in the new century, has called into question the conventional journalism school practice of having separate tracks-print, broadcast, etc. Journalism educators around the country also are trying to figure out what they should do, if anything, to better prepare students for the converged media. For instance, should journalism educators consider merging different sequences such as magazine, newspaper, broadcast, and photojournalism, or still teach all such courses as if they were unrelated media?

"Traditionally defined segments of the communications industry are less and less distinguishable for technological and market convergence," observed Moon (2001). Are college journalism educators themselves both theoretically equipped and technologically prepared to teach their students for converged media? What do media companies expect from future news practitioners? What do current news practitioners in converged media feel is lacking? For both news practitioners and professors, the two most urgent questions cry for answers: Should journalism schools train specialists or fit for-all generalists?

And how should college journalism education balance the teaching of critical thinking and technical skills? Apart from all these education-related questions, we are also interested in finding out what are the driving forces behind the media mergers, who are regarded as the beneficiaries of this trend, and how people's political beliefs are related to their attitude toward teaching media convergence in colleges? These questions pertain closely to college journalism education, which has been the subject of debate and criticism for two decades.

A national survey was conducted among colleges, daily newspapers, and commercial television stations to explore the issue of how journalism schools should prepare students for the trend of media convergence from the perspectives of news editors, news professionals, and journalism professors. The study measured the level of general support for convergence education and determined if a new model of journalism education was called for.

If so, it examined whether consensus existed among the three groups on the direction educators should take when revisiting programme designs. Where consensus was not apparent, divisions among the sample of educators, editors, and reporters were defined. The goal of the study is to provide evidence that will help journalism educators make informed decisions about how to respond to media convergence in their curricula and courses and lay an empirical foundation for further discussions and conversations about media convergence.

The search results show that media convergence is a comparatively new topic in media research, though articles about it have inundated the Internet, magazines, and newspapers. Most research writings appeared no earlier than 1998. Articles about the relationship between media convergence and higher education are rare and have shown up more recently in trade magazines such as Presstime, Quill, and Journalism Education Today and in Web sites. A few research writings were found in academic conference (i.e., AEJMC) proceedings.

Many writings have addressed one of the toughest questions: What is media convergence? How to define "media convergence" had a direct bearing on how we conducted this study. Out of these writings, we identified four categories of media convergence that directly affect how journalism will be taught in colleges.

CONTENT CONVERGENCE

As Tremayne noted, decades ago, the term media convergence referred to the content convergence between competing newspapers and even among newspapers, magazines, and television.

Today, pure content convergence continues on the Internet. For instance, the St. Petersburg Times has incorporated local Channel 10's TV news into its online newspaper though they are independent business entities. In other words, media convergence may not necessarily be tied to media merger.

Form convergence (or technological convergence). Around the mid-1990s, as Tremayne and Wurtz (2000) noted, computer technology and Internet technology made possible the convergence of all forms of mediated communications including video, audio, data, text, still photo, and graphic art for "on-demand" audiences.

Using these different forms to tell news stories on the World Wide Web has been widely regarded as the future of mass communication regardless of the fact that most online news sites have had a hard time making ends meet, let alone making a profit. Form convergence, often called technological convergence, has been a fundamental force to guide and lead convergence in the market, industry, and regulation.

CORPORATE CONVERGENCE

Since the late 1990s, media convergence has been escalated to the level of media mergers. The News Centre located in Tampa, Florida, owned by Media General, and the Tribune Interactive, owned by the Tribune Company, for instance, are the products of media mergers.

In The News Centre, WFLA-TV, The Tampa Tribune, and Tampa Bay Online operate out of the same building. They share daily tips and information, spot news, photography, enterprise reporting, franchises, events, and public service. Each of the three entities in The News Centre has its own independent newsroom, but they issued a joint statement of coverage principles, titled "News Centre Pledge".

The Tribune Interactive has brought together the interactive functions of the company's four newspapers and more than a score of television stations including WGN-TV and CLTV. The individual media outlets have their own newsgathering staff, but their coverage is enhanced by their multimedia desks in the Chicago Tribune newsroom and the Tribune Media Centre in Washington.

"A synergy-team of print editors and TV news veterans at the Chicago Tribune work together to manage resource sharing and the relationship". Media merger has made both content convergence and form convergence handy.

Corporate convergence via vertical and horizontal integration, mergers, alliances, and acquisitions will make traditionally defined segments of the communications industry less and less distinguishable.

ROLE CONVERGENCE

Russial identified several examples of role convergence in newsrooms. For instance, the roles of reporter and librarian, the roles of copyeditor and compositor, the roles of graphic artist and Web designer, and the roles of photo editor, darkroom technician, and photographer are all converging in different media. In more recent years, content convergence, form convergence, and especially corporate convergence have sparked more in-depth role convergence among news practitioners.

For instance, Victoria Lim from The News Centre in Tampa revealed at a February 2002 conference on media convergence at the University of Florida that she primarily works as a television reporter for WFLA-TV, but she also has to write for the company's newspaper, The Tampa Tribune, as a senior consumer investigative reporter and for the Web company TBO.com on a daily basis; at the time of the conference, she was working on 31 stories.

A newspaper reporter may also produce a newspaper in QuarkXPress or serve as a TV news anchor, while a newspaper photographer may shoot video stories or produce interactive online stories in Flash. Role convergence requires that both reporters and editors re-equip themselves both journalistically and technologically.

Of the four types of convergence, role convergence has the most direct effect on future journalism education. Within the media industry, there are serious doubts about whether training cross-media journalists are possible or desirable. When asked whether reporters of the future must be equally skilled in print, TV, and online, Forrest Carr, news director of WFLA-TV at The News Centre in Tampa, said no.

He said he believed that there would always be areas of specialization and students may still choose specialties, but said that it no longer makes any sense to pretend print journalists and electronic journalists are in different professions.

On the other hand, he said that journalists who have skills in TV, print, and online media certainly will be more valuable to their employers; and he emphasized that prospective employees must be willing to work in an environment where reporters cooperate across platforms. In most cases currently, he said, cooperating across platforms simply comes down to the sharing of tips and information.

Charles Kravetz, the vice president for news and station manager of New England Cable News (NECN), the largest regional news network in America, concurs with Forrest Carr. When asked "Do you see a time when all journalists will have to be able to file stories on all platforms (print, TV, radio, online)?" Kravetz said: "I am not sure that is the way it is going to work out.

This notion we had that one-journalist-fits-all-media is perhaps not that realistic.... There are very few people we will talk about in the future that are TV/newspaper/internet reporters". Gates (2002) agreed, "The 'backpack journalist'-a superhack master of multimedia who can do it all and who routinely packs a laptop and a video camera along with the tape recorder and steno notebook-may be the subject of avant-garde j-school courses, but it's not likely to become the norm."

Some other media executives have tried to define the extent to which role convergence is expected. Gil Thelen, executive editor and senior vice president of The Tampa Tribune, for instance, gave suggestions to journalism educators based on his two years of experience in The News Centre.

"The fully formed, all-purpose, multiplatform, gadget-laden journalism grad is NOT what we're looking to hire.... Journalism schools must continue to produce graduates who are competent in one craft area: reporting, design, producing, directing, editing." However, Thelen encouraged journalism schools to train writers to write for print, online, and broadcast and train print photographers to learn how to shoot and produce TV packages. Thelen said that cultural resistance is the biggest hurdle for converging newsrooms, and that employees or current journalism students need to learn to cooperate and collaborate across newsrooms.

What is unclear is whether these media administrators' predictions are limited by the status quo of the current generation of news practitioners who might not be very well prepared for convergence or who might even resist the notion of media convergence. At Brigham Young University, students with multiple skills are more valued and feel more comfortable in the converged media environment.

In addition, sharing tips and information does not entail convergence. Reporters have been doing this for decades. It seems that keeping convergence only on the level of sharing tips and information can hardly justify the high cost of rebuilding infrastructures like The News Centre. We are interested in finding out what expectations media companies have for future journalists. From news professionals' self-evaluations of their preparedness for media convergence, we should also be able to infer what is most desirable in the media industry nowadays.

In the face of increasing demand for technically skilled journalists-conversant with QuarkXPress, Photoshop, Avid, and Dreamweaver and able to crunch statistics using spreadsheets and other statistical methods in order to uncover the hidden story-should longstanding staples such as ethics, law, and theory remain at the heart of journalism curricula?

Or should such materials, commonly grouped together as "critical thinking", share equal hilling with technology or "skills" training? In other words, how should journalism schools balance the teaching of professional skills and that of critical thinking in an era when technology penetrates every facet of news gathering, preparation, editing, production, and delivery?

Convergence further complicates this age-old battle in journalism education. Abraham noticed that the goal of most restructuring in journalism institutions is to provide an integrated skills environment where students would get the chance to practice the skills of multimedia production. Abraham argued: "The role of journalism academy should be very different from that of the industry. Its role should not simply be to inculcate skills that will help students to flag down jobs. They should aim to provide a scholarly background for a deeper intellectual understanding of our lives, media forms and of communication in general".

The dean of the University of Nevada at Reno thinks the ability to use multiple media skills is essential. Brigham Young University, which has built a working converged newsroom into its curriculum, expects students to graduate with multiple skills. University News Director, Dean Paynter, said, "We expect our students to more than anchor, more than report, and more than produce. The best ones can do it all, including write for the newspaper".

Mitchell Stephens, professor of journalism and mass communications at New York University, holds up the other end. "In a world where corporate pressures on 'content providers' seem to be increasing and civic affairs decreasing, the argument for emphasizing the basics does have much to recommend it."

Thomas Kunkel, dean of the Philip Merrill College of Journalism at the University of Maryland, sums it up:

"Today's journalists, first and foremost, must be strong critical thinkers who know enough about geography, history and the human condition to understand why events play out as they do. They must be intellectually curious.

They should speak a second language. They should read something other than Jim Romenesko's MediaNews site. They ought to have a world view."

A controversy in late 2002 at Columbia University demonstrates how volatile the argument is currently. The debate arose when the graduate school of journalism at Columbia University halted its search for a dean. The new university president, Lee Bollinger, wanted to re-evaluate the school's mix of craft versus theory, and the move created a flurry of opinion about the journalism school's existing curriculum.

This critical curriculum question is often reflected in the questions of whether and how new technology classes should be included in the existing curriculum and how they should be taught. Some journalism schools are preparing to embrace the wave of media convergence in their new curricula by converging print and electronic media sequences to adapt to the industrial trends and the new technological environment.

Blanchard and Christ warn that universities with limited resources will no longer tolerate duplicating specializations with separate courses such as writing for television, writing for newspapers, writing for public relations, and writing for advertising. Blanchard and Christ add that the communications revolution (the media's convergence and related trends) is making journalism and mass communication's traditional sequences obsolete.

Actually, Blanchard and Christ's opinion is not something new. Early in 1972, the University of Iowa School of Journalism already eliminated its sequences but at the expense of being denied reaccreditation by ACEJMC. About thirty years later, their decision seemed to be finding more sympathy.

Many schools are still exploring where to go. In October 2001, seventeen professors and leaders of new media from thirteen journalism programs across the country gathered in Berkeley, California, and had a discussion about new media in journalism education. The University of Nevada, Reno, offered several different elective courses in new media, but it did not have a special sequence.

It was struggling with how to incorporate them in other classes. The University of Florida had a concentration in online media, which was equivalent to other concentrations such as reporting and editing and photojournalism. Students who were not in that concentration couldn't always squeeze in the online media courses because they did not have any leftover électives they could take in the school. American University had three divisions, journalism, public communication, and visual media, but they did not work together very well most of the time. The University of South Carolina was restructuring its graduate masters programme in newspaper leadership and was focusing it on convergence. The University of Maryland had an online curriculum, but it was not formally structured as such. Northwestern University had an introductory New Media course at the undergraduate and graduate level, which was offered as an elective.

It was packed with everything from new skills training to wrestling with the business issues of new media to actual production. After three admission cycles, enrollment declined. The University of Minnesota established the Institute for New Media Studies, which merged broadcast journalism and print journalism programs to make them a concentration with the idea that future journalists would work in a multi-channel environment and should know how to operate within all those channels.

Although editors and academics sometimes agree on the qualifications a journalism student needs, an ideal curriculum doesn't always include convergence preparedness courses. In a 2000 poll, editors and educators agreed "on the same five of 14 types of knowledge considered most necessary for journalism graduates and listed them in the same order of importance". Technical skills were not mentioned in the top five, surpassed instead by "understanding of a journalist's responsibility to the public, understanding of the ethics of journalism, knowledge of current events, broad general knowledge, and knowledge of government".

With so much variance across universities, we are interested in finding out how many journalism schools have revamped their curricula to prepare students for the trend of media convergence, what professors' attitudes are toward teaching critical thinking vs. teaching technical skills and training generalists vs. training specialists, and what editors' and news professionals' attitudes are toward the same issues. In this regard, several scholars and news practitioners have tried to give advice to journalism professors and students in the context of media convergence.

In 2002, David Bulla from the University of Florida presented his "Media convergence: Industry practices and implications for education" to the AEJMC annual conference in Miami. This is the first research writing of its kind. The theme of the paper is the closest to that of this study. Bulla's study looked at the changing nature of contemporary mass communications practices, focusing on multimedia or converged journalism.

It described what scholastic journalism scholars are doing to prepare their students for these changes and provided recommendations to educators about how to update curricula to account for convergence.

The research questions for that study were:

- What are journalism educators currently doing to incorporate convergence into their curricula;
- What abilities, skills, and attitudes do professional journalists expect from their newest employees?

Media convergence in Bulla's study was defined as multimedia journalism, which means reporting, writing, and disseminating content in two or more media platforms.

Because of the controversy about media mergers, Bulla tried to find answers to some hot issues concerning democracy including: Does corporate media merging reduce public discourse and hinder democracy? Will it ultimately mean the need for fewer and fewer reporters, as the development of other technology has meant a decline in the number of employees in other areas of the production process? All these questions pertain to our study.

Bulla obtained a sample of 114 news practitioners working at newspapers, television stations, wire services, magazines, radio stations, and online publications in the United States. The sample was randomly selected from Editor & Publisher and Yahoo lists of media companies in the U.S. Media Web sites. With a response rate of 36 per cent, Bulla interviewed 41 news practitioners. Bulla also interviewed college educators, but he did not state how he sampled them.

What is unclear is the extent to which the Yahoo list and Editor & Publisher list overlap each other and if a sample from two potentially overlapping lists is any longer a random sample. In addition, since Bulla's questions were almost all unstructured, that is, he conducted interviews,10 he did not really need a random sample. Researchers strive for depth rather than breadth and don't mean to claim external validity in the statistical sense by conducting interviews. Finally, if he did need a random sample, a sample of 114 people with a 36 per cent response rate could be statistically defective because of big statistical errors. Bulla needed a better research design to make his study valid and reliable.

Some scholars doubt whether journalism school professors are theoretically and especially technologically prepared to teach media convergence. In an article written for Journalism Education magazine, John Irby, a professor from Washington State University and a veteran newspaper editor and publisher, for instance, was concerned about the disconnection between the newsroom and the classroom. Irby (2000) asked:

Are universities and educators effectively preparing students for the work force? Do educators understand what newspapers are looking for in future reporters and editors? Does the newspaper industry have a responsibility in the division between educators and professionals? Are journalism educators "discounted" by professionals who believe those who teach couldn't succeed in newspapers?

Irby said older generations of newspaper reporters also appeared on radio and television periodically though they had no training; they never even felt like it was part of their job and thus did not take it very seriously.

But now, he continued, print journalists do need to take it seriously; journalism educators need to re-evaluate, and probably modify, the separatetrack approach in training print and broadcast journalists.

Irby believed that there is still a need for specialization, but he told students to take both broadcast and print courses and told them that computer literacy is as crucial as the old-fashioned kind.

A study about the impact of media convergence on journalism education without consulting Robert J. Haiman's article "Can convergence float?" (2001) should be considered incomplete.

Haiman's fervent talk against media convergence raised some challenging questions that educators must face. Haiman, president emeritus of The Poynter Institute, argued that the converged media world is one from which good journalism, and good journalists, are going to be in great need of defence.

He stuck to his notion of the mission of good journalism he stated 40 years ago: "To inform the public about the public's business, creating a society that is equipped with the knowledge it needs to make the right civic decisions more often than it makes the wrong civic decisions, and thus helping to perpetuate self-government and democracy."

Expressing his deep concern for journalism, Haiman said: "I think that convergence may end up being good, maybe even very good, for media companies. I fear, however, that it is going to be bad, and maybe even very bad, for journalism." He continued to explain:

I think it is going to be bad for journalism because, even if it goes as well as it possibly can, I believe that it is going to distract journalists, journalism teachers, and journalism students away from that single most important imperative of the craft - to create an informed society capable of intelligently governing itself.

And if it does not go well, I fear it is going to subject journalists to time, resource, craft, and ethical pressures, all of which will be bad for journalists, bad for journalism, and bad for the country. In his talk, Haiman mentioned a top education reporter who had done a"superb job" for more than 18 years. Now, he had to do short reports for the TV station with which that newspaper was converged.

However,"he's not exactly ready for prime time." After this reporter retires, Haiman is afraid that that he will be replaced by"someone who may not report like a buzz saw and write like a dream, but who probably will report and write education okay and who will also look good and sound good on television.""When that happens," he continued,"the journalism quality of all of the education reporting coming out of that converged news operation is going to go down."

We believe that few people would disagree with Haiman's point that quality content is the king, to use his own words, but Haiman's above comment could be limited, again, by the performance of the current generation of reporters who are not prepared for media convergence.

Haiman was suggesting that a future reporter who has been trained to work for different media platforms and who has learned more about reporting would produce reporting of less quality.

In our study, we would like to find out to what extent Haiman's concern is shared by editors, news professionals, and professors.

While convergence is still in its infancy, Haiman suggested that journalists, journalism students, and journalism teachers do three"terribly important things":

- For journalists who want to keep good journalism alive in the converged world to take a blood oath to fight, scrap, kick and scream whenever any attempt is made to dilute good journalism values.
- For journalism schools and journalism teachers to offer students the right curriculum to function best in that converged world, and this does not mean offering new courses in convergence.

- For journalism students to emphasize the right areas of study and take the right courses so they will be able to defend themselves against the evils of convergence, prosper in that new world, and contribute to the effort to sustain informed self-government.

Haiman said,"If we decide to teach anything about convergence at Poynter, that is the lesson I hope we'll teach."

To students, Haiman said that the journalists who will be the most successful in the converged world are the same ones who are the most successful today, and they are the ones who are best trained in six areas: reporting, writing, editing, ethics, and media law, research techniques and specialized knowledge such as business, finance, law, science, health, aging, and the environment.

Since the top reporter in education Haiman mentioned can hardly survive the converged media world, our question is whether gaining knowledge in these six areas is sufficient and what else, if any, students need to learn. Do students need to learn any new skills? What new skills do news practitioners need?

Also, we would like to see how the attitudes of the respondents from these three groups toward media merger affect their views of how to train future journalists. As South and Nicholson (2002) commented,"If the industry doesn't agree on what new skills journalists need, it will be hard for journalism schools to know what to teach."

LARGER CONTEXT OF THE STUDY

The questions concerning teaching skills vs. critical thinking and training specialists vs. generalists are not new. They have been contextualized in ongoing conversations across disciplines over decades on many campuses in the United States. But such conversations take on new meanings in journalism schools when many reporting jobs today are becoming high-tech-oriented and many news companies are demanding high-tech skills from new hires upon their graduation.

The impact of such industrial demands on universities brings us back to the core issue-the role of the university in the shaping of the young souls in its charge. In other words, how should a university achieve the desired product-a truly educated human being for newsrooms.

The question of teaching skills vs. critical thinking winds down to a perennial competition between acquiescing pervasive vocationalism with its emphasis on skills training in an attempt to enable college students to survive outside academic institutions and establishing the relevance of the broad spectrum of knowledge to the career goals and lives of individuals. E. D. Hirsch argues: "Narrow vocational education, adjusted to the needs of the moment, is made ever more obsolete by changing technology... What is required is education for change, not for static job competencies".

Probably no one has better expressed than Joanne G. Kurfiss the importance of imparting critical thinking as skills of analyzing and constructing arguments, as construction of meaning, and as the manifestation of a contextual theory of knowledge. "Critical thinking can result in a new way of approaching significant issues in one's life or a deeper understanding of the basis for one's actions. Or it might result in political activity".

Along the similar line as Kurfiss's critical thinking theory and unlike Allan Bloom, who condemns the introduction of non-Western materials into the university curricula so as to protect the curriculum from the contamination of ideological conflict, Jerry Herron also highly promotes the teaching of critical thinking by calling on faculty to bring their conflicting ideologies into open engagement so that students can discover what is at stake in different ideas and can see their representational meaning.

The questions are whether universities should totally give up the teaching of skills today and how the needs of the job market and the goal of college education can be in harmony. In other words, can the teaching of common traditional content and the teaching of higher order skills join forces? Patracia Graham, ex-dean of the Harvard Graduate School of

Education, argues that we need both commonality and flexibility in American education and there is no reason we cannot have both at once.

The question of training specialists vs. generalists is an extension of a larger conversation about reforming the fragmented curricula in higher education. Often classified as "cultural right," Ernest Boyer, Allan Bloom, and E. D. Hirsch share similar views about the problems in higher education. They point out that the university now is anarchistic. There is no vision of what an educated human being is. The curriculum is disjointed and disciplines are fragmented into smaller pieces.

Undergraduates find it hard to see patterns in their courses and relate what they learn to life. Careerism conflicts with the liberal arts. And finally, schools have failed to thoroughly carry out the educational goal of promoting mature literacy for all our citizens. They all agree that an educational reform is needed to teach more common traditional content apart from the higher-order skills that are commonly emphasized.

Boyer calls for a balance between individual interests and shared concerns while the actual priority is given to the latter. To promote a liberal education, Boyer advocates the "integrated core" or "enriched major"-a programme of general education that introduces students not only to essential knowledge, but also to connections across the disciplines, and, in the end, to the application of knowledge to life beyond the campus.

Boyer points out, knowledge becomes important only when we use it and apply it to humane ends; therefore, the undergraduate experience should not only generate new knowledge, but channel that knowledge to the service of the society. It is a matter of invigorating "the claims of community while protecting with full vigour the dignity and origins of each individual," to use Boyer and Kaplan's words.

In a similar vein, Bloom calls on teachers to look toward the goal of human completeness and to provide students a liberal education, in which learning is both synoptic and precise. To Bloom, liberal education feeds the student's love of truth and passion to live a good life. It also requires that a student's whole life be radically changed by it.

Bloom offers an ivory tower vision of the university-"the good old Great Book approach"-undergraduate students spend four years reading certain generally recognized classic texts for answers to philosophical questions of personal and human identity and aspirations. Bloom thinks that man may live more truly and fully in reading Plato and Shakespeare than at any other time because then they are participating in essential being and are forgetting their accidental lives.

In accordance with Boyer's and Bloom's points of view, Hirsch argues that "the greatest human individuality is developed in response to a tradition, not in response to disorderly, uncertain, and fragmented education" and "only by accumulating shared symbols, and the shared information the symbols represent can we learn to communicate effectively with one another in our national community".

However, Hirsch places emphasis more on the content of education, ensuring that students acquire all the "right" elements of knowledge that will enable them to get along in the Real World.

He believes that neither the content-neutral curriculum of Rouşseau and Dewey nor the narrowly specified curriculum of Plato is adequate to the needs of a modern nation.

Hirsch calls for a curriculum, including extensive curriculum and intensive curriculum with an emphasis on the former, which is traditional in content and provides students with a common core of cultural information. "The conception of a two-part curriculum avoids the idea that all children should study identical materials" Hirsch says.

Based on our literature review, media convergence in our study is defined as the assimilation of media content for multiple media platforms. Media convergence may involve any combination of the convergences of media contents, media forms, media companies, and roles of news practitioners.

Our general research question is how college professors should prepare students to cope with media convergence. To be specific, should college professors prepare generalists who can competently work in multiple media platforms or prepare specialists who know inside out how to work for one particular medium platform? And how should journalism schools balance the teaching of critical thinking and technical skills?

Corresponding to these two questions, we also would like to find out if college journalism educators themselves are both theoretically equipped and technologically prepared to teach their students about media convergence. The study serves both as an attitude finder and a fact finder.

We believe that professors, editors, and news professionals are the best candidates to answer these questions. Editors represent the media companies to hire news staffers with news reporting abilities desired by the company. News professionals work in the forefront of news reporting and know best about what news reporting abilities they need.

The attitudes of the editors and the current generation of news professionals toward media convergence will have a great implication on future journalism education. Professors run journalism schools, and they have the final say about where their schools are going. Their attitudes toward journalism education in terms of media convergence will have the most direct influence on the kind of education journalism students will receive and how the students will perform in tomorrow's media.

Editors include daily newspaper editors in charge of newsroom operations or online news operations and news directors in charge of newsroom operations in a commercial TV station with news content, both in the United States.

News professionals refer to non-management news staff, such as reporters, anchors, photographers, designers, producers, Web staff, etc., working in American media companies. Journalism professors are defined as full-time instructors with any academic rankings who teach journalism courses in a U.S. journalism school, department, programme, or division, which could be administratively affiliated with an institution with a name like College of Communications or Department of Communications Studies.

To obtain opinions about media convergence, we could have targeted our survey only at those editors and news professionals in a converged media environment. The opinions obtained from those editors and news professionals, however, could be biased. Those media companies that have not gone through convergence must have a reason for not doing so. We also wanted to find out what they are doing about convergence. Balanced views both from the converged and un-converged media companies will better assist colleges in their strategic planning.

We conducted a national survey among editors, news professionals, and journalism professors with three different versions of online survey questionnaires posted on a school Web site. Respondents were asked to fill out the questionnaire online and submit answers online as well. The answers went through a commercial form handler and reached the primary investigator's email address. By doing so, the primary investigator had no way to detect who answered the questionnaire unless the respondent voluntarily revealed his/her email address to request the findings from the study.

There were twenty-two questions in each of these three questionnaires. Almost all questions were close-ended. About half of the questions used a 5-point Likert Scale from "Strongly Agree" to "Strongly Disagree." Some questions across the three questionnaires shared similarity, so that comparisons could be made when analyzing data. A text field was created for respondents to provide feedback to the survey freely.

The textual answers in the text field will be reported along with the statistics to illustrate and explain the quantitative findings. All questionnaires went through pilot tests. The unit of analysis was each participant.

In order to conduct a systematic random sampling of editors and news professionals, we needed a list of newspaper editors and TV news directors in the United States and a list of newspaper and TV news staffers. We found that such lists did not exist, though lists of newspapers and lists of TV stations did exist in multiple places online like Editor & Publisher Yearbook and Broadcasting Sr Cable Yearbook. Therefore, we decided to construct our own.

To do so, we went through two steps. First, we constructed a combined list of daily newspapers and TV stations so that we could sample these news institutions. Second, we visited the Web sites of all sampled news institutions to find the email of the editor/news director and the email of one news professional randomly chosen.

After further research, we decided that newslink.org's daily newspaper list was the most comprehensive and workable list for sampling daily newspapers. In total, 1,190 U.S. daily newspapers with a valid URL were listed alphabetically by state. We sampled one out of every four dailies. Then, we visited each of those Web sites to find the email address of the managing editor, chief editor, online editor, or equivalent in each of those dailies and sent out a survey invitation email to him/her. If an individual email address was not available, we replaced it with a generic email address listed on their Web site and specified that the email was for the editor.

In total, there were 1,093 companies ordered alphabetically by state. From the list, we removed PBS network companies, which mostly did not provide staff information, companies that did not generate news content such as WB network companies and UPN network companies, religious TV stations, and foreign language stations. In total, we extracted 674 TV stations with a valid URL. Since this population is smaller than that of the newspapers, we over-sampled it. Instead of sampling every other four, we sampled every other station.

Then, we visited each of those Web sites to find the email address of the news director or equivalent in each of those TV stations and sent out a survey invitation email to him/her. If an individual email address was not available, we replaced it with a generic email address and specified that the email was for the news director. In total, we successfully sent out invitation emails to 523 newspaper editors and TV news directors as our sample.

We also sampled one news professional out of each of the sampled U.S. dailies and TV stations for the survey. Since there was always more than one professional in a company, we simply randomly clicked on one name and picked him/her and made sure that s/he was on the news staff.

Then, we sent him/her a survey invitation email. If an individual email address was not available, we replaced it with a generic email address and specified whom the email was for. S/he was asked to fill out a questionnaire that was worded in a slightly different manner. In total, we successfully sent out invitation emails to 398 news professionals.

We also needed to conduct a systematic random sampling of college journalism professors, but we were disappointed that all lists we found had many J-schools, even major ones, missing. Therefore, a new list was built upon the existing lists and upon the findings from a more careful search in the Yahoo U.S. Colleges and Universities site. In total, the new list contains 205 alphabetically ordered U.S. J-schools that contain 2,194 journalism professors.

We sampled one out of every four professors from the virtually running list of all journalism professors across the schools. For instance, if a school had six journalism professors, we picked the fourth one; then, the second journalism professor from next school was picked. We sent an invitation email to every professor in the sample. In total, we successfully sent out 500 emails.

The three samples of editors, news professionals, and professors included 1,421 cases.

We understood that nonresponse had been a serious problem with online surveys in recent years. In order to counter possible low response rates in our survey, we created three samples for editors, news professionals, and professors containing roughly 500 people for each group, which were much larger than the sample sizes for populations recommended by Mildred Patten (2000) in her book

Understanding Research Methods: An Overview of the Essentials so that, if low response rates occurred, we could base our confidence limits on the actual number of responses themselves. We also sent out one reminder email to the samples, which drastically boosted the response rates, especially for professors and news professionals.

After two weeks of online data collecting in November 2002, we received 223 responses from professors (a 44% response rate), 151 responses from editors (a 29% response rate), and 142 responses from news professionals (a 35% response rate).

The overall response rate is 36%. As Singletary notes, returns of 30% to 40% are common in mail surveys. The response rates of this online survey seem typical. However, the response rates are still comparatively low. A response bias is potentially present. Many respondents (41%) left textual answers to explain and illustrate their answers to the close-ended questions and/or made comments on the topic.

- What is the status quo of media convergence in the industry?

By the end of 2002, 19% of the newspapers and commercial television stations with news content in the United States had gone through media mergers. Being merged or not has to do with the size of a company. Larger companies tend to have been merged while smaller ones have not.

Roughly half of the news professionals surveyed (48%) reported that they produced news content for multiple media platforms on a routine basis; that was true both in merged media (50%) and non-merged media (48%). In other words, media merger is not the precondition for practicing news for multiple media platforms. The pressure on news professionals to learn to produce multimedia content is also felt in many non-merged media companies. This finding confirms that media convergence is not necessarily related to media merger.

A typical editor or news director was a man (71%) between 36-45 years old (42%) with a bachelor's degree (76%) who had worked for at least two media (57%) for more than 20 years (53%). A typical news professional was either a man

(52%) or woman (48%) between 26-35 years old (43%) with a bachelor's degree (84%) who had worked for at least two media (60%) less than ten years (62%).

Editors had generally worked for more years than news professionals, but they did not have more multiplatform experience than news professionals. As more news companies are practicing cross-media reporting with or without their companies being merged, it is important that editors with multiplatforrn experiences are chosen to direct newsroom businesses. Many editors need cross-media training more urgently than news professionals do if the news company they work for produces news contents for multiple media platforms on a daily basis.

- Should J-schools train specialists or generalists?

Gil Thelen (2002) said that writers should learn how to write for multimedia and still photographers should learn how to shoot videos, but he was not interested in hiring people with multiple sets of skills. We designed four questions to test how popular Thelen's opinion was.

The majority of the respondents (84%) agreed or strongly agreed with Thelen that journalism students should learn how to write for multiple media platforms. One-way ANOVA shows significant difference among the means for professors (4.35), professionals (4.05), and editors. Tukey HSD post hoc tests show that professors were more positive on this statement than editors and professionals, while no significant difference existed between editors and professionals.

A similar number of respondents (85%) agreed or strongly agreed with Thelen that journalism students with a visual emphasis should learn how to produce and edit photos, videos, and online interactive images. One-way ANOVA shows significant difference among the means for professors (4.55), professionals (4.22), and editors. Tukey HSD post hoc tests show that professors were more positive on this statement than professionals, while professionals were more positive than editors.

Most respondents (78%) agreed or strongly agreed that all journalism majors should learn multiple sets of skills, such as writing, editing, TV production, digital photography, newspaper design, and Web publishing.

Oneway ANOVA shows significant differences among the means for professionals (4.28), editors (3.99), and professors (3.86).

Tukey HSD post hoc tests show that news professionals who worked in the forefront of news production felt this need more deeply than other respondents. Editors also had such an expectation for them.

There is no significant difference between editors and professors. These findings support the growing evidence that news professionals are being asked to wear multiple hats. The findings also indicate that Thelen's view has its market at this moment when news professionals with multiple sets of skills are highly desirable but not easy to find. Such a view may change as more journalism graduates equipped with multiple sets of skills enter the job market.

The professors' textual answers show that some of the difficulties J-schools have come across include the lack of a friendly curriculum, lack of credit hours to include the components of convergence content, lack of willing cooperation among faculty from different sequences, and lack of expertise, interest, or even time for some professors to develop new courses on convergence.

When asked whether journalism students should still have a specialization, such as writing, photojournalism, broadcasting, and new media, over half (63%) of the respondents agreed or strongly agreed. Over a quarter of the respondents (28%) were negative and 9% were not sure. Oneway ANOVA mean comparisons show no significant difference of attitude among professionals (3.42), editors (3.51), and professors (3.72).

Comparing the support rate for this question to those for the first three questions, it is fair to argue that editors, news professionals, and professors emphasized the importance of cross-media training more than that of specialization, though they believed that specialization should not be neglected either. Currently, students in many J-schools specialize in one area by subscribing to a sequence such as news-editorial, magazine, photojournalism, and broadcast. When asked whether sequences should be reorganized considering the trend of media-platforms merging in the industry, 56% of the professors agreed or strongly agreed, 22% were not sure, and another 22% disagreed or strongly disagreed.

The concept of sequences is being shaken among professors though it is still being accepted as a legitimate means of training students in various specialization areas in some J-schools. Speaking on behalf of herself and her colleagues, Professor #93 offered some special insight on this issue: We can't teach for the"now." We have to prepare students for when they graduate...which in most instances is now five years out. And, we feel a commitment to expose them to all types of writing in all platforms so they can be flexible about their career choice at the front end of their academics. Then, they can apply the skills to a specialty area where they are totally proficient.

"Flexible" is a key term repeatedly seen in editors' and news professionals' textual answers as a suggestion for future journalists. Editor's statement is typical:

Our job descriptions are open ended and new hires understand that they are being hired for their skills. They may be hired today to cover the city beat. In six months or in two weeks, if necessary, a person with Quark skills may be asked to fill in or shift duties to include pagination of a particular section. It is important that hires stay flexible.

The new hires, wrote Editor, "need to understand that the information they gather and process can have many different uses, audiences and shelf lives. They need to understand the complexities of the audience mix and be able to respond." "Those unwilling to be flexible may find themselves in a difficult scenario later in their careers".

From a different perspective, Professional concurred: "Students must be flexible, have a vigorous skill set and be prepared to get laid off and move around in the changing media arena." In short, "young journalists must be prepared to fill a variety of roles if they hope to succeed". "The most successful journalists are those that take on assignments willingly, can learn and want to learn".

Specialization in journalistic jobs is still honored, but is losing its favour to cross-media capability in converged media. Today, professionals with different specializations team together to work on multiple media projects. Tomorrow, it is likely that one-man bands will be more and more desired in newsrooms.

- How should J-schools balance the teaching of critical thinking and that of technical skills?

Most respondents (93%), especially professors, agreed or strongly agreed that journalism students should both learn technical skills, such as online information search and Web design, while learning critical thinking skills in media law, ethics, etc.

One-way ANOVA shows significant difference among the means for professionals (4.35), editors (4.38), and professors (4.76). Tukey HSD post hoc tests show that professors were more positive on this point than editors and professionals, while no significant difference existed between editors and professionals.

But, should journalism students spend more time on learning critical thinking skills than on technical skills? Opinions were divided.

More than half of the respondents (62%) believed that should be the case, but 19% of the respondents were not sure and another 19% of them did not agree. Oneway ANOVA shows significant difference among the means for professors (3.21), professionals (3.87), and editors (4.3). Tukey HSD post hoc tests show that editors were more positive on this point than professionals, and professionals were more positive than professors.

Throughout all the answers from the three groups of respondents, critical thinking was highly regarded as being more important than technical skills. Editors, news professionals, and professors all liked to see good stories, and good stories come from good thinking ability. An editor said: "Journalism graduates need to have a broad, well-rounded education; be critical thinkers; have the ability to write clearly; have a serious work ethic; and know computer basics - in that order".

"You can teach a monkey to type," echoes a writer. Therefore, he strongly suggested that J-schools "get more critical thinking skills pounded into the skulls of the students". While highly emphasizing the importance of critical thinking ability, editors did not mean to neglect the importance of teaching technical skills in schools.

We will develop this point when we discuss the next question. Comparing the professors' highest mean for the first question and their lowest mean for the second question, it is clear that professors saw critical thinking as highly important, but preferred a comparatively balanced approach for the teaching of the two sets of knowledge. One professor's comment illustrated this observation:

Knowing technical skill alone will not make you a "good" journalist. Critical thinking is vital not just to a career but to life itself. Without developing your ability to discern and evaluate, you will become "the prey" of society. Next, a technical skill is critical to a career in journalism today.

Even print Journalism is very high tech these days and all electronic media require extensive computer knowledge as well as other technical skills. I would place critical thinking skills first on your list of things to do because a developed mind will make it that much easier to develop a creative and technically sound understanding of the technical side of the business.

From a holistic view, there was no substantial disagreement between classrooms and newsrooms when we examine the issue of teaching critical thinking vs. teaching technical skills.

Compared to Terry's 2000 poll, this study shows that professors gave a higher status to technical skills in journalism curricula in 2002 than they did in 2000.

This is a period during which media convergence garnered its momentum. In short, all respondents generally agreed that J-schools should place emphasis on teaching critical thinking, but at the same time, should not neglect teaching technical skills.

- Should technical skills be learned at work or in school?

News professionals were asked, "If you wish to possess the technical skills you don't have now, do you prefer to learn them at work or wish you had learned in school?" Editors were given the same question with a slightly different wording.

Chi-Square test shows that the difference between editors and news professionals is significant. This finding well supplements the findings from the preceding questions. It suggests that editors not only looked at future journalists' critical thinking ability, but also hoped that future journalists would already possess the skills needed in a converged newsroom when they are hired.

On the other hand, most professionals preferred that they spend most of their school time on gaining critical thinking ability and learn skills largely at work. The professionals' general preference, to some extent, also reflected their need for technological update at their current positions, so that they can better qualify for multimedia productions.

Many editors and reporters said that school is the best place for journalism students to explore every facet of the media and acquire basic technical skills, though some advanced skills can only be learned on the job.

Learning skills while in school, they said, can build confidence and an expansive and broad understanding of the entire field and help with damage control and communication in newsrooms.

"If editing and the technical skills were more prevalent in college courses," wrote a multi-tasking editor, "I think I could stave off a lot of headaches when the students become professionals."

An internship was the news professionals' and editors' most recommended venue for enhancing and learning more technical skills and gaining other practical experience. Reporter said: "While I value my college education, my internship and first job provided me with the most valuable skills today."

Another reporter said: "While education is great, students who work in media while in school fare much better in the real world." Some editors had complaints about graduates with a 3.5 GPA but no practical experience and no published news work. An anchor/reporter said that it is important even "for a freshman or sophomore in college to visit a newsroom and shadow someone. So many students wait until they are juniors and seniors to do this and then they realise they made a mistake in selecting their major. You will learn more by watching and doing". One reporter said, "To remain competitive, education must continue throughout a career".

The implication of the discrepancy from this finding suggests that Jschools should place emphasis on teaching critical thinking, expose students to new technology, and design a comprehensive internship programme for students to gain real-world knowledge and further develop their crossmedia technical skills.

- What skills do news professionals need to learn most at their current positions?

Both editors and news professionals were given this unstructured question with slightly different wordings. We read through all the answers, and categorized them into the following nine facets in random order:

Multimedia production: producing and editing news stories on video, for the Web, and for print; re-purposing the same story for different media.

New technology: knowledge of software for producing video, Web sites, graphics, newspapers, and magazines; knowledge of how to operate a computer and use the Internet.

Good writing: knowing how to write to make people remember and/or take action, write about the beats with an expert's view.

Good editing is also expected:

Critical thinking: Having good news judgment, understanding what is legal and ethical, knowing how to report with insight, knowing how to crunch statistics.

Computer-assisted reporting: Expert's knowledge of conducting online information search, database knowledge.

On-camera exposure: How to report like a TV news anchor before a camera for a newspaper reporter.

Visual production: A newspaper writer must know how to take photos, or a TV reporter must know how to shoot video.

Second language: Knowing how to fluently speak and read a foreign language.

Time management: Well organizing time to work for multiple media platforms; the ability and willingness to work as a team to produce multimedia news stories.

Then we ranked these facets according to the percentage scores each facet got separately from the editors and the news professionals:

This ranking shows more agreement than disagreement between editors and news professionals. No matter how technology changes and whether media are converged, editors and news professionals believed that learning how to write good stories is still the top priority and writing is the very basic skill all news professionals should learn.

One editor pushed the importance of good writing to the extreme:"I've worked in markets 170 to 20, and having training in multiple media will not help you get a job, but being a good writer will".

Most editors and news professionals, however, did believe that learning multimedia production, new technology, and computer-assisted reporting are also among the top priorities."I would strongly urge students to prepare themselves to the best of their ability to be able to report/edit the news in a variety of platforms and to learn how to truly engage readers/listeners/viewers in what they are writing about," said Editor.

Editors and news professionals both believed that it is not very important for a newspaper reporter to learn how to talk like an anchor in front of a video camera.

This skill was even regarded as being less important than knowing how to speak a second language. Some editors and news professionals also mentioned learning how to manage time for producing multimedia news stories. Editor hoped that journalists in a converged environment would learn to avoid"extra" work by working"smarter" and with greater awareness of the requirements of the different publishing media. This finding, again, shows that editors valued critical thinking ability more than news professionals did. Editors wanted news professionals to be good thinkers first, and the latter wanted most to learn how to express their thinking in different media.

- If news professionals have to re-purpose their work for multiple media platforms, will the quality of their work suffer?

Since some authors such as Haiman expressed the concern about the possible decline of work quality if news professionals have to "re-purpose" stories for multiple media platforms, we tried to find out to what extent this concern was shared by editors and news professionals. Opinions split.

Thirty-eight per cent of the editors and professionals agreed or strongly agreed that the quality would deteriorate, 40% disagreed or strongly disagreed, and the other 22% were not sure. Editors and professionals showed no significant difference on this attitude T-test. Such a concern was not prevalent in the news industry.

In response to such concerns, the news director from a converged media company wrote: "When reporters do cross platforms we give them the time to finish the project for all three platforms. Quality does not suffer. If we were to try to force reporters to cross platforms while operating under daily deadlines then quality could suffer depending on the nature of the story and the extra time consumed".

Another editor summed up this issue: "Some employees can capably handle multiple media and tell stories effectively. Others cannot. Certainly strong technical skills and training can help, but it's not just dependent on that; it depends more on the attitude and aptitude of the journalist".

Quality multimedia work also involves a solid understanding of different cultures in different media. Editors both for and against media convergence noted the difficulty of merging different media with different cultures, and editors in those merged media called for flexibility in aptitude and willingness to cooperate across platforms. For instance, Editor wrote: Clarity of what convergence means to the news organization is vital and often lacking. This causes unneeded anxiety. Managers have to realise that each medium has its own culture, language, skill set and timetable and is naturally skeptical of anything unfamiliar. It is also true that these same journalists' stock in trade is learning a new culture, language, skill set and timetable-on a daily basis. Therein lies the hope for an efficient news operation running on all cylinders and an effective -maybe even happy-staff.

If most editors and news professionals are not concerned about the quality of the work prepared for multiple media platforms and if news professionals are given enough time to complete their cross-media work, there is little reason to worry that future journalists, if well trained both theoretically and technologically for multiple media platforms, will produce work of poorer quality.

Training students to practice news in multiple media platforms will help bridge newsroom cultures from different media and eventually erase such differences.

We have noticed that no significant statistical differences existed between the editors and news professionals from the converged media companies and their counterparts from the not-yet-converged media companies when they answered the questions reported above.

- How are J-schools coping with media convergence?

From 1998 to 2002, about 60% of the J-schools in the United States redesigned their curricula or developed new courses to prepare students for practicing news in multiple media platforms.

A typical journalism professor was a man (71%) between 46-55 years old (42%) with a doctoral degree (63%) who worked in news media for one to ten years (48%), may still be practicing news (45%) in one way or another, and conducted academic research (66%).

More professors claimed that they were theoretically equipped (81%) than technologically prepared (53%) to teach students how to report news in multiple media platforms.

More than half of the professors (57%) had not taught any journalism courses in the last five years where skill sets were beyond their own expertise; 25% of the professors taught one such course and 11% taught two.

Nevertheless, the majority of the professors (84%) added content about media convergence either to their existing courses or to new courses or participated in cross-media team-teaching in the last five years.

Worries, concerns, and, sometimes, misconceptions about media convergence appeared in professors' textual answers. For instance, a professor from Montana said: "convergence is not happening". A professor who no longer practiced news said, "In my judgment, the writing portion of preparing news for print and for the Web is exactly the same".

Another professor maintained that it was not necessary to teach cross-media news practicing because "few 'want ads' for newspaper reporter and editor positions specifically listed multimedia platform skills as required or preferred experience for new hires". Many professors worried that media mergers would restrict the number of voices in a community. They regarded media mergers as a grand experiment in the profession and waited for the FCC's ruling on the cross-ownership of different media in the same market.

Wait-and-see-that was the strategy some universities took for teaching media convergence. One professor said that he needed to see the substantive contribution media convergence could make before he would be more serious about this phenomenon. He said that J-schools should be cautious about embracing convergence. Some other universities didn't have the time and resources to teach convergence courses or make major curriculum changes.

Most professors, however, did believe that media convergence was a reality; and "anybody serious about practicing media needs at minimal an acquaintance with various media and at best multiple competencies," as

Professor said. Many professors (and editors and news professionals as well) had a clear opinion as to which comes first, teaching critical thinking or teaching technical skills.

While acknowledging the need for incorporating media convergence content in curricula, especially the technological components, professors cautioned against sacrificing conceptual and theoretical courses such as law, ethics, history, cultural studies, critical perspectives, etc. Professor analogized critical thinking as meat and potatoes and technical skills as dessert and side dishes and argued that "the meat and potatoes need to come before one begins to worry about the dessert and side dishes (or side shows)." This viewpoint was popular. Professor wrote:

It's the message, not the medium, that is of paramount importance. If students cannot understand and appreciate the underlying concepts, principles and ethics of journalism, then they cannot produce the type of content that will be of value to a free society. A thorough grounding in journalism must come before any training in tools. The tools are means to an end, not the end in and of themselves.

Incidentally, a reporter had similar thoughts: The medium isn't the message, the message is the message. In short, the fundamental analytic and synthetic skills of the news writer are paramount to the message.

The medium does not alter the reporter's craft of interpreting news events in the context of the society in a way that will make sense for the receiver of the information.... Additional skills may be desirable, but for the most part they can be learned on the job.

Obviously, the more skills one can offer, the better the employment opportunity. Those ancillary skills should not come at the expense of thorough proficiency as a news writer.

We fully understand why these respondents emphasize the teaching of critical thinking and the fundamentals of good reporting over the teaching of technical skills, and we strongly agree with their opinions. But, we also see the danger of over-stretching the point by treating the two sets of knowledge as two opposing poles.

Those arguments are based on the presumptions that message and medium can be easily separated, content and form can be detached, and readers for different media are from the same population. But, is that right? It is true that content is the king. It is true that "the medium does not alter the reporter's craft of interpreting news events."

News practice, however, is not only about news-gathering and writing. It also includes production, editing, and delivery. Without a solid grasp of grammar and style, how can a writer effectively express his/her good analytical thinking? Without knowing the available features and limitations of online news delivery, how can messages be constructed to their fullest potential?

Without understanding the technical difference between video news and print news, how can messages be constructed appropriately? In the digital era when almost all steps of news transmission involves technology, if professors don't teach students technical skills, will the computer majors, who know little about news practices, be expected to produce newspapers, TV news, and online news?

Writers, for instance, do not necessarily have to be conversant in constructing news reporting with Flash for online presentation or know how to operate a video camera to shoot video stories.

But knowing the principles and rules of news videotaping and what Flash or other software can offer will surely help writers more effectively convey their messages and better cooperate with visual reporters. Creativity distinguishes artists and artisans. Critical thinking ability distinguishes master journalists and technical writers. But artists must first know what artisans know and a master journalist must possess all that a technical writer knows for a living. Skills are intrinsic instead of extrinsic to ideas.

Teaching critical thinking and teaching technical skills are not mutually exclusive. Teaching journalism students how to express their critical thinking with conversant technical skills in different media seems to be a big challenge for J-school professors in the years to come.

From the professors' textual answers, we have observed different philosophical approaches to teaching convergence. Unlike some professors who took the wait-and-see approach, a professor from the University of Texas at Austin claimed that "convergence is already happening, and journalism schools should be leading the parade and not following it".

A popular viewpoint was that "skills across platforms must be taught, but more importantly storytelling, ethics, and critical thinking skills should be even more important in the journalism school curriculum".

One professor from Texas Christian University said that it maintained the existing sequences but required broadcast students to take print courses and vice versa.

Team-teaching was an often-used approach in some J-schools such as Indiana University for courses involving multiple sets of skills while professors learned from each other. Another professor, from the University of Colorado at Boulder, said convergence meant that "students work together to produce multimedia content for the Web-not that each individual should attempt to become proficient in all media".

To overcome the hurdle of the ratio limited by the ACEJMC accreditation standards between journalism courses and liberal arts courses, a professor from Bowling Green State University suggested that journalism undergraduate students stay for five years and devote the fifth year entirely to practice.

Some professors said that journalism students only need to know a little about the practices in media other than their own while some other professors firmly maintained that students should "be the master of many arts and the explorer of all".

- Who benefits from media convergence?

All respondents were asked, "Do you think that merging media companies such as television station, newspaper, radio station, and online news from a local area will benefit any of the parties listed on the left? Check all entries that apply." The entries included "The general public," "News professionals," "Media companies," "Nobody," and "Not sure." We designed this question about the legitimacy of media merger as a barometer for testing the respondents' political view on media convergence. We presumed that a respondent's answer to this question could be related to his/her way of answering other questions regarding teaching media convergence or requirement for new hires.

Most respondents (66%) from all three groups pointed to media companies as the beneficiary of media mergers. In comparison, only 37% of the respondents said that media mergers also benefit the general public, and even fewer (27%) said that media mergers benefit the news professionals.

By reading the percentage numbers horizontally, we can find that consistently fewer respondents believed that media mergers benefit the general public or news professionals; also consistently more respondents believed that media mergers benefit media companies. It is also noticeable that 47% of editors believed that media mergers benefit the general public while the other 53% didn't. Editors' opinions on this point were roughly equally split. This finding indicates that media merger is a grand experiment in the media industry. Its benefits to the general public, which can better legitimize media mergers, are to be explored in the years to come.

By reading the percentage numbers both vertically and horizontally, we also find that editors were the most positive about the benefits media mergers could bring to all three parties while professors were least sure of such benefits. It is logical to reason that management personnel, such as editors and news directors and the companies they represent, are the primary forces behind today's media merger movement.

The question is that, since most professors, editors, and even news professionals believed that media mergers do not benefit news professionals and hardly benefit the general public, why do most news professionals still want to be trained to be cross-media practitioners and why are so many Jschool professors enthusiastic about training such graduates?

Considering the editors' most positive attitude toward media convergence, we wonder if news professionals are under the pressure to do so, and J-school professors are under the pressure to follow the industrial trend. Our surmise is partially corroborated by some textual answers. A news anchor from a merged media company agreed that new hires should have received cross-media training in writing and visuals and should possess multiple sets of skills. She showed her understanding for media mergers:

The merging of media companies is almost a daily occurrence. The pool of entities providing news services is shrinking. I think there is a danger that the public will lose in this race for media giants to accumulate wealth. At the same time, with the amount of competition in the industry from cable networks, the Internet, DVD's etc., I see the financial need for companies to merge to survive.

A newspaper reporter also from a merged media company expressed a similar feeling: "I am not all for the media convergence... At the same time I find it quite beneficial to be savvy in all branches of the industry. It helps the journalist become more knowledgeable about her or his job". News professionals were not alone in having such feelings. Here are two excerpts from two professors who have expressed similar feelings:

It's a harsh reality that I checked the box saying that news companies are the ones that are sure to benefit from media convergence. It may not be great for the public or even for news professionals who are going to be asked to bring more and more skills to the table and to have more and more responsibility on the job. Even so, convergence in one way or another is gonna happen and we need to prepare our students. Finally, my answer on merging media companies... reflects my disdain for the corporatization and concentration of control in the media. I think we ought to train mass communicators for a converged world, but as professors we ought to fight like hell against media mergers.

Very few respondents (19%) believed that media mergers benefit all three parties, the general public, news professionals, and media companies, but about one third of the respondents (35%) believed that media companies are the only beneficiaries to such a practice. These 35% respondents, who were almost equally proportionally found in editors, news professionals, and professors groups, could be regarded as the most critical toward media mergers.

We compared these 35% respondents with the rest of the sample and found no significant difference in their answers concerning the necessity of teaching journalism students cross-media writing and visuals and teaching multiple sets of skills. Always, more respondents believed that professors should teach all those things. In short, the respondents' political view was not directly tied to their views of teaching students cross-media practices.

Chapter 2

The Influence of Layout

In the history of the press, publishers have always made decisions about the presentation of news, following prevailing custom and the advice from skilled craftspersons. During the past twenty years, that advice, and the day-to-day implementing of decisions, came less often from typographers and printers in the "back shop" and increasingly from designers and editors in the newsroom. One of the key decisions in the adoption of newer styles of newspaper design has been whether stories should appear laid out vertically or horizontally.

Long, chimney-like articles predominated in the so-called Victorian style of the nineteenth century and have reappeared recently, while horizontal articles became a shibboleth for the wave of modem news layout that surged in the 1970s. Although newspaper designers and editors express strong loyalties to one form or another, the difference may amount to nothing more than a matter of taste. Does it make any difference to the reader's understanding of the content?

Answering that question can shed light on a broad range of decisions about the form of public communication. In health, education, art, and advertising, as well as in journalism, practitioners routinely select ways they deem most appropriate to attract attention, convey information, enhance comprehension, facilitate learning, and effect change.

Media buyers choose between competing forms of media, editors decide the particular mix and organization of verbal and visual material, and art directors select colour and illustration effects. Even government publications and academic journals use position, emphasis, and other subtle cueing devices as strategies to accomplish their communication goals. The relationship between form and content in newspapers thus addresses an important issue in designing all sorts of communications. Does the appearance of a message affect how people perceive and process its meaning? If so, how?

PREVIOUS RESEARCH

During periods of communication design change, empirical research takes up the salient issues. Within the field of visual communication, researchers during the years when modern layout reached its peak examined the effects of such elements as type, colour, and printing mode. Studies of overall design measured reader reactions to different newspaper styles. Like these studies, most subsequent design research oriented itself to the applied decisions of practitioners, without much attention to theory (with some exceptions).

In cognitive science during the same period, research on instructional design began to focus on how learning occurs. For example, Solomon analysed media as symbol systems that elicit different types of mental processes and recommended that these could guide media research and practitioner decisions.

Within aesthetics, scholars also tried to understand the motivation and cognitive context for viewers of art, as well as the representation of motion and space among viewers of video and film. In the emerging field of marketing communications, researchers recently began to examine the effects of colour and music to study the affective and cognitive processes underlying attitude change.

This nexus of the formal visual properties and the perceived content of communication also emerged in the study of newspaper design. Barnhurst's began analyzing layout decisions within the context of applied art, proposing that the traditional rules of thumb for newspaper make-up can be interpreted as applications of basic principles from art and design.

Individual news articles have an underlying structure of visible and implied points and lines that produce three well-known patterns of layout: vertical, horizontal, and brace (right angle). Furthermore, these forms convey a mood or tone: "horizontal lines express stability and repose... the vertical in art expresses life and reaching.... Diagonal lines express the greatest visual energy."

An understanding of the theory underlying news layout could lead to more effective news design. A vertical layout could express the liveliness of hard news about politics and business, and a horizontal layout could express the tranquillity of softer news such as positive human interest stories and coverage of the arts.

Two empirical predictions can be made from this rudimentary theory of article design. First, the layout of the article should affect the perceived tone of the article's content, and, second, the effects of layout on perceived tone may interact with the content characteristics of the article. The latter prediction refers to the normative dimension of the theory, that judges a layout "good" or more effective when the form is consonant with the content.

No previous empirical work on newspaper design has examined article layout, and most of the general research on the perception of form and on experimental aesthetics is not relevant. These studies take up principles such as symmetry, complexity, novelty, and organization to study much more complex stimuli.

By contrast, newspaper articles, no matter what the layout, are regular, rectangular forms. The work that has considered simple forms and/or spatial direction focuses on how perception and cognition occur, not on how form affects meaning, higher cognition, and affective processing.

Earlier work, however, did consider the emotional tone or affective value of simple forms, including a comparison of horizontal and vertical orientation. Hollingworth suggested that vertical lines convey simplicity, firmness and dignity, and rigid formality; horizontal lines, ease, quiescence, and repose; and diagonal lines, action and motion.

He offered two potential explanations: the imitative movement tendencies produced in the observer and the associations learned through encounters with lines in the natural and built environment.

Later Valentine similarly argued that lines and forms attain meaning through suggested movement-the vertical having the power to stand up and the horizontal stretching out and letting go.

Empirical studies of these ideas do associate horizontal lines with adjectives such as gentle and quiet, and both vertical and diagonal lines with joyful, uplifting, and powerful (when perceived to move upward) or sad, lazy, serious, and weak (when moving downward).

The theoretical notion of design conveying messages more or less consonant with content has antecedents in typographic research. Zachrisson proposed the term congeniality for "the correspondence between content with visual form" and showed how the principle was used in the history of typeface selection. Harrison and Morris suggested that typographic form works at the level of metacommunication.

The typographer encodes the connotations of a message to:

- Reinforce these connotations,
- Provide new and independent connotations,
- Offer neutral, or at least minimal, connotations,
- Introduce conflicting connotations.

Ample empirical evidence shows that typefaces do communicate connotative meanings, but a review of this work points out that respondents rated each typeface itself, without reference to their perception of the content or message conveyed.

The Study: The larger issue, whether the theorized relationship between form and content is open to empirical study, can be illuminated by examining the specific case of vertical versus horizontal layouts for news articles.

This study proposes to determine whether readers perceive the content of an article differently if it appears in a different layout and whether the effect demonstrated empirically matches the moods proposed in theory. If so, then the study can explore what type of effect the layout will produce for different news content.

Two hypotheses will be examined:

- That the horizontal layout will differ from a vertical layout, with respondents perceiving the tone of the horizontal as tranquil and the vertical as lively,
- That the effect of the layout will differ depending on the content of the article.

We began by creating two layout formats, one horizontal and one vertical, with otherwise identical typography. The headline type was set in 24/30-point Helvetica, and the text was 9/10 Times New Roman. The column measure ran 12.5 picas wide. Each format was reproduced on a legal size sheet, the vertical layout occupying one long column and the horizontal occupying three shorter ones.

We then selected four news articles for study: two examples of hard news, a New York Times article on Catholics lobbying state government and a USA Today article on the Lotus Development Corp. alliance with IBM, and two of softer news, a New York Times article on the discovery of a plaster model thought to be Michelangelo's study for the David sculpture and a Chicago Tribune article about the weather on an unusually warm day in early March. Two of the articles were edited slightly to make them all the same length. Each article was then formatted vertically and horizontally, to produce a total of eight experimental stimuli.

Participants were randomly assigned to one of these eight experimental conditions. The participants were 154 male and female undergraduate volunteers from an introductory advertising course at a major midwestern university. They came from a wide variety of fields within the university, were almost all freshmen, and had no formal training in either design or journalism.

This experiment, completed as part of a two-hour session devoted to television content and advertising, lasted about ten minutes. Each participant read one of the four articles in only one format, either the vertical or the horizontal layout. After reading the article, participants indicated their perception of the article by rating "the article I just read" on a series of bi-polar items.

The perception of the article, the dependent variable, was assessed using the semantic differential technique. This technique is a common one used to elicit the meaning of a target, such as a concept, object, or behaviour, by presenting a series of bi-polar adjectives as endpoints on a seven-place scale and asking participants to rate the target on the adjective pairs. The technique can be used in situations where little is known about the appropriate dimensions of meaning. The responses, indicating which place on each scale describes how people feel about the target, are particularly useful to establish the connotative, as opposed to the denotative, aspects of people's reactions, a focus of this study.

Twenty-nine adjective pairs were used in this study. All but five of the pairs were selected from the first four factors of factor analyses of previous work on the measurement of the meaning of communications. Since no previous work had examined news article layout, we added several items pertinent to newspaper design.

Three items were selected to assess the perceived importance and value of the article. One item asked for a rating on the horizontal-vertical continuum, as a check on how well the stimuli matched the intended layout, and another item, hard news/human interest, was used to check whether the article content did indeed vary along a perceived hard-news continuum.

The twenty-nine adjective pairs used in the study were first grouped into composite scales based on a factor analysis. That is, composite measures of perception were created by combining individual items that were conceptually related to develop measures that were more reliable than individual scores. To determine conceptual similarity, we conducted a principal axes factor analysis using squared multiple correlations to estimate the commonalities with varimax rotation. A parallel analysis, comparing the obtained values to those produced in random data, yielded five factors that account for 88% of the common variance across the pairs.

To arrive at the five composite measures of perception of the article, we calculated a simple average of the items loading on each factor (not weighted by factor coefficients). The first composite, labeled the comfort measure, consisted of nine pairs.

The second, the dynamism measure, comprised six items, and the third, the clarity measure, comprised five items. The importance measure emerged from three items, and the uniqueness measure from two.

Besides these composites, we used four items to construct three other measures of the perception of the article. Two items (good-bad and I like— I dislike) were averaged into an evaluation measure and were grouped together because they loaded moderately on four of the five factors but had the highest correlation with each other. The final two items were our separate checks on the layout stimuli (horizontal-vertical) and article selection (human interest-hard news). None of these four was a defining item in the factor analysis.

Where available, the matrix provides the diagonal estimates of internal consistency reliability: simple correlation for measures with two items and Cronbach's alpha for measures with more items. The reliabilities are all adequate, ranging from a low (.63) for the two-item uniqueness measure to a high (.91) for the nine-item comfort measure.

Among the first four factors, the comfort measure does not relate highly to the other three. That is, the correlations of comfort with dynamism, clarity, and uniqueness are all fairly low (less than.30). However, the perception of how dynamic and fast the article is moderately associated with how clear and unique it is rated (both.44). From the middle of the matrix, the evaluation measure is associated with the importance measure (.52).

This suggests that articles rated as good and liked were also perceived as important and valuable. These two factors, importance and value, relate to several of the first four factors. They are related strongly to dynamism and clarity and also slightly to uniqueness. The comfort measure relates moderately to evaluation but is independent of importance.

Other correlations, further down the matrix, run much lower. A moderate relationship does emerge, however, between perceptions of how comforting and gentle the article is and where it falls on the hard-news continuum. The correlation between comfort and human interest (.44) means that the more the article fits with human interest (as opposed to hard news) content, the more it was rated as comforting, pleasant, and nice.

Also, a small negative correlation between human interest and importance suggests a perception of softer news as less important, profound, and valuable. Finally, rating the article as horizontal (as opposed to vertical) was slightly but significantly related to the comfort (.19) as well as human interest (.16) measures.

These results clearly indicate that the measures of perception of the content of the article are adequate. They are reliable and relate to each other in sensible ways. Furthermore, in normative judgments of news, what makes articles good is quite complex. Good can mean not only interesting and active but also comforting and pleasant as well as logical and clear.

We next considered the effect of the two independent variables, article content and layout, on the eight dependent measures of the perception of the article. For each of the eight composite measures as dependent variables, 4 (article) x 2 (layout) analyses of variance were conducted.

Not surprisingly, the articles differed significantly on almost all measures. Most important, the rating of the articles proved consistent with expectations along the human interest versus hard news scale.

The respondents rated two of the articles (warm weather and the Michelangelo sculpture) as human interest articles. The other two (Catholic lobby and the Lotus deal with IBM) were perceived as significantly harder (although the rating was close to neutral on the scale).

This consistency is strengthened by the fact that each respondent read only one article and had no opportunity to compare it with another.

The articles also differed on all but one of the remaining measures. The Michelangelo article had the highest mean on five measures; it was rated the most dynamic and interesting, clear and logical, unique and unusual, liked and good, and important and valuable.

The weather article was the most comforting but least dynamic, clear, and important. The Catholic article was the least comforting and liked. The Lotus article was perceived to be average on five of the measures and, consistent with this, was rated as the least unique.

Next we turn to the results on the dependent measures by article layout. Most important here is the effect of layout on the horizontal— vertical scale. Clearly, when presented with a horizontal layout, the respondents rated it more on the horizontal side of the scale (4.31); when presented a vertical layout, they rated it more on the vertical side (3.43), with mean responses falling on opposite sides of the neutral centre point (4.00).

This result would seem obvious except that each participant rated one and only one article and the instructions asked for a rating on "the article I just read," not on the design or appearance of the article.

There was also a statistically significant effect of layout on one other measure, the comfort scale. Overall, when presented a horizontal layout, the respondents rated the articles as more comforting, pleasant, nice, and so forth than when the same article was presented in a vertical layout.

However, the layout did not significantly affect how dynamic the article was perceived to be. Although the horizontal format did lead to a more comforting perception of the article as predicted, the vertical layout did not produce the anticipated lively tone. Thus, the horizontal versus vertical form of the layout did have the predicted effect on one aspect of the perceived tone of the content.

Last we turned to the most intriguing question of how the two independent variables of content and layout interacted with each other in producing a perception. For those three measures, the effect of the layout depends on the content of the article. In other words, the difference made by the vertical and horizontal formats changed from article to article.

Consider first the results on the comfort scale. Here Scheffe post-hoc tests comparing the four pairs of horizontal and vertical means revealed that horizontal layouts were perceived as more comforting, gentle, and pleasant than the vertical layouts in two of the cases, the articles on Catholics and on warm weather, but not for the other two. For the Lotus article, layout made very little difference. For the Michelangelo article, the vertical layout resulted in slightly more comforting ratings than did the horizontal.

Statistically significant interactions occurred on two other measures, the ratings of clarity and human interest. Here post-hoc comparisons revealed no statistically significant differences, although the pattern of differences in direction is interesting and consistent. Overall, the Catholic, Lotus, and weather articles were rated more clear, precise, logical, accurate, and insightful in the horizontal than in vertical layout. Once again the Michelangelo article differed: the vertical was considered the clearer of the two layouts. Similarly, the Catholic, Lotus, and weather articles were rated higher on human interest (as opposed to hard news) in the horizontal layout in comparison to the vertical layout.

Readability is one possible explanation for the different results from the Michelangelo article. Perhaps the vertical seemed more comfortable when readers confronted challenging writing. To test this explanation, we did a post hoc calculation of readability. The Michelangelo article was difficult (a Gunning fog index of 13.30), but the other article from the New York Times, covering the Catholic lobby, was just as difficult in the readability test.

It is beyond the scope of this study to resolve the readability issue, but the results for the Michelangelo article make it clear that the layout affected the perception of content in complex ways. The results of the study support our first hypothesis, that the horizontal layout would produce different perceptions of the articles from those the vertical layouts produced. However, the specific descriptions of the differences were only partly supported.

Overall, the participants who read articles in horizontal layout did perceive the content as more tranquil (comforting, gentle, light, pleasant, sweet, beautiful, and so on) than did those who read the same articles in vertical layout. Vertical layouts, on the other hand, did not induce the lively tone predicted, at least when measured by how dynamic, active, fast, interesting, and so forth the participants found the article.

Perhaps the lively effect would have emerged from different stimuli, such as an additional format with the diagonal forms of brace layout, or from other articles more strongly hard news in content. Or perhaps the meaning of vertical in art does not transfer to the readerly context of newspaper design. In light of previous research on emotional tone, which found that the meanings of vertical and diagonal depend on whether lines are perceived to move up or down, perhaps the act of reading downward negates any upward motion of the layout. These possible explanations suggest avenues for further research.

The results also support the second hypothesis, that the effects of the layout would depend on the content of the article. Changing the format from vertical to horizontal produced significant shifts in how participants perceived the content. Although the article layout and content appear to interact, the nature of that interaction is not simple.

Differences between vertical and horizonal were in one direction for some of the articles, but the opposite way in the case of the Michelangelo article. The contrary example suggests that the relationship between form and content involves other dimensions (such as readability) that are inherent in all news articles as well as other media content.

This study provides an initial attempt to operationalize the distinctions news professionals make between vertical and horizontal layouts and between hard news and human interest articles. Just as the content of news differs in a wide variety of ways, and any articles (whether from real-world newspapers or not) introduce many possible confounding factors, the visual forms of news likewise differ greatly, and with similar consequences.

Even the basic distinction between horizontal and vertical arrays of type contains other factors. For example, horizontal articles have shorter columns, fewer jumps from line to line in headlines, and more jumps from column to column in running text.

At the other extreme, full pages of newspaper content in either layout present a multiplicity of confounding factors. This study strikes a balance between the abstract forms used in pure perceptual and aesthetic research and the rough-and-tumble forms found in professional practice. It begins the process of mapping the finer dimensions of news forms.

The results are especially noteworthy because the design variable (the horizontal or vertical form of the layout) influenced the perceived content of communication. That is, the participants were asked to rate the article as read, not as it appeared.

The effect emerged from a method that was also in other ways relatively nonreactive and unobtrusive. The between-subjects design exposed each participant to only one article without any chance to compare other layouts.

The study also took place as a brief segment during a longer session devoted to other, quite different media content. The effects on perception would be less surprising if the method had focused attention directly on the layout of the article by asking questions about its appearance, had used a within-subjects design that exposed participants to both layouts, or had taken place along with related experiments on visual form.

Finding a link between news articles and their layout has implications for the larger issue of the relationship between form and content in public communications. At the practical level, it suggests the possibility of mapping in detail the ways media forms influence the perception of content.

The findings reported here show that it is possible to demonstrate the effects of subtle manipulations of the form of communication on empirical measures of perception of content. The results contribute to a practical understanding of textual material used in all printed and visual media.

Our results cannot be reduced to simplistic rules of thumb for practitioners (such as "Always use horizontal layouts for calm stories") but instead teach that those small decisions do have an effect on readers. In plain terms, professionals are justified in arguing, based on this research, that design decisions matter. Because the interactions of form and content in the news are complex, practitioners need time for at least some thoughtful consideration of design decisions. This research may support their efforts to develop work routines that allow that extra margin of time to that end.

At a theoretical level, this study demonstrates the usefulness of theory-based empirical research on design issues. The effects of layout we found are consistent to an extent with theory35 and help confirm a tradition that has suggested the impact of forms on content for almost a century. Of course, a fully developed theory of the effects on communication from formal characteristics would need to take into account the perceptual process by which the impact occurs, as well as its openness to learning and change. As it develops, that theory seems likely to show that far from being a separate or trivial aspect that follows the function of communication, form is content.

Chapter 3

Critical Analysis of Visual News

That the news media can be seen as a forum within which institutions, groups and individuals struggle over the definition and construction of social reality is now something of a sociological truism. This process sees certain issues and events become the foci of collective concern or anxiety, that is, defined as "social problems," not by virtue of the objective severity or frequency of the isssue or event in question, but as a result of the organization and process of people talking and writing about them. Social problems become "visible" to mass publics, then, only when they are socially defined within "knowledge or knowledge-processing" institutions such as the mass media.

As a claims-making arena where the cultural meanings of circumstances and events are constructed, news discourse provides a rich source of data for examining how everyday issues or events come to be defined as "social problems," and offers clues as to how meaning will be negotiated and understood by the public.

Claims about putative "problems" may be constructed in numerous ways. In focussing upon the discursive accomplishment of social problems, we find a distinction routinely made by scholars between verbal or written claims (e.g., speeches or media reports), and visual claims (e.g., posters, graffiti, advertisements). Scholars who examine the role that news media play in the construction of social problems argue that different modes of discourse are likely to register different kinds of attitudinal or behavioural "effects."

For instance, distinctions are often made between how audiences will interpret "hard" news discourse, which is purportedly grounded in such uniform criteria as the preclusion of personal bias, fact—opinion separation, and the inclusion of opposing viewpoints, and "opinion" news, which are intentionally biased accounts of social phenomena that proclaim the status of the news outlet as a participant in debates pertaining to matters of cultural or political importance.

The vie wpoints expressed in opinion discourses are important when considering the role that news coverage plays in the process of social problems construction because, unlike hard news reporting, opinion discourse blends normative prescriptions and factual beliefs.

- Whilst scholarly attention has centred mostly on the examination of written or verbal discourse, visual news discourse has remained relatively unexamined.
- This study examines political cartoons, a form of satirical journalism and a type of visual opinion news discourse, and theorizes on the role of cartoons in the construction of social problems.

Political cartoons offer newsreaders condensed claims or mini-narratives about putative "problem" conditions and draw upon, and reinforce, taken-for-granted meanings of the world.

By doing so, political cartoons provide metalanguage for discourse about the social order by constructing idealizations of the world, positioning readers within a discursive context of "meaning making" and offering readers a tool for deliberating on present conditions. Cartoons "frame" phenomena by situating the "problem" in question within the context of everyday life and, in this way, exploit "universal values" as a means of persuading readers to identify with an image and its intend ed message.

In addition, political cartoons have a transitory character. This temporality, as far as the meanings of cartoons are concerned, is due not to the notion that an assertion or inference will lack meaning for some people, but that they will be more persuasive with people living under a particular set of social, historical, political, economic and cultural circumstances.

The ideological appropriation of cartoon discourse as a "mental framework" for rendering social life intelligible concerns the question of how various conceptions of the world influence and modify courses to action on which individuals and groups move and therefore depends crucially upon the situated context occupied by the reader in everyday life.

FRAMING AND TEMPORALITY IN VISUAL NEWS DISCOURSE

In what is now a classic treatise, Goffman argues that human beings organize or "frame" everyday life in order to comprehend and respond to social phenomena. When applied to studies of news, "media frames" allow readers to "locate, perceive, identify, and label" the multiple happenings of the social world in a way that will be meaningful to them.

Media sociologists have found the framing metaphor to be of heuristic value for understanding how journalists process and package large quantities of information, quickly and routinely.

For instance, Gitlin argues that media frames are "largely unspoken and unacknowledged [and] organize the world both for journalists who report it and, in some important degree, for us who rely on their reports."

According to Gitlin, media frames "naturalize" the social world apropos certain discursive conventions. In other words, media frames function as the centre or core of a larger unit of public discourse and are intelligible beca use they are "tacitly presupposed within a particular linguistic practice". According to Snow et al., media frames have the capacity to do more than merely organize experience for newsreaders—frames also serve as a "guide to action".

Conceptualized in this way, framing essentially involves selecting "some aspects of a perceived reality [to] make them more salient in a communicating text, in such a way as to promote a particular problem definition... frames, then, define problems... diagnose causes... make moral judgements... and suggest remedies".

Political cartoons operate as frames for the organization of social knowledge insofar as they make use of various rhetorical devices— metaphors, catch phrases, depictions, etc.—that purport to capture the essence of an issue or event graphically As Gamson and Stuart have argued, cartoons "offer a number of different condensing symbols that suggest the core frame" of the issue.

Cartoons help to render infinite amounts of detail into practical frameworks that are relevant and appropriate to social actors understanding the everyday world. In this sense, political cartoons channel the discursive possibilities for making sense of social phenomena; they legitimate (and thus facilitate) the grounds upon which some things can be said and others impeded.

The structural organization of knowledge about the world within visual discourse may lead to what Mumby and Spitzack (1983) call "metaphoric entrapment": "The way in which a concept is understood becomes so tied up with a particular metaphoric structure that alternative ways of viewing that concept are obscured, or else appear to make less sense".

The visual image, its caption and the accompanying label or "punch line" provide clues to the preferred meanings and the types of outcomes or consequences that the artist feels may legitimately result from the activity, issue or event being depicted.

Despite offering a rather useful framework for examining the selectivity, partiality and inclusion or exclusion of particular claims, the "framing" metaphor is theoretically limited in terms of being able to properly capture the temporal or unfolding character of social reality.

Indeed, Goffman readily acknowledged that the rules of a frame are analogous to the syntactical structures of language, a position which led some observers to critique frame analysis as far too static a model for capturing social process as it actually unfolds.

To account for the shifting and temporal character of the social world, our understanding of it and how political cartoons capture this process, Mead's theory of temporality may be useful as a complementary framework to the approach developed thus far.

According to Mead, neither the past nor future exists as an objective social fact in the sense that there is no definitive claim to universal understanding about what has already happened, what is currently going on or what is likely to happen in the future. Rather, for Mead, "every conception of the past is construed from the standpoint of the new problems of today".

Furthermore, to find justification in a permanent or "irrefragable past" is, according to Mead, an endeavour hampered by awareness that "different minds within a generation will discover different pasts".

In Mead's view, the definition of the present is always subject to change in light of the claims-making activities of social actors in the real world. Moreover, as real world events change over time, news frames must become "flexible to accommodate new contents and perspectives, and to rearrange what is already [embedded] within the frame".

When applied to studies of media discourse, this suggests that news coverage organizes our understanding of everyday life in its temporal sense, i.e., it structures our awareness of the past in ways that are shaped by, and become meaningful for, claims about current or future needs.

Indeed, as Schudson argues, journalistic accounts of the past not only legitimate the authoritative status of newsmakers as storytellers but they al so provide newsmakers and readers alike with analytic tools for describing and constructing meaning about future problems.

The temporal dimension of visual news discourse is of sociological importance not only because cartoons provide a lens through which an implied version of the past may be examined vis-a-vis present conditions but also because media accounts of social phenomena have repercussions for how societies relate to their own histories.

The claims constructed in political cartoons are illustrative of whether a society will see itself as a collective or a mosaic of different groups, whether it will interrogate its past critically or accept it as given, and whether and how it will see the past as relevant to the needs of the present and future.

Thus, political cartoons not only grasp the way in which visual discourse conveys social experience, but cartoons also help constitute the subjectivities and identities of social subjects, their relations, and the field in which they exist.

Of course, this is not to say that political cartoons causally affect how individuals and groups will define themselves in moments of stability or crisis. Rather, in speaking of visual discourse, it is probably more accurate to refer to "the persuasion to attitude, rather than persuasion to out-and-out action". Political cartoons are an optic to a "timely topic that exploits commonplaces of a transitory nature". Political cartoons are thus both informative and persuasive.

Cartoons render normative judgements about social issues by employing a variety of journalistic conventions, such as figures of speech, metaphors and irony As Savarese notes, persuasive techniques such as the aforementioned are used either "deliberately or unwittingly to convince the public of a certaln point of view (for or against something) without being explicit."

As the empirical portion of this study will endeavour to show, the persuasiveness of any claim about a given "social proble m" will resonate only when the audience being addressed is living in and experiencing a set of socio-historical conditions that enable those claims to make sense," that is, when the temporal positions of social actors correspond to the structural organization of discourse about phenomena in a meaningful way.

This chapter employs a hermeneutic framework for the analysis of political cartoons as visual news discourse. In doing so, it takes seriously Thompson's statement that discourse analysis should involve "a synthetic construction, a creative projection, of a possible meaning".

A word of caution: the political provenance of an approach of this sort requires methodological clarity, for as Purvis and Hunt state, "the discursive practices through which subjects are constituted... may have, but do not necessarily have, ideological effects."

Thus, visual discourse analysis does not reveal how newsreaders will actually interpret the content of a cartoon in the context of everyday life.

Rather, hermeneutic analysis of political cartoons allows the analyst to describe the "materiality" of discourse at the point of reader contact and provides clues to the range of possible readings readers may construct. Though a reader may be able to decipher, in whole or in part, the preferred interpretation of t he cartoon, this is not to say that s/he will accept it ipso facto.

Whereas most studies of social problems construction criticize news media for amplifying the situation and exaggerating the general public's level of anxiety, significantly less attention has been paid to examining the visual signs and symbols that accompany written news reports.

A hermeneutic analysis of political cartoons and its relation to social problems construction acknowledges the role that cultural and symbolic representations, myths, narratives and meanings play in organizing everyday experience and the interpretive process that ensues. Such a framework "accords to the various levels of human consciousness a fundamental role in the ontology of social problems".

In making a case for the sociological import of political cartoons, this study draws upon the methodological schema developed by Morris's sociology of visual rhetoric. Morris argues that cartoons capture the endless binary oppositions that organize social representations about the world and provide, as it were, a "cognitive map" for understanding everyday life.

According to Morris, cartoons establish social goals and devise the division of labour needed to attain these by:

- Establishing the source of the cartoon (i.e., artist, newspaper) as an authority or expert in relation to the event or problem in question and identifying, locating and labelling certain "other" elements as "troublesome";

- Constructing a specific frame and setting an agenda that will "create or excite interest in a problem, generate a sense of intellectual crisis, identify the nature of the crisis, pinpoint its symptoms, and propose a course of action as the effective remedy";
- Constructing a normative agenda against which newsreaders may evaluate the cartoon's characters in moral terms; and
- Promoting the "desire for action" by ensuring that the preferred message resonates with the lived experiences of the audience.

Morris also argues that four rhetorical devices will affect the contents, intended meanings and negotiated meanings of political cartoons. First, condensation involves the compression of disconnected or complexly related events to a common, singular frame. Second, combination involves the construction and organization of various elements or ideas from different domains with numerous and perhaps conflicting meanings. Third, opposition is a process whereby the complexity of a problem or event is reduced to a binary struggle. And fourth, domestication occurs when distant events remote from the everyday experience(s) of the reader are translated into concrete happenings that can be experienced as close and familiar.

To enrich Morris's schema, it is instructive to consider the ways in which visual discourse of the world transfers meaning and causal blame along a referential chain of signifiers within a particular image. Thus, I propose an additional analytic device: the notion of "transference."

Transference normally operates in an implicit way that absolves the cartoon's actors of their absurd actions or commentary by displacing blame to another, normally non-visible, actor. The notion of "transference" fits neatly within the rhetorical framework of opinion discourse in that it not only evaluates social phenomena and social process, but it also explains these events in ways that have first and foremost to do with the allocation of blame and attribution of responsibility.

One final caveat is worth mentioning here, which is that when performing empirical analysis, each of these processes—condensation, combination, opposition, domestication and transference—should not be treated independently but, rather, as strategies of "meaning-making" that operate within a broader "repertoire of cultural evaluation".

THE PUTATIVE "PROBLEM" OF ILLEGAL IMMIGRATION

Crucial to the analysis of discourse is an awareness of the broader context within which a "social problem" is constructed. During the summer of 1999, four unmarked boats in near-abysmal condition arrived at the coast of British Columbia, Canada, transporting 599 undocumented, would-be refugees from China's Fujian province.

From the arrival of the first boat, tension mounted among media observers, politicians, immigration advocacy groups and other non-governmental organizations, nationalist groups, academics, citizen groups and others, concerning Canada's commitment to provide humanitarian aid to those in need without appearing, at the same time, too lenient to unqualified, would-be refugees. Although upwards of 30,000 refugees from around the world attempt entry to Canada every year, news coverage of these events suggested that these Chinese migrants were posing a unique and significant threat to law and order and national security Consider the following quotes from some of Canada's daily news papers:

If people can get around all of those [immigration laws], then you expose yourself to all of those dangers... criminal elements and people with violent political habits and communicable diseases.

There are so many things that depress me about... the near anarchy and chaos... inflicted upon the country's immigration system that I hardly know where to start. Perhaps the best place to begin is with the debasement of our citizenship which all this entails. If all one has to do to gain this prized citizenship is jump ashore in Canada and holler "refugee," then we obviously do not think it is that valuable.

Those chinese women who find themselves paying off their passage in the whorehouses of Vancouver and Toronto will I'm sure, be gratified to know that the federal government regards them as the moral corrective to the dark stain of Canada's history.

In order for political cartoons to be cognitively persuasive, they must address a timely topic that exploits transitory, common-sense ideas. Given this, even an exceptionally humorous cartoon exploiting the subject of "migration waves" (If, in fact, readers find such a topic humorous) would have a hard time getting published during periods when fewer migration attempts are made by asylum seekers, such as during the winter months when sea voyages to Canada are a climatic impossibility. Thus, the above quotes are offered in order to provide a sense of the discursive context from which the cartoons that comprise the next portion of the study can be seen to make sense. It suggests that as "part of the gallery for news accounts", political cartoonists draw upon, reinforce and reproduce the commentary of opinion columnists, editorial writers and other claims-makers or "opinion formulators" featured more prominently in media discourse.

ANALYSIS: TWO ILLUSTRATIVE EXAMPLES

The two cartoons shown below illustrate some of the theoretical imperatives and methodological processes discussed above. To varying degrees these cartoons illustrate the rhetorical processes of condensation, opposition, combination, domestication and transference in accounting for some of the responses and reactions to the migrants' arrivals by political, media and lay audiences alike.

The primary agent of folly in both cartoons is the federal government, whose immigration and refugee policies are held up to be not only intrinsically flawed but also negative in their consequences for Canadian citizens. This supports Press's argument that satirical art in liberal democratic countries tends most often to involve appraisals of state performance, which emphasize the foolishness of government rather than private citizens and corporations. However, this criticism of government is implicit in this instance since "government" does not have a visible presence in either cartoon.

The first cartoon, "Farmers and Immigrants", was published in the Vancouver Sun—a middlebrow family newspaper catering to a socio-economically diverse readership—and shows four farmers devising a strategy for gaining financial assistance from the state. Depending on the reader's situated position in social life, s/he may find it difficult to identify with these "simple folks," leaving the question of ideological appropriation uncertain.

However, given that the cartoon has been published in a major newspaper that circulates in one of the country's densest urban areas, and especially due to the prominence of a "crisis" in farmer incomes as a salient issue in the Canadian news media at the time of the boat arrivals, it is quite possible that although the reader may not relate personally to the farmers' frustrations, s/he may do so empathetically.

Having established the farmers as comical characters, the artist then attributes to one of them a common-sense utterance suggesting that the first responsibility of the state should be to take care of its own citizens before attending to the wants of others. News coverage of these events indicated that among lay and expert communities there was widespread belief that the United Nations human rights convention enabling asylum seekers to more easily claim refugee status was too lax and opened the immigration and refugee systems up to abuse by criminals, thereby harming Canadian citizens and negatively affecting the ability of the state to meet new demands.

While the artist is not presenting himself as a purveyor of "truth" by providing information that the reader lacks, he is telling the reader what the public is already presumed to know, which is that non-citizens are getting state assistance while "needy" Canadians are not. While mocking the absurdity of the farmers' plan, the arti st indicates no disagreement with their general viewpoint or with the emotional rationale motivating their plan for action.

The prescription of action is implicit in the causal connection that changing the refugee determination process will mean that farmers can now receive help from the state. The image suggests that the federal government's priority of addressing the needs of "legitimate" citizens is so out of whack that it is more willingly attending to the demands of "illegitimate" foreigners.

Evoking emotion and promoting a desire for action is articulated here through the extreme ends to which the farmers are willing to go in order to gain the help they feel is rightly deserved. In this sense, the farmers' extremism is portrayed simply as a reaction to or mirror image of the government's absurd policy priorities. The ends to which the farmers are willing to go are also a measure of the distance between their priorities, i.e. the implied priorities of "real" Canadians, and the artist's appraisal of the state's priorities.

The absurdity of the farmers' scheme is also transferred implicitly to the absurdity of the migrants' arrivals. In this sense, transference operates as a mechanism of meaning construction that, on the one hand, travels along an articulatory chain of referents while, on the other, making this articulatory travel possible. The artist condenses the entire refugee process to a rather simple scheme, showing that if refugees can have it this easy, so too should farmers. Rather than working to change the government's stance in terms of restoring previously cut expenditures on farmer income, the characters seem convinced that a loophole in the refugee law is the surest and only means of obtaining their goal.

The clearest indication that the cartoon employs the process of combination is the linkage of increased transnational population movements with decreased government funding to Canadian farmers, insofar as the image blends into a single and complete frame, containing both the crisis in immigration and the crisis in farmer income.

The reader is invited by the cartoon characters to see the immigration and refugee system as the "cause" of (and solution to) the problems facing farmers.

The implications are numerous, but three are especially noteworthy: first, the suggestion is made that making a refugee claim is an easy, seamless process that offers great riches; second, the speaker suggests that the government bureaucracy is glaringly ineffective, i.e., the system is broken; and third the cartoon is "blind" to the positive characteristics of the country's policy so far as the presence of refugees is concerned.

The cartoon does not address claims pertaining to the miserable material realities and deprivations that normally motivate refuge-seekers to flee their homelands, and it reduces the issue of farmer funding to a binary struggle ("us" versus "them"; "our" needs versus "their" wants). One may argue that what results from this is a dialectical construction of "self" and "other" that depicts a traditional conception of Canada under threat by a surge or wave of illegal migration, an interpretation consistent with Clarkson's (2000) textual analysis and Greenberg and flier's (2001) content analysis of press coverage of these events.

This interpretation also suggests the importance of Burke's assessment that a key principle of rhetoric is "identification": "that kind of clation wherein the audience feels as though it were not merely receiving, but were itself creatively participating in the [artist's] assertion."

The second cartoon, "Brain Drain," published just after the third boat arrival (7 September) in the National Post—a right-of-centre highbrow paper with a national distribution that addresses Canada's political and business elite—establishes the artist as among a faction of Canadians profoundly concerned about the future prosperity of the domestic labour force and the economy. In this case, the federal government is again the target of blame and the agent of responsibility.

Illegal immigration, however, is used as a lightning rod for public anxiety about other pressing "social problems," in this case the current state of tax policy and the problem this has created in terms of retaining an upwardly mobile class of young professionals. While the rate of tax reduction in Canada remains much slower than in the United States, sharp drops in personal income tax rates and stimulated growth in the high technology sector in the U.S. are believed by many elite claims-makers to entice highly educated and skilled Canadians away from home.

In the second cartoon, a massive ship carrying Canadian citizens is shown to be sailing to the United States. The Canadian passengers are gesturing rudely at the small tugboat of illegal immigrants who, we are to assume given the direction of the boat, are on their way to "freedom" in Canada. In framing this issue, the cartoonist suggests that the negative effects of immigration policies are compounding the negative effects of taxation policies.

The relationship of these two issues may be interpreted in three ways: first, that problem A (immigration) has a direct and causal relationship to problem B (brain drain); second, the relationship between these problems is ridiculous, and the cartoon is intended to be ironic; and third, while the public is becoming so upset over a small number of migrants whose wish is to come to Canada, no one is bothered by those citizens who, trained and educated by Canadian tax dollars, wish only to leave the country.

The cartoon implies that, on the one hand, the economic situation at home is so bad that the government cannot keep its own citizens from seeking a better life abroad—a "good life" is thus equated with economic prosperity. Seen this way, the "mooning" can be interpreted as being directed not at the migrants per se but the government. At the same time, the cartoon implies that less skilled, illegal immigrants, who are also in search of the good life, will fill the jobs that have been vacated by the brain-drainers.

Whereas the first cartoon omits the material deprivations likely motivating asylum-seeking voyages abroad, missing from the primary frame in the second cartoon are the numerous other ships from all over the world (including the

U.S.) bringing skilled and educated foreigners to Canada.

The artist does not appear to be offering the reader concerned about the "brain drain" any direct prescriptions to action (except maybe that it's time to leave) which is to say that there is no ind ication about what should be done to resolve the double problem of too many migrants arriving whilst too many Canadians are leaving.

Not all of the rhetorical processes discussed so far are as apparent in this cartoon as in the first one. The clearest processes at work appear to be those of transference and combination: the government's foolish immigration policy is combined with and linked to the foolishness of its taxation policies; and the problem of emigrating skilled Canadians is transferred onto the problem of immigrating unwanted foreigners.

By framing the situation in this way, the cartoon is reinforcing a binary logic that positions "our" problems on the same plane with "their" presence. Moreover, the second cartoon appears to be interpolating readers across both nationalistic and economic axes, calling into question the country's ability to compete in the global marketplace, a concern rooted in the "reality" that desirable citizens are leaving in search of low-tax havens whilst undesirables are taking their places.

DISCUSSION

It is instructive at this point to recall the usefulness of Mead's notion of temporality for investigating how news discourse conceptualizes contemporary "social problems" in terms of past events, situated presents and future goals. In relation to framing analysis, the symbolic construction of temporal awareness is of paramount interest to sociologists interested in the ways in which the contours of public discourse are organized.

It is important, then, to interrogate which topics the media present to the public for consideration and debate, and how claims about these topics are presented. Part of the standard critique of mainstream news coverage of social problems is that the news fails to adequately contextualize (historically, politically, culturally and otherwise) the events on which it reports.

In Gitlin's terms, newsworthiness is measured according to "traditional assumptions in news treatment: news concerns the event, not the underlying condition; the person, not the group; conflict, not con sensus; the fact that "advances the story," not the one that explains it" (emphases in original).

This is to say that when news coverage focusses explicitly on immediacy (hundreds of illegal migrants from unknown regions of the world have arrived and declared refugee status) at the expense of examining the broader historical and political (i.e., push/pull) forces that have given rise to this (e.g., the capitalist world system is widening the gap between rich and poor countries, thereby creating a global environment more amenable to illegal transnational population movements) it is doing so in relation to a certain, taken-for-granted understanding of how the world works.

The implication of this is that fragmented or partial accounts of an event contribute to a fragmented or partial picture of the situation. The lack of historical and social context creates a discursive space where readers are less likely to fully appreciate, understand or interpret the implications of events and issues.

Mead argued that the social construction of the past is of sociological concern because of the political, ideological and material implications it poses. The image of the destitute farmer, coupled with the implicit proposition that migrants and refugees "have it easy," connotes the gradual or eruptive collapse of what were previously shared perceptions about basic certainties, that is, old modes of capital accumulation and relations among citizens are being supplanted by something new and unknown.

Such depictions situate or place "readers qua subjects" within specific discursive contexts. For example, the interpellation of the "law-abiding citizen" brings into play a certain configuration of discourses which are presupposed to motivate such subjects to celebrate "hard work" and "respect for the law," and which set up the possibility of opposition to "rule breakers" and others who eschew these normative standards.

When public debate is inflected with normative linguistic terminologies, such as referring to refugees as "illegals," "queue-jumpers" or "aliens," this attribution precludes analysis of the concrete ideological, political and economic conditions refuge-seekers might experience in their homelands.

The extent to which graphic depictions of "migrant waves" will resonate with readers and precipitate attitudinal change or the desire to act is an empirical question which requires a methodological schema different from that employed here.

Whether we are referring to visual or verbal/written journalistic texts, discourse "provides a vehicle for thought, communication and action". That is, visual news discourse has both an ideational and material quality that confronts readers and poses possibilities for changes in consciousness and calls to action.

The imaginary worlds that are depicted in political cartoons utilize comedic conventions to provide newsreaders with views of everyday life. The cartoons discussed here, addressing the "social problem" of "migrant waves," emphasize how the mundane discourses and rhetorical style germane to satirical journalism are illustrative of the discursive insinuation of concern and anxiety into daily life.

Thus, while cartoons are normally understood by readers to be satirical depictions of real events, they nevertheless draw from an available stock of public knowledge and reproduce a common-sense view of the world.

In much the same way that newspaper editorial writers attempt to pressure political decision-makers to act in a particular way, the claims embedded within political cartoons have the capacity of persuading readers toward attitudinal change.

Thus, cartoonists draw on timely topics that have already been established in the mainstream media as worthy of public attention. Though the y speak of the world in hyperfigurative terms, political cartoons are but one mode of opinion news discourse that enables the public to actively classify, organize and interpret what they see and experience in meaningful ways. Limitations to the approach developed here deserve mention. First, as a primarily textualist analysis of cartoon discourse, the approach to visual discourse undertaken here may be seen as overly speculative, that is, offering no grounded views on what audience responses to such discourse would actually be.

Whilst research into audience reception of these cartoons would no doubt strengthen the analysis, it is by no means a requisite stage through which all discourse analysis must proceed.

A broader research agenda examining lay opinions about immigration and the construction of social problems generally needs to explore not just symbolic and metaphorical representation, which has been left largely unexplored by scholars but is attempted here, but also the microcontextual contexts in which opinions about immigration and refugee issues are generated and experienced by newsreaders. Second, it may be objected that the cartoons discussed here have been misinterpreted altogether.

Satirical journalism in democratic countries is most often directed toward the decision making of government officials and so a political cartoon that targets the official state apparatuses (e.g., the Department of Immigration) is normally carried out as a "friendly gesture to ensure democracy lives up to its own ideals".

This having been said, there should be little disagreement over the general interpretation that these cartoons depict the current immigration/refugee and taxation policies as "not normal" and in need of change before things get any worse—and as attributing direct blame for the ensuing chaos to the federal government and, if less directly, to the migrants themselves.

And third, the attachment of meaning to the actions and opinions of the characters in each cartoon depends on a "cultural familiarity" and awareness of current events that is assumed by both the artist and analyst. That is, the reader who is sensitized by an awareness of Canada's historic maltreatment of Chinese immigrants will likely reach entirely different conclusions about the meanings of these cartoons than a person with no such understanding of Canadian history.

This suggests that political cartoonists will construct their accounts of "news" against a backdrop of assumptions about the social world, assumptions they expect to share with an implied readership community. Thus, whether we are talking about "food scares", "terrorism" or "migrant waves," storytellers (journalists, cartoonists, novelists, etc.) shape the form and content of their accounts with a particular understanding about who their readers are and what they will find interesting, informative and humorous.

Chapter 4

Bridging Newsrooms and Classrooms

The study examined newspaper reporting of anabolic steroid use in the six months before and after a haggard-and now deceased-football player named Lyle Alzado appeared on the cover of Sports Illustrated in 1991, attributing his inoperable brain lymphoma to abuse of anabolic steroids during his NFL career.

Scientific evidence never connected the steroid use with the lymphoma, and some of the most reputable experts on anabolic steroids have expressed considerable doubt that such a relationship existed.

Yet, journalists appear to have concluded, a priori, a relationship between the drugs and the cancer, and indeed Alzado continues to be cited as an example of what can happen from the usc of anabolic steroids. Thus, in the present study:

H3: A significant relationship will emerge between exposure to mass communication and estimates of self-inflicted harm caused by anabolic steroid use, with higher media reliers estimating greater harm.

Additionally, the ICPSR research instrument included an item asking respondents about the frequency with which they had seen anti-drug spots on television or heard them on the radio. Because the questionnaire item addressed "drugs" in general, the present study poses the following three research questions:

*RQ*1: How does the frequency of exposure to anti-drug

spots on television and radio relate to estimates of illicit drug use among professional athletes?

*RQ*2: How does the frequency of exposure to anti-drug spots on television and radio relate to attitudes toward anabolic steroid use?

*RQ*3: How does the frequency of exposure to anti-drug spots on television and radio relate to estimates of self-inflicted harm caused by use of anabolic steroids?

The following section describes how each of the hypotheses and research questions were addressed.

METHOD

SAMPLE

Funded by the National Institute on Drug Abuse (NIDA) and conducted by the Inter-University Consortium for Political and Social Research (ICPSR) at the University of Michigan, Monitoring the Future: A Continuing Study of American Youth enters the field each spring, gathering data from a national probability sample. The Monitoring the Future project seeks to identify "values, behaviours, and lifestyle orientations of contemporary American youth," monitoring changes and consistencies across time.

The present study draws on the 2003 ICPSR Form 6 data file, produced for scholars in October 2004. The following sections describe the variables extracted from the larger study.

DEMOGRAPHIC CONTROLS

Because many individuals react to questions about illicit drug use, and risk in general, from the standpoint of religion, the analyses here included a variable measuring importance of religion, in addition to standard demographic controls of sex and race, which have the potential to affect perceptions of both risk and ideal physical appearance.

The religion question asked, simply, "How important is religion in your life?" A four level response variable included "not important, a little important, pretty important, and very important." The race demographic had been collapsed by the

ICPSR into a dichotomous measure indicating Whites and members of minority races. Given the potential influence of sociological variables on normative behaviours and risk perceptions, additional controls indicated whether respondents grew up in rural or urban environments, the presence of a father and a mother in the household, and the education level of the father and the mother.

As indicated, the study also measured participation in sports, athletics and/or exercise, with the survey asking, "How often do you actively participate in sports, athletics, or exercising?" A five level response measure included "never, a few times a year, one or two times a month, once a week, and near daily."

MASS COMMUNICATION PREDICTOR VARIABLES

The 2003 ICPSR data set included items measuring exposure to the following: Magazines, movies, newspapers and television. It also included an item addressing exposure to radio or television anti-drug spots. Questions about media exposure asked, "How often do you read magazines... go to the movies... read newspapers... watch TV?" Response options included "never, a few times per year, once or twice a month, once a week, and near daily."

The question addressing anti-drug spots read as follows: "The next questions ask about anti-drug commercials or 'spots' that are intended to discourage drug use. In recent months, about how often have you seen such anti-drug commercials on TV, or heard them on the radio?" Response options included "not at all, less than once a month, 1 to 3 times a month, 1 to 3 times a week, daily or almost daily, more than once a day."

DEPENDENT VARIABLES

Questions about anabolic steroids and other illicit drugs included, first, "How many [professional athletes] would you guess use illicit drugs?" Response options included O-10%, 11 -30%, 31 -50%, 51 -70%, 71 -90%, 91-100%, and no idea. Due to relatively few observations in the 91-100% category, it was collapsed into 71-90%, thus creating a 71-100% fifth and final category (with "no idea" eliminated due to a similar lack of observations). second, "Do you disapprove of people taking steroids for body-building or improved athletic performance?"

Response options included "don't disapprove, disapprove, and strongly disapprove." Third, "How much do you think people risk harming themselves if they take steroids for body-building or improved athletic performance?"

Response options included "no risk, slight risk, moderate risk, great risk, and can't say." The last option, "can't say," was eliminated due to lack of observations, and thus the response options for the first and third questions were ordinal in nature (i.e., ordered categories of percentage estimates such as 0-10%).

Statistical analyses were therefore performed using ordinal logistic regression. The second question contained a three-level categorical response option, without order, and therefore multinomial logistic regression tested predictor effects. In all statistical operations, demographic and athletic-participation controls were entered first and tested for explanatory power, followed by exposure to the various forms of mass communication.

REGRESSION EQUATION ONE

Variables retained in this model included sex and race of respondents, as well as whether respondents grew up in an urban or rural environment. Additionally, exposure to magazines proved highly significant as a predictor of drug use estimates.

While exposures to movies, newspapers and television did not prove significant, the significance of magazine reading lends limited support to H1, moving in a direction that reflects earlier scholarship on which the hypothesis was based; that is, the greater the exposure to magazine content, the higher the estimates of illicit drug use in professional sports.

Of course, one cannot simply assume that respondents had read Sports Illustrated, or only Sports Illustrated, but the relationship moves in the anticipated direction, nonetheless. Additionally, males and members of minorities also estimated higher percentages of illicit drug use.

While significant and well suited for the model, the variable measuring whether respondents grew up in an urban or rural environment did not reveal a uniformly ordered pattern.

REGRESSION EQUATIONS TWO AND THREE

The second hypothesis focused on whether respondents disapproved of steroid use; to this end, multinomial logistic regression tested predictor effects. Importance of religion, sex of respondents, and whether respondents grew up in an urban or rural environment all showed significance as predictors, as did exposure to newspapers.

Of those who indicated that religion was not important to them, one in five said they did not disapprove of steroid use; closer to one in 10 who said that religion was very important to them did not disapprove.

Similarly, approximately one in five males said they did not disapprove of steroid use, compared to fewer than one in 10 of females. Finally, those from rural areas did not express as much disapproval as those who grew up in urban settings or suburbs.

Regarding newspaper exposure, reveals a pattern similar to the pattern for magazines; that is, respondents who indicated that they never read the newspaper expressed significantly less disapproval than those who read more regularly, especially those who read the newspaper every day.

Mirroring that, those who read the newspaper more frequently expressed greater disapproval than did those who never read the newspaper, thus lending partial support to H2. Additionally, while magazine exposure did not prove significant in the controlled regression model, a bivariate cross-tabulation did indicate that those who never read magazines expressed slightly less disapproval than did those who read magazines more frequently, again showing limited support for H2. No effects were found for exposure to movies.

Here, 21.5% of respondents who said they seldom, if ever, watch television did not disapprove of steroid use, compared to 14.4% who watched on a daily basis. On the second and third levels of the dependent measure-disapprove and strongly disapprove of steroid use, respectively-those who viewed more television expressed greater disapproval, thus adding television exposure as a variable supporting the second hypothesis.

REGRESSION EQUATION FOUR

The third hypothesis examined self-inflicted risk estimates, which displays the results of an ordinal logistic regression, indicates significant predictor effects for sex of respondents, the importance of religion in the lives of respondents, as well as newspaper use.

Here, females estimated significantly greater risk than males did, and those who said that religion played a very important role in their lives expressed greater estimates of risk than did those who indicated lower levels of importance for religion.

Additionally, while 17.4% of those who reported never reading the newspaper estimated only a slight physical risk from steroid use, 9.2% of those who read the newspaper daily indicated the same. Mirroring that pattern, those who read the newspaper daily estimated higher levels of moderate and great health risk than did those who read the newspaper less frequently and not at all. Results revealed, then, lend support to H3, which suggested that newspaper readers would estimate high levels of risk.

Exposure to magazines, movies and television did not show statistical significance in controlled regression models, but the results of bivariate cross-tabulations reveal that those who never read magazines tended to estimate the slightest risk from using steroids, as did those who said they seldom, if ever, watched television. Higher levels of exposure to both forms of mass communication tended to yield slightly higher estimates of risk. Once again, exposure to movies showed no effects.

Lastly, three exploratory research questions examined exposure to anti-drug spots and whether such exposure showed an association with each of the three dependent variables.

Cross-tabulation and chi-square analysis revealed a significant bivariate relationship between exposure to anti-drug spots and estimates of illicit drug use in sports, with those who had seen very few spots estimating slightly lower levels of use. Ofthose who had been inundated with spots, seeing more than one each day, 21.4% said that 71-100% of athletes use illicit drugs-the highest percentage of any exposure category.

With respect to the second dependent measure, disapproval of steroid use, a significant bivariate relationship again emerged, and it lent support to scholarly literature that has shown how anti-drug spots reach a saturation point and actually may become counterproductive. Specifically, those who had been inundated with exposure to anti-drug spots and those who had not seen any spots were the least likely to express disapproval.

With regard to estimates of self-inflicted health risk, those who had not seen anti-drug spots at all estimated the slightest levels of risk, followed by those who had been inundated with anti-drug spots. Respondents in the middle ranges once again tended to estimate more moderate levels of risk, indicating that moderate levels of appeal tend to be most effective in persuading adolescents to take the issue of drug use seriously-not dismissively-appreciating that such use comes with physical and psychological risks. The study now turns to a discussion of its numeric findings.

Despite being classified as a Schedule III Controlled Substance for the past 15 years, anabolic steroids continue to be used by adolescents, with about one in every 20 individuals of either sex experimenting with the drugs at some point. Proceeding conceptually from second-level agenda setting-that is, proceeding from an assumption that media have the capacity to tell people how to think about certain issues-the present study sought to identify potential effects of mass communication on attitudes toward anabolic steroids among adolescents.

In the first regression equation, both males and members of minorities estimated higher levels of illicit drug use among professional athletes than did females and Whites. From the standpoint of sport sociology, this pattern may reflect the fact that many young men, especially young men of colour, are socialized to view professional sports as a viable career option.

Sport has long been touted as a source of upward social and economic mobility for African Americans, and adolescents often communicate with athletes in the college and professional ranks about scholarship opportunities, effective training practices, nutrition supplements and so forth. Thus, they may be more familiar with the realities of drugs in sports. At the time the data analysed in this study were gathered-in 2003-steroid precursors such as andro-stenedione were still for sale in the marketplace. Additionally, in 2002, Sports Illustrated published its widely discussed Caminiti article.

Based on a previous study that identified major fallout from the Sports Illustrated report, the present study anticipated that a relationship would exist between magazine exposure and estimates of illicit drug use among professional athletes.

The study found support for this anticipated relationship, and it therefore suggests-as the earlier study did-that Sports Illustrated may serve an agendasetting function in the sports world, and particularly the youth sports world, telling people not only what to think about with regard to otherwise unobtrusive issues, but also how to think about them.

The present study does not assume that the ICPSR variable necessarily reflects exposure to Sports Illustrated; however, it does note consistency in the direction of the significant relationship. Had the ICPSR asked respondents to estimate the percentage of black-market steroids that prove to be phony, if not toxic, there likely would have been no association with magazine exposure, as that was not emphasized in 2002. Readers, in sum, were told to think about the decaying integrity of professional baseball, as well as professional sports in general, and the subsequent need to consider all performance accomplishments suspect.

The second set of hypotheses focused on whether respondents disfavored the use of anabolic steroids for performance gain. In the United States, the press has characterized illicit drug use as morally wrong, and media have characterized the use of steroids as a threat to competitive integrity and broader ideals of fairness in American society.

It therefore came as little surprise that among demographic controls, importance of religion emerged as a highly significant predictor of attitudes toward steroid use. Additionally, female respondents disfavored use in higher numbers than did their male counterparts, and exposure to both newspapers and television predicted adolescents' attitudes; that is, the greater the level of exposure to each form of mass communication, the more likely individuals were to disfavor steroid use.

As indicated, sports journalists had spent the previous year assailing professional baseball, in particular, for failing to rid itself of performance-enhancing drugs, and it appears plausible that such coverage played a role in telling adolescents and others not only to consider the issue of drugs in sports, but how to consider the issue.

As Schudson has observed, news stories rarely, if ever, challenge fundamental moral assumptions, and given the role of celebrity as a fundamental news value, the prospect of suggesting moral failure among multi-millionaire professional athletes-especially athletes thought to be egomaniacal or arrogant-would appear ideal for media companies seeking to attract attention, and in so doing, maximize profit. Mass media have long blamed individuals and their purported moral failures instead of addressing institutional explanations for the presence of certain behaviours, and the current study appears to demonstrate that pattern.

In this study, the third dependent variable measured estimates of self-inflicted harm caused by anabolic steroid use.

Consistent with studies that have addressed hyperbole in press reports, results here indicate that, in addition to demographic controls of sex and importance of religion, exposure to newspapers predicted risk estimations.

Certain journalists, like certain policymakers, often focus on the need to protect young people from drugs, typically including dramatic anecdotes and extreme side effects in media reports.

Be it the brain lymphoma of Lyle Alzado or the suicide of a teenager who had experimented with steroids, news reports sometimes assert far more than scientific evidence can substantiate, and that may explain the significant effects for newspaper exposure in the current study.

A similar phenomenon appears to have occurred with respect to anti-drug spots and attitudes toward anabolic steroids. Respondents who reported seeing more than one spot per day appeared to grow weary of the message, sometimes reporting attitudes that were more similar to those who saw no spots whatsoever than to those who had seen the spots somewhat regularly.

The study thus identified patterns consistent with studies that have addressed boomerang effects and the counterproductive nature of message saturation. "Threats of death, illness, injury or other serious harm should play a limited role in health campaigns," Atkin stressed, noting that with overly negative appeals, respondents tend to focus the most on controlling their fear, not on controlling dangers associated with a behaviour.

Overall, then, the present study demonstrates that high school seniors do pay attention to differing forms of mass communication, and that the attitudes these adolescents express tend to be consistent with attributes emphasized in media reports. Not all media outlets proved significant in this study (especially movies), but enough emerged at highly significant levels to conclude that media outlets do have the capacity to affect the perceptions of young people, and that journalists who report for such outlets must attempt to report as factually and as accurately as possible the scientific and statistical realities of performance-enhancing drugs such as anabolic steroids.

Young people appear to discount anti-drug messages that contain hyperbole and are broadcast on a seemingly constant basis. Put another way, they cannot be frightened into not experimenting with drugs. Data analysed in the current study point to education based on accurate, factual representations.

Finally, the study offers suggestions for researchers who plan to explore the subject of adolescents and use of anabolic steroids. Movie and television exposure indices had to be collapsed in the current study due to lack of variance, and scholars should follow Slater and others in continuing to explicate the concept of media use, identifying what "exposure" to visual media, in particular, actually means.

Additionally, participation in competitive sport could be a valuable covariate in identifying media effects, but competitive sport would need to be addressed independently of "exercise." In the present study, the variable measuring participation in sports, athletics or exercise showed a heavy skew toward adolescents who did some form of activity every day; it thus failed in maximizing variance and in making the important qualitative distinction between recreation and competition.

Additionally, continuous measures for the variables under study might lead to more parsimonious explanations of relationships and allow for parametric tests such as the multivariate analysis of covariance, which requires interval-level dependent measures, to examine media effects with categorical and continuous controls already in the model.

Ultimately, scholars are encouraged to pursue additional research studies that focus on mass communication and knowledge acquisition among adolescent populations, specifically with regard to anabolic steroid use and attitudes about performance-enhancing substances.

Adolescents are not curbing their use of these substances, and in fact are using them for both competitive and cosmetic purposes. As this study has demonstrated, media have the capacity to affect knowledge as well as normative attitudes about steroids, and journalists should therefore move beyond the dramatic anecdotes and narratives, emphasizing scientific findings in a more factual manner.

As an experimental industrial trend, media convergence in the sense of media mergers is still in its formative stage. Whether it will sustain its momentum to reach popularity in the nation and how its advantages balance against disadvantages are yet to be seen. While there seems to be a good deal of support for cross-media education, on some questions, professors are more gung-ho than editors and news professionals about the trend.

The legitimacy of media mergers needs repeated tests before such mergers can be truly accepted as a healthy development and a full-force education of media convergence can be seen in many in J-schools.

Media convergence, however, is not tied to media mergers. Media convergence, initiated and made possible by digital technology, is more than media mergers propelled largely by financial considerations. More pervasive is the media convergence in the senses of content convergence, technological convergence, and especially role convergence, which have occurred not only in merged media companies but also more in non-merged ones. No matter whether media mergers will continue, the other three forms of media convergence, which are not subject to the FCC regulations, are likely to continue to develop.

Most editors and news professionals in this survey are not from merged media companies. Many editors, news professionals, and professors do not yet see media mergers as beneficial to the general public and news professionals. But, their backgrounds and political views do not prevent them from sharing with other respondents with different backgrounds and political views many opinions regarding where future college journalism should go. Such common understanding is shaping a force to push forward the education of media convergence in campuses nationwide.

To better direct newsroom businesses in a converged media environment, many editors need cross-media training.

Many opportunities are out there for news companies and universities to work together to explore the issue of media convergence and provide mid-career professionals and editors cross-media technological training. It seems sensible that opportunities for learning multimedia skills should be made available both on campus and through off-site continuing education programs that are geared for midcareer news professionals as technological developments continue to evolve.

Multi-dimensional news reporting in multiple media platforms will be tomorrow's way news is presented. Therefore, dealing with media convergence in college journalism education is an urgent necessity. The wait-and-see strategy will place a Jschool in a disadvantaged position over the long run.

These findings tell us that J-schools do need to provide cross-media knowledge and experience to their students, so that the latter can better qualify for cross-media jobs in the future. Media convergence poses both challenge and opportunity to J-schools for them to reconsider their current curriculum design, sequence setting, faculty composition, teaching methods, and internship approaches.

Many professors, editors, and news professionals have expressed concern that media mergers will eliminate voices in a community, thus potentially eroding democracy. However, media mergers did not start only these days. As a TV reporter wrote in the textual answer, when she first went to Philadelphia years ago, there were five daily papers.

Now, there are two; and they are both published by the same company. Philadelphia is not alone in such media reduction.

The question is whether the general public feels that it is less well-informed than it was thirty or forty years ago and that democracy has been eroded by such media reduction prior to media convergence. This is a topic for another study. Nevertheless, students should be exposed to such a legitimate concern and learn to take a critical look at the phenomenon of media mergers.

J-schools should continue to teach critical thinking courses and meld critical thinking components into the teaching of all courses. Critical thinking is the cornerstone of journalism education. However, technology courses or course components should also be given the status they deserve. In other words, there should be a balanced curriculum to include both kinds of courses, and many cross-media related courses should contain both components.

An ideal curriculum should balance the load of technical skill-based courses and critical thinking courses, weighting toward the latter. Critical thinking and technical skills can go hand in hand rather than being competitors for class time. A balanced curriculum can help students better gather, produce, edit, and deliver quality news; more creatively and professionally materialize their ideas; and make them better fit into the market, especially in an economic downturn.

University of Florida professor Melinda McAdams, one of the Washington Post's first online editors, told colleagues that if colleges don't teach journalists the technical skills they will need, no one else is likely to take on the responsibility. "[T]he reality they'll face in the world is they'll have to teach themselves". The classroom should be the first stop for students to at least get exposed to and get familiar with the technology for cross-media practices, though they can become more proficient with such technology through internship and their future jobs.

With all that said, technology courses should not dominate journalism students' education, and technology should not be taught for the sake of technology. Technology must serve the purposes of doing good journalism. Apart from teaching students multimedia productions, new technology, and computer-assisted reporting, J-schools still need to place good writing-the very basics of being a journalist-as the top priority for all journalism students regardless of sequences or specializations.

Many respondents point out that the teaching of technology should not be at the expense of the teaching of critical thinking. Many J-schools have no more elective hours for students to learn cross-media technology within the existing parameter of curriculum. For such schools, curriculum redesign is a necessity.

Though some J-schools such as Indiana University School of Journalism have eliminated sequences to provide a comprehensive education to all journalism students, we expect that sequences will continue to exist for some time in some other J-schools. However, it has become increasingly important to encourage students from all sequences to learn technology and reporting skills from other platforms.

Sequences in many J-schools are regarded as dinosaurs because it no longer makes sense to teach broadcast and newspaper, for instance, as two unrelated bodies of knowledge in the era of media convergence and students can opt for a specialization without sequences but with professors' advice.

Most respondents expect that future journalists will be competent in producing news in multiple media platforms while being particularly strong in one area. It appears that students will be prudent to opt to specialize in either print or television and take several electives in a secondary platform, either radio or online journalism. Versatility and specialization should be equally important.

The majority of the editors do expect that future writers will be able to and willing to write for multiple media platforms, and photographers and designers will create multimedia visuals, though such expectations will not be converted into requirements in job ads for a while because "too many newsroom dinosaurs have to die off first," as Editor put it. But chances are they will, as Nelson (2002) predicted. Most editors even expect that new hires will possess multiple sets of skills to become "superhack masters of multimedia," to use Gates's term.

The needs are out there, but whether the training of such superhack masters will become the norm, as Gates questioned, largely depends on whether J-schools are willing and able to develop those "avant-garde" courses. Apart from the technological aspect, students also need to learn to cooperate and collaborate across newsrooms so as to bridge different newsroom-cultures. Students need to be both theoretically and technically prepared for media convergence.

The findings from this study show that more than half of the J-schools in the United States have redesigned their curricula or developed new courses to cope with media convergence, but professors need to be better prepared technologically.

Team-teaching is one approach to solve the problem, but will the teaching of media convergence be more effective if a professor at least knows as much as a student in a convergence class will learn? Does the Gestalt psychological principle "the whole is more than the sum of its parts" also apply in such a context?

Professors normally learned little or no technical skills while studying in a J-school doctoral programme. Their technical knowledge inherited from their previous media experience is easily dated. More than half of the professors (54%) no longer practiced news after they began to teach, as we found out in this study. In some cases, professors know less technical knowledge than their students do. Therefore, in the middle of heavy teaching and research, updating and learning more technical knowledge for teaching convergence is a big challenge for many professors.

Learning from each other during team-teaching is, of course, a good way of learning, but professors also need to find time to do self-teaching to gain more in-depth knowledge. J-schools should provide financial support for professors to attend new technology workshops. Being exposed to or involved in community news reporting in a multiple-media-platform environment, if possible, is an even better way of learning new technology for professors.

Attitude and aptitude, together with time management ability, will be the key to producing quality work in newsrooms. Since editors and news professionals are not prevalently concerned about the quality of work currently re-purposed for multiple media platforms, there is no reason for them or professors to be concerned that students being trained on multiple media platforms will be jacks of all trades but masters of none.

Students need to learn how to re-purpose their work in a timely manner and control the quality of their work in a professional manner. One editor said it best: "To sum things up, journalists need to be prepared to hit the workplace running. With limited resources and cutbacks across the country, the new hire will be the person who is the most skilled, coupled with energy and willing to be flexible as needed."

Media convergence is a comprehensive topic. Many sub-topics related to this study are yet to be explored. For instance, how can the general public benefit from media convergence? Does the general public in markets where media are converged think that they are less well-informed and that democracy has suffered in their areas? How can news professionals benefit from media convergence? What are the typical differences between the career lives of the news professionals in converged media and the career lives the same news professionals led before the media were converged? We call on mass communication scholars to continue to study media convergence to shed more light on this phenomenon that will affect every one of us.

Less than a decade ago, there was a growing concern among corporate executives, scholars, and even many editors about the future of the newspaper industry.

Newspapers faced stiff challenges on every horizon: circulation was stagnant, and a smaller percentage of the public was reading newspapers than at any time in the past half-century; the Internet was competing for the populace's time and advertisers' money; the costs of doing business were rising and unpredictable; and, for public companies, profit pressures were increasing as corporate managers sought to maintain control over their companies amidst waves of hostile buyouts and takeovers.

The message to those leading the industry was clear: change or fall victim to the forces redefining your environment.

There were also rumblings within the industry for change. Some influential editors and journalists became outspoken critics of how newspapers had lost sight of their public service mission and lost touch with their communities. These critiques often focused on the insular nature of journalism, emphasizing that journalists are "insider-oriented" elitists.

This inner directedness could be understood in at least two ways: first, journalists tended to assess the value of their work in relation to how it is viewed by other journalists, not the public; second, working close to politicians and other powerful sources resulted in reporting more focused on power struggles and personal political battles than the issues that affect the daily lives of average citizens.

Some editors - buoyed by support from scholars, a small body of research, and philanthropic organizations - became convinced that if journalists were able to get closer to readers, reconnect with their democratic mission, and begin framing stories from the centre of their communities, then newspapers would reclaim their relevance.

It is within this framework that newspaper executives - addressing both internal and external issues - re-evaluated the goals and practices of the industry and set out to put it back on course.

In 1994, the American Society of Newspaper Editors created a Change Committee, a group of editors given a 5-year period to develop and experiment with initiatives that would ensure the long-term viability of the industry.

Founded on the heels of a recession that had lingered since the late 1980s and resulted in smaller newsroom staffs and budgets, the committee focused its attention on exploring ways to:

- Reorganize newsrooms for better efficiency
- Realign journalists' values more closely with those of readers and citizens.

Change initiatives emerged that attempted to transform the culture of the newsroom, making it more externally focused on markets and readers, while internally changing the nature of work by abandoning the century-old beat system of news coverage and replacing it with collaborative teams.

"Change" became the mantra of many leading editors and executives, and the new, restructured approach to producing newspapers was labeled "strategic," "reader-driven," or "market-driven" journalism. Newsroom managers, recognizing that they lacked the organizational background to plan, execute, and monitor fundamental change, increasingly looked to outside consultants to guide their efforts and alleviate employee resistance. The process of change, seldom easy in any organization, became a target of skepticism for journalists, who worried that initiatives jeopardized core journalism values and credibility.

Organizational development (OD) is the study of how organizations evolve, learn, and adapt. This lino of inquiry is well suited, although it lias been rarely used, to explore and understand the process of change in the newspaper industry. The research reported in this monograph uses OD theory as a framework for assessing the perceptions and attitudes that top newsroom managers and rank-and-file journalists have about initiatives aimed at changing the newsroom culture.

This study also explores the impact of two newer, largely unstudied variables that have been a part of change initiatives - newsroom restucturing and the reader-oriented redefinition of news values - to better understand how journalists perceive change and its impact.

Organizational development scholarship is rooted in social psychology and management. OD scholars concede that because organizations vary in size and resources and have different goals, OD research has generally focused on one organization at a time. Argyris acknowledges that this situation-by-situation approach, which relies on on-site observations, in-depth interviews, and situation-specific variables, makes the task of generalizing results and theory building more difficult.

This study takes a different approach than most OD research and attempts to advance OD theory building and the practical understanding of ongoing newspaper change by surveying a relatively large probability sample of rank-and-file journalists and a census of top newsroom managers from 17 newspapers most experienced in ASNE-sanctioned change initiatives.

The logic of the approach is that journalists working at newspapers that have experimented with similar change initiatives create a population of cohorts who have clear perceptions regarding change based on their common experiences.

This commonality should permit valid research that extends beyond single organizations and site-specific variables, producing results that can benefit newsrooms embarking on change initiatives. Accordingly, this study extends newspaper change research by addressing the problem differently, both in terms of its theoretical framework and methodological design.

The extent to which change initiatives can be tied to economics is uncertain. By 2001, a recessionary national economy led the nation's largest public newspaper companies to downsize their workforces between 5 and 10% to maintain profit levels attractive to investors.

However, the late 1990s, a period of a strong economy and fast and furious change, saw the same high profits that had characterized the industry a decade earlier. Publicly owned companies, which account for nearly half the nation's daily circulation, returned an average profit of 20.7% in 1998 and 22.2% in 1999. Advertising revenue was also at record levels, reaching $46.3 billion in 1999, the eighth consecutive year of record highs, casting doubt on prognosticators who only a half-decade earlier had predicted the Internet would spell doom for newspapers.

Following the lead of the Change Committee and continuing today under the rubric of change, newsrooms are being reorganized, news values are being redefined, and the nature of newspaper journalism work is changing. The seriousness of prominent editors leading this effort can be understood by their numerous references to the need to "blow up" the newsroom and its associated routines and values;

another editor, using a less violent metaphor, claims his goal for change is "cultural transformation".

However, a large body of organizational development scholarship indicates that changing an organization's culture (its values and beliefs and form and function of work that supports them) is not easily accomplished, and understanding the need for change is not often enough to convince employees, and even members of management, to accept change.

CHANGING ORGANIZATIONAL STRUCTURES

Following a national manufacturing trend, by the mid-1990s, newspaper managers began disassembling the assembly line, creating instead self-contained work teams. The team-based structure flattened the traditional top-down manufacturing hierarchy, grouping editors and reporters into 6- to 10-member teams responsible for reporting, writing, editing, and packaging news in their coverage areas.

The most controversial changes have come in those newsrooms using cross-departmental teams. section development teams at The Los Angeles Times include people from advertising, classified, editorial, marketing, and research. Former Times Publisher Mark Willes said these teams are necessary to create a stronger marketing consciousness at the newspaper.

Journalists and scholars have questioned whether cross-departmental teams compromise the traditional "wall" between the news and business sides of news organizations. This controversy was fueled in October 1999 whon the Times created a special Sunday magazine promoting the new downtown Staples Centre. Written by journalists, the section garnered nearly $2 million in advertising, which the paper split with the Staples Centre.

Perhaps more indicative of the direction the industry is heading is that 63% of the editors responding to a 1999 Editor & Publisher survey agreed that there should be more cooperation between news departments and business/ marketing departments, while 29% disagreed. Clearly, editors are becoming more active in marketing. A 1998 study found that 57% of the 192 newspapers surveyed have marketing teams that include editorial members.

A less controversial change that none the less has had an impact on the nature of newspaper work has been the reorganization from a beat system to a team system of news coverage.

Some of the reorganization plans of newspapers in this study are described briefly. After a year of planning, the Si. Louis Post-Dispatch scrapped the beat system in 1999 for topic-driven teams. Staff had to reapply for jobs, 19 general assignment positions were redefined in the team structure, and editors became team leaders. Each team created a mission statement and set its goals.

At The State, the news and features desks were abolished to facilitate a team structure. The paper also created an "office of the managing editor," which at any given time could be staffed by one of five different people. At many newspapers, changes in newsroom structure have brought with them new job titles that many news veterans would not recognize, including duty officer, maestro, circle editor, news manager of public life, and change facilitator.

At the Grand Forks (N.D.) Herald, editor Mike Jacobs said the change to reporting teams was initially resisted. He learned that change requires people in leadership positions who believe in change and are committed to executing it. To help staffers work through their problems with change initiatives, Jacobs brought in a marriage counselor to serve as "a listening post" between staff and upper management.

The Dayton (Ohio) Daily News adopted a "newsroom without walls" concept. Conceived by an architect, the reorganization eliminated departments and placed newsroom staff in gathering and producing teams. Managing editor Steven Sidlo said the model is "a system that breaches our walls of tradition, encouraging a more effective, fluid use of our resources".

In Portland, The Oregonian's "warp-speed nine" initiative prompted managing editor Peter Bhatia to joke

"Reorganization 'R' Us." More than 80 jobs were posted in the newsroom as open assignments. Nearly every writer, regardless of experience or seniority, had to reapply.

The final result was 10 teams, with a flattened newsroom hierarchy that saw former editors become team leaders. Bhatia, aware that the flattened hierarchy offers fewer career advancement opportunities, said, "The satisfaction that people will get from this system is in the quality of their work and what they put in the paper as compared to a traditional careerpath".

Flattened newsroom hierarchies have resulted in some editors returning to the reporting ranks. In Tacoma, Wash., editor David Zeeck's reorganization of The News Tribune resulted in 34% of his staff changing jobs, and 23% of the editors becoming reporters. At the Wichita (Kan.) Eagle, the copy desk was eliminated in 1995 and copy editors were assigned to reporting teams.

Former managing editor Janet Weaver said "blowing up the copy desk" resulted in eight more staff reporters. Weaver said the reorganization took the Eagle from a six-tiered hierarchy to just three tiers: editor, managing editor, and three equal teams - content, organization, and presentation.

Stepp writes the goal behind eliminating the editors at many papers was not only to cut payroll, but to simplify chains of command and reduce the number of news managers resistant to change.

CHANGING NEWS VALUES

Aware that their readership is stagnant and influence declining, newspaper managers and journalists have been reexamining their news values.

This introspection has manifested itself in several ways: an increased marketing consciousness, a desire for more credibility, the involvement of readers in deciding news and how it should be reported, and a sense the media are failing to live up to their historic democratic role of informing people of issues important to successful governance.

American Journalism Review, in a 2000 cover story titled

"Reader Friendly, " reported that the emerging culture of restructured newsrooms around the country is characterized by:

- Enthroning readers as the "invisible giants," elevating them to near equal partners in decision making;
- Erring on the side of caution rather than aggressiveness, rejecting stories that might offend readers as lacking compassion or sensitivity;
- Promoting cooperation with everyone, from City Hall to the paper's advertising departments.

The long-time taboo of "pandering" to readers has been swept away by an attempt to reverse what some editors have called a "disconnection" between newspapers and the public. Following a series of meetings called the Journalism Values Institute in which 30 editors from around the country debated the problems of the industry, Peck (1996) wrote, "The essence of these evaluations comes down to this: American journalists continue to say they practice good journalism in the public's interest - but the public doesn't believe we deliver".

Editors left the meetings agreeing that newspaper content includes too much gossip, not enough substance, bias but no balance, and a preoccupation with conflict and few solutions. The Oregonian's Bhatia summed up the problems: "Our comfort zones are painting the world in black and white. And our comfort zones are seeing the traditional good side and evil side of whatever issue it might bo. We've got to blow that up".

Many of the editors most active in the ASNE Change Committee borrowed ideas from and adopted the language of civic (or public) journalism. Civic journalism broadens the concept of journalistic social responsibility into a more active role, with the goal of journalism becoming a catalyst for the revival of civic life by promoting citizen engagement and dialogue.

Merritt insists the practice of civic journalism requires journalists to abandon several common and traditional practices, including: valuing conflict as the primary narrative device, framing issues at extremes, maintaining an adversarial role with institutions, treating the readers as audiences rather than participants, and insisting that journalism credibility arises from detachment.

Stopp (2000) wrote that a cross-country tour of newsrooms left him impressed by how many newsrooms were using the language and techniques of civic journalism. he notes that when he raised this issue many editors and journalists dismissed it, suggesting civic journalism is a project-driven formula that they don't understand. Stepp, however, concluded: "Perhaps the resistance to the civic journalism label simply underlines how much some of the techniques have seeped into the newsroom groundwater".

CHANGING THE NEWSROOM CULTURE

Nearly all editors who have involved their newsrooms in change initiatives have suggested the key to making change work is to create a new culture. Weaver said changing the newsroom culture requires "getting the staff to think of the whole paper, as opposed to their own story or small piece they contributed." She said that reporters need to be trained to work in a new system, as many lack the editing, headline writing, and design skills required in the team structure.

Managers, too, have more pressure, as the staff is often competing for the attention of fewer bosses. And, because of the changing nature of journalism work, job performance evaluations need revision to reflect the standards and goals of a new system. She admits that "newsroom stars" under the old system often fool stifled by the team structure. Teams require a "new breed" of journalist with different personality traits and skills than the "lone wolf" who worked well alone and often produced breakthrough stories.

Sue Deans, editor of The (Myrtle Beach, S.C.) Sun News, said for change initiatives to work staff members need to understand that change is a constant; it will not go away after a short time or a few experiments. The two "core issues" of change are continuous product improvement, and keeping aware of what readers want and the market demands. She said changing the newsroom culture requires emphasizing "passion" for the newspaper business and:

- Impressing on people who do not want change that they must change or leave;
- Eliminating "silo" thinking by creating cross-departmental approaches to work and evaluating work quality;
- Staying focused on strategy and on the market.

Campbell, who resigned in April 2000 as Si. Louis Post-Dispatch editor after a stormy 3 1/2 years, had embarked on an ambitious attempt at "cultural transformation" at the paper. He claims the existing newsroom "judgmental culture" is part of the problem with American journalism, and he attempted to change the Post-Dispatch's culture from one based on "judgmentalism" to one based on "collaboration."

By the millennium, the ideas for change that began in a couple dozen newsrooms in the mid-1990s were becoming the industry norm. Stepp (2000) wrote:

"From civic journalism to New Directions for News, from credibility reforms to the Committee of Concerned Journalists, a host of foundations, trade groups and other forces have been pouring millions of dollars into attempts to remodel how journalists think and act".

IMPACT OF CHANGE ON MORALE

Change initiatives have required journalists to rethink some fundamental principles of their work: their sense of news, audience, organization, and even the purpose of journalism. Signs of eroding morale were present before change began in the mid-1990s, and morale problems in relation to change initiatives have been reported in trade journals.

Columbia Journalism Review, in a 2001 cover story, reported that its national survey found 84% of the responding journalists indicate that low morale is widespread in their newsrooms. This finding is supported by a 2001 ASNE study that found 54% of the respondents saying they weren't sure if they would remain in the newspaper business.

Among the reasons for low morale: ineffective leadership, management and editors who don't listen, not enough opportunity to be creative, and increasing budget pressures that arise from the drive to maintain high profits.

Underwood wrote that the mid-1990s layoffs and a widespread belief that management used downsizing as a way of getting rid of unhappy journalists - many of whom were aggressive, good journalists in a traditional sense - have left "a deep and growing cultural divide between newsroom managers and their reporters".

Many veteran reporters think that change initiatives - and associated reader-driven, marketing consciousness - made newspapers look needlessly desperate in the late 1990s when newspaper companies were posting record profits.

Stepp wrote that changes in management goals may mark a historic period of journalism. Journalists always considered themselves bestowed by the First Amendment with special status, feeling they were public servants who value social responsibility; however, he writes, "You feel it in virtually every newsroom, the sag, the deflation, the suspicion that a special way of life is teetering".

The frustration is not limited to rank-and-file, but includes editors who face the challenge of leading changes they may not understand or support.

Stepp (2000) wrote that editors are no longer seen by their staffs as in control of the newsroom, as publishers look for top editors who understand "a different approach" based on what the market needs and the reader wants.

This leaves editors less time to focus on journalism and interact with their staffs, further widening the gulf between managers leading change and rank-and-file.

The Newspaper Association of America surveyed more than 2,600 newspaper journalists who left their jobs in the mid-1990s, trying to find the factors that caused journalists to leave the profession.

The NAA found, beyond the expected reasons of stress and long hours, that people left newspapers because of low morale, lack of advancement, and perceived inequities in pay and promotions. The authors conclude all of these reasons are issues that management can control.

ORGANIZATIONAL NEWSPAPER RESEARCH

In the past half-decade, a line of organizational newspaper research has looked at the impact of public ownership (companies that publicly trade stocks) on corporate goals and identifying the level of newspapers' market orientation. This section reviews three areas of research that were relevant to the conception of this study: early organizational studies, the recent profit and market-orientation research, and the few attempts in recent years to study the process of managing change in the nation's newsrooms.

Breed and Argyris (1974) were pioneers in newspaper industry organizational research. Breed, a sociologist, suggested that role theory provides a model that explains the organizational relationships in newsrooms. he asserted that all newspapers, whether management and journalists admit it or not, operate under the influence of a publisher policy.

The publisher, as a representative of ownership, has the authority to set and enforce the policy. Journalists learn the policy, which is often covert because it betrays journalistic values, through experience and observation. The social norms and conventions of the newsroom teach journalists how and when to conform or deviate from the policy. Breed concluded:

Thus the cultural patterns of the newsroom produce results insufficient for wider democratic needs. Any important change toward a more 'free and responsible press' must stem from the various pressures on the publisher, who epitomizes the policy making and coordinating role.

Argyris, an organizational development scholar, studied one of the nation's largest newspapers for 3 1/2 years, exploring the paper's internal dynamics and how they related to problems of press credibility. he also provided the paper an organizational development programme and advised during its implementation. In his book, Behind the Front Page, he concluded the internal system at the paper helped create policy clashes, one-upmanship among reporters, and fear of authoritarian bosses. He found the greatest resistance to new ideas came from mid-level editors and managers, who, despite acknowledging the need to change, would not participate in organizational efforts at change. Discussing his frustration about why the problems his systems analysis identified were not addressed, he wrote:

The reason is not (italics Argyris) a lack of motivation to solve them on the part of top management. The problems will not be solved because the individuals and groups behave in ways that create a living system which teaches them (they become acculturated) to be hard of hearing, to be unable and unwilling to take action on threatening issues.

Gassaway used observation and survey to study the social construction of a journalist's reality. he found news judgment decisions were most often the result of "preordained news," determined by coverage beats and how editors decide to use their resources. Editors and reporters struggle for control of information because they often disagree on what should be communicated to the public. Editors' authority is derived from organizational hierarchies, but reporters can deny editors' authority by controlling information obtained in iiewsgathoriiig. Gassaway concluded editors and reporters negotiate for control to prevent confrontations and reduce resorting to power.

Jeffers and Lewis studied organizational communication at a midsized newspaper and found rank-and-file journalists perceived their communication with their immediate supervisor and publisher as poor. They suggested the organizational climate could be improved by increasing the amount and frequency of communication at all levels. The authors concluded their study supported the findings of Pincuss, Knipp, and Rayfield, who found rank-and-file employees' communication relationship with their immediate supervisor is a predictor of job satisfaction; however, employees' sense of having meaningful communication with top-level managers was as strong a predictor of satisfaction as immediate-supervisor communication.

In the mid-1990s, several scholars began to assess organizational structure and goals, often considering profit motive and its impact on normative journalism values.

Deniers integrated organizational and economic theory in his book, The Menace of the Corporate Newspaper: Fact or Fiction?, to define the corporate newspaper, its characteristics, and organizational dynamics. Demers asserted that corporate newspapers are complex bureaucracies controlled by trained managers, not owners. These managers are best understood as innovative professionals or "technocrats" who are morn interested in professional, organizational, and technical goals than profit goals.

Demers juxtaposed the roles of managers to those of owners, defining the latter as "capitalists" most interested in returns on their investments. In the 20th century, managers replaced owners as the driving force; in corporations because llie organizations had become complex bureaucracies that required professional management.

Further aiding the transition was the death of the original owners, whose influence was dispersed over time and divided among heirs. Deniers wrote the result is that corporate newspapers are efficiently managed and structured to maximize profits, but they place less emphasis on profit than non-corporate newspapers, which tend to be family-owned, less bureaucratic organizations. In two studies, his results indicate that newspapers become more rigorous editorially as they become larger, more complex organizations.

In studies that both support and refute Deniers' work, Beam studied the conditions that influence newspapers' market orientation and whether market orientation affects content. To define and measure market orientation, Beam explored the extent that newspapers:

- Have one or more departments active in understanding customer needs and the factors affecting the needs,
- Share this information across departments,
- Have various departments engaged in meeting select customer needs.

He found that ownership by a large group is the most important predictor of a newspaper's market orientation, suggesting the corporate parent may not be involved in specific content decisions but is more likely to require certain general processes be followed in making content decisions. he concluded that traditional journalistic values are important at market-oriented papers, and while more market-oriented newsrooms are more committed to special interest and visual content, they are not less committed to traditional content, including public affairs.

Beam (2000) has also found that newspapers that are part of privately owned companies are more market oriented than those of public companies.

Using his survey data, Beam (2001) then chose 10 newspapers for a content analysis - 5 papers with strong market orientation and 5 papers with weak market orientation. he found the majority of items on page one of both orientations was "public sphere" content, which includes government affairs; however, the percentage of public sphere items on page one for weak market orientation newspapers was significantly higher (65.6%) than for strong market orientation papers (54.9%).

Overall, Beam analysed the display pages (section front or topic lead page) and found papers with strong market orientation have proportionately more items devoted to private life, coping, and sports, while proportionately fewer items about government and public life.

Martin (1998) compared profits earned by 15 public newspaper companies to profits of publishing companies and yields from corporate and government bonds over an 11-year period. For the entire period, newspaper profits averaged 90% higher than publishing companies, 78% higher than government bond yields, and 54% higher than interest payments from corporate bonds.

Using a scale created by an economist that labels profits 50% above those of comparable measures as "excessive," Martin found that in 23 of 33 annual comparative indices (70%) the newspaper companies in the sample earned excessive profits. In some cases, these excessive comparative profits occurred in the early 1990s during what an analyst called "the biggest advertising recession since World War II".

After newspapers embarked on broad, and in some cases bold, change initiatives in the 1990s, a few researchers began to study these initiatives through the lens of organizational development. Gentry observed while a small California daily embarked on several change initiatives aimed at better aligning its content with community interests.

The year-long efforts, orchestrated by New Directions for News, led Gentry to conclude the following elements were essential for successful newspaper organizational change:

- Strong leadership;
- Management communication about: why change is needed, management's vision, and new performance standards;
- Staff involvement in the change process;
- Management rewarding correct behaviour and extinguishing improper behaviour;
- Anticipating problems of acceptance and implementation.

Working a few years later with the American Press Institute, Gentry developed a model he calls "A Roadmap for Change" that added several variables, including:

- Prechange analysis of the current culture to determine the extent and types of changes needed;
- Use of mission statements to clarify core values for employees;
- Flexible management strategies and putting people in the proper roles to execute them;
- Enabling structures, such as job training;
- Creating visible symbols of the new culture.

Testing the model, Gentry surveyed management and rank-and-file at six newspapers and found management thought it was doing a better job than the staff thought it was doing on all 10 elements of change the study addressed.

In a longitudinal case study, Gade and Perry measured newsroom employees' perceptions of change initiatives led by editor Cole Campbell from 1996-2000 at the Si. LOUJS Post-Dispatch. Over 4 years, Campbell, known as an industry innovator, had some success making news values more reader driven, but the 1999 reorganization of newsroom coverage from beats to teams left much of the staff confused about their roles and job responsibilities.

Campbell's embrace of public journalism did not resonate with a majority of the staff. Morale declined and was lowest among respondents with management duties. Respondents consistently indicated they wern open minded toward change until after reorganization, which apparently was the last straw in a series of changes that underscored Campbell's tenure as editor (he resigned under pressure in April 2000). Over the course of the study, respondents consistently indicated that they failed to see how change initiatives contributed to better journalism.

At a time when cross-departmental teams were still new to the industry, Sylvie studied how department heads of news, advertising, and circulation perceived their identity and ability to cooperate with each other. News managers named advertising as the most difficult department, while the advertising directors named the news editors as least cooperative.

News editors showed a significantly greater tendency to say more cooperation between departments is needed. Sylvie concluded the news managers exhibit a "surprising sensitivity" to market-oriented concepts, which gives credibility to journalists' anecdotal claims that the newspaper industry is moving toward a greater market orientation.

A meager amount of research exists on newspaper team performance. Russial studied changes in health and science content at The Oregonian after that paper created a Health and Science team. He found that the team produced more coverage that received better play (Al or Metro section front) than before the team was created. Russial suggested that although his study did not measure coverage quality, the creation of a team-based system represents a realignment in the use of newsroom resources that may have important consequences on news content.

Neuzil, Hansen, and Ward surveyed Minneapolis Star Tribune and St. Paul Pioneer Press journalists working in teams and found most thought they had less authority and less success getting story ideas in the paper than before teams were created. Those who thought they had less authority also said they were unsure of the chain of command, worked on larger teams, and wore reporters more than editors. The researchers concluded if a goal of team work was to "empower" journalists by granting them more autonomy to be innovative, this goal was not being met.

In sum, trade journals and a developing body of research provide evidence that newspapers are changing in some fundamental ways: flattening organizational structures, replacing traditional beats with teams, revising job descriptions and required skills, rethinking organizational values, and redefining news judgment.

USING ORGANIZATIONAL THEORY TO MAKE SENSE OF CHANGE

The study of "organizations" is a relatively new discipline. Drucker wrote that "no one in the United States - or anyplace else - talked of Organizations' until after World War?" Drucker said that the modern idea of an organization - as a purposely designed and specialized entity that is defined by its task and is distinct from society's other institutions - emerged in the second half of the 20th century with what he calls the "management revolution." Initial theoretical assumptions of this revolution were largely shaped by turn-of-the-century scholars: Taylor's views on "scientific management" and Weber's ideas on the rational and specialized bureaucracy. This organizational model is characterized by a hierarchical division of labour where managers are the "thinkers" and laborers are the "doers". Employees develop highly specialized skills that increase performance and productivity, while management's job is to ensure the conditions exist for the organizational "machine" to run smoothly.

Recognizing that organizations must evolve and adapt to survive in changing environments, Lewin suggested a "natural" (as opposed to mechanical) metaphor to explain organizational dynamics; change, he wrote, can be best understood and managed through a process of "unfreeze, change, refreeze." These early attempts to understand organizations and their dynamics prepared the intellectual soil for the growth of organizational development, which attracted the interest of U.S. scholars and corporate managers in the last quarter of the 20th century as the changing global marketplace threatened U.S. dominance.

Although Taylor's and Weber's (and to a lesser extent Lewin's) ideas are considered outdated, they have proven resilient and modest adaptations of them are still very much alive in both theory and practice. Bergquist wrote that most organizational theorists have conceived organizations as pendulum-like mechanisms, which value "simplicity in motion" and homeostasis. When organizations experience turbulent times, they tend to seek equilibrium by returning to their previous form and function.

However, the structured and predictable environment in which U.S. companies once thrived no longer exists, and Bergquist contends a more accurate metaphor in the postmodern world is that of the organization as a liquid, "poised on the edge of order and chaos". The liquid system, he wrote, contains at the same time both elements of stability and change, especially along the edges, or shifting boundaries.

In an organizational sense, it is the shifting boundaries that offer potential for understanding the change process. It is these places on the "edge" where innovation occurs and where organizational traits such as mission, communication, and leadership become integral to success.

In perhaps the seminal book on organizational change and development, Kanter wrote American companies that value "innovation" are better placed to use their employees' creative capacities and stay ahead in changing environments. Interviews with 65 corporate executives led Kanter to conclude the innovative companies are integrated (my italics); they grant power to individuals to encourage fresh thinking and create opportunities for new ideas to cross organizational boundaries.

She juxtaposed integrated companies with "segmented" companies, which are characterized by an "ovorspecification" of resources and consider themselves successful when every segment works well independently, without much need for communication. Segmented companies, Kanter wrote, seek stasis, because they are constantly looking to the past to define the future; accordingly, habits and routines that maintain the course are valued.

Kanter identified five major building blocks in change initiatives that increase the company's capacity to meet new challenges:

- *Departures from tradition*: Activities or ideas that require the organization to think and behave in new ways.
- *Crisis or galvanizing event*: A critical event that cannot be solved by traditional means. This allows a non-traditional idea to be pushed forward.
- *Strategic decisions*: The opportunity for management to create a vision by articulating a deliberate and conscious direction.
- *Individual "prime movers"*: People who push the innovative strategy through the organization by communicating strategic decisions and manipulating the symbols of the organizational culture toward the direction of change.
- *Action vehicles*: Mechanisms that allow new action. These include training programs, successful results for people using new practices, new organizational rewards that support new practices, and ongoing messages of the benefits experienced by individuals using the now practices.

Kanter wrote that managers need three new sets of skills to operate effectively in integrated, innovative environments: "power skills" used to persuade others to invest in new initiatives; ability to manage problems associated with teams and greater employee participation; and understanding of how organizational change is designed and constructed. She concluded that "the art and architecture of change" requires managers to abandon their reliance on traditional analytical tools, which measure what already exists or has occurred.

"Change efforts have to mobilize people around what is not yet known, not yet experienced... they require a leap of faith that cannot be eliminated by presentation of all the forecasts, figures, and advance guarantees that can be accumulated". Accordingly, the paradox of managing changes, she wrote, is "there needs to be a plan, and the plan has to acknowledge that it will be departed from".

Most attempts at organizational development involve efforts to transform an organization's culture. Schneider, Brief, and Guzzo wrote that the values and beliefs that are the foundation of an organization's culture can be changed by focusing on the tangible things - such as practices, policies, and procedures - that define daily life in the organization. It is these tangible phenomena that comprise an organization's climate, and for real cultural change to occur, management must change the climate in which the employees exist.

The authors contend that many efforts at cultural change are focused on "macro" issues such as values and beliefs, while overlooking the more tangible issues that create the organizational climate in which employees experience everyday life. They wrote: "Sustainable organizational change is most assured when both the climate - what the organization's members experience - and the culture - what the members believe the organization values - change".

Successful companies have increasingly educated workforces, and they are creating cultures that are more innovative and flexible. The new, desired culture is one in which power and accountability are shared between managers and employees in a manner that allows companies to respond quickly to challenges and opportunities. The goal of these efforts is to unleash and channel the power of employees' knowledge in an organizational "culture of contribution."

Fisher acknowledges that this is a major cultural shift for most U.S. companies because - unlike the Japanese, whose collective society adapted easily to a team-building, egalitarian corporate model - "America's professional workers value their individualism and often express it in counterproductive ways". Corporate America also clings to some values that work against creating a culture of contribution; most prominent among these, Fisher wrote, is the corporate view on job attachment.

Workers are expected to accept such surprises as downsizing, job reclassification, or relocation with quiet stoicism, which contradicts companies' claims they are striving to empower employees as co-partners with management. Fisher contends that U.S. managers need to be aware that there is no single ideal corporate culture; rather, corporate culture is better understood as a combination of macro and micro cultures.

Many senior managers claim to embrace a culture of contribution, but Fisher contends that few have ideas about how to put a programme or process in place to let the transformation occur. On the other hand, the changing nature of professional work, driven by new technology, has organizations acting as though they are horizontally constructed even though most corporate organizational charts still reflect a vertical hierarchy.

If management is to be successful creating the culture of contribution, it must cede some of its "span of control" and forge a "span of relationships," with workers and managers acting more as "learners than knowers, listeners than tellers, partners than adversaries". Fisher cautions that management should not be too optimistic that a reorganization into teams will solve the ills of the company; rather, a culture of contribution is more likely to develop in a climate where workers are trusted and have the freedom to think and act like owners.

At the core of many organizational development efforts over the past two decades has been the restructuring of organizations from vertical hierarchies into more horizontal, "flattened" designs where most of the work is done by self-directed teams. In theory, teams "empower" employees by giving team members more decision-making authority and eliminating vertical chains of command.

However, empowerment efforts not only require management to share power, they also demand that individual team members think differently about the nature of work. Labianca, Gray, and Brass (2000) found that empowerment efforts require a change in "schemas" - cognitive frameworks that give meaning to experience - for both management and lower level employees. The authors analysed a 2-year organizational development project involving team building and increased participation of lower level employees in decision making.

Before the project, the "schema-in-use" for organizational decision making was that management should maintain control of events and decision making, and this schema was understood by both management and employees. The expected new schema for management included: making the organization more team oriented and collaborative, empowering lower level employees, aligning organizational structure effectively, and keeping current workers.

For the ruiik-aiid-filu, the expected new schema was characterized by working on team building, creating more avenues of communication, and encouraging employees to air their "beefs." The authors found: a great amount of employee skepticism at the outset about the likelihood of real change; despite a series of organization-wide meetings, interviews revealed both managers and nonmanagers were unclear about the project's goals; resistance was heightened when managerial behaviour failed to conform with its stated expectations; and management incorrectly assumed that employees would postpone judgment of the reorganization plan until after it was implemented. The authors concluded that employees' resistance to the empowerment plan was motivated less by intentional self-interest than by constraints of well-established, ingrained schema.

Randolph (2000) wrote that few managers or employees fully understand how empowerment affects traditional patterns of corporate hierarchy and behaviour. Management confuses empowerment as "giving people the power to make decisions," and this perception misses the essential notion of empowerment, that a great amount of power already exists in employees' knowledge, experience, and motivation.

Rank-and-file perceive empowerment to mean they will be given the freedom to make all major decisions about their jobs. Randolph wrote that empowerment efforts do require a cultural shift; however, the shift is from one person making decisions to team-based shared decision making. he asserts that empowerment makes employees more accountable than the older, hierarchical culture, and it is best understood as a strange combination of opportunity and risk.

An organization moves toward team-based empowered culture through three stages:

- Starting and orienting the process of change,
- Making changes and dealing with discouragement,
- Adopting and refining empowerment to fit the organization.

Each stage utilizes three "interlocking tools" - sharing information, creating autonomy through boundaries, and replacing the hierarchy with self-directed teams.

Hirschhorn, a management scholar whose work focuses on team-based organizations, wrote that the entire philosophy of management is changing as corporations flatten hierarchies and adopt new team environments. Successful managers develop roles for team members and "manage the boundary," communicating the company's needs to the team and the team's needs to the company. Managers lead by creating a structure in which the team can be successful and by positioning themselves to defend the team's efforts.

Managers must realise they are both cause of and solution to many team problems. To be successful, managers must show their vulnerability (a traditional management faux pas) and willingness to learn from team members. Exhibiting these traits shows that managers are open to new ways to solve problems and encourages team members to respond to challenges that can enhance team performance.

Although development efforts are characterized by dispersing power throughout an organization, management's ability to provide leadership remains a key to organizational success. Kets de Vries, a psychologist who focuses on the "psychodynamics of organizations," wrote that organizational culture depends on the psychological contract that exists between its leaders and followers. Effective leaders need to: articulate a vision of the future; create symbolic impressions to communicate the vision; build networks; empower followers; make choices (often painful ones); and keep perspectives of the followers based in reality.

He wrote that the leader/follower relationship a process of social comparison that involves power, authority, hero worship, flattery, ambition, and attention seeking - provides tremendous opportunities for distorted management reasoning. The key is for managers to "preserve their hold on reality."

Trust is essential for a healthy organization, and trust is dependent upon communication, support, respect, fairness, competence, and consistency on the part of the leaders. he concluded, "In order for the leader to understand the meaning of these words, it is important that he or she realise what it means to be a follower, how it feels to be in that position".

The importance of communication in organizations, especially during times of change, has spawned its own discipline of study. Lewis wrote that a growing body of empirical research indicates that the communication process and organizational change efforts are "inextricably linked processes".

Communication plays an important role in several aspects of the change process, including: creating and articulating a vision; soliciting input and channeling feedback to and from all levels of the organizational hierarchy; and propelling and altering the paths of change. The organizational communication literature reveals that communication has been shown to reduce uncertainty associated with change efforts, increase accuracy in perceptions about the reasons and goals of change, and increase willingness to participate in planned change.

Studying the methods and channels organizations use to communicate change, Lewis found change agents consider themselves to be the primary sources of change-related information, and they solicit input much less frequently than they disseminate information. She suggests that management's lack of use of channels of communication, especially upward channels, limits feedback from lower level employees who do the work of the organization.

This approach can affect the success of change efforts, as "changes in status, reward structures, job descriptions, roles, work methods, work relationships, and procedures bring significant organizational issues to the surface" that increase rank-and-file employees' need to communicate with their supervisors.

There is a small body of literature; on organizational attempts to initiate market-oriented cultural change. Narver and Slater described a market-oriented culture as one that most effectively and efficiently creates superior customer value. Harris defined a market-oriented culture as "the dominant, dynamic segment of an organization whoso orientation, attitudes and actions are geared towards the market". Harris contends that most reseachers err when they assume an organization has a single, unitary culture. This approach ignores the dynamic interaction of many aspects of an organization's culture and denies the possibility of the existence of multiple cultures.

Generally, developing a market-oriented culture can be understood as a means to improve organizational efficiency and effectiveness. However, Piercy maintains the success of developing such a culture is largely dependent on internal power relationships and organizational politics, which - at least in the short term - do not necessarily lead to high levels of organization-wide motivation, commitment, or satisfaction.

When understood in this context, developing a market-oriented culture can be seen as one of many ways that an organization can impose cultural control over the attitudes, actions, and behaviours of its members. Overall, Harris and Ogbonna (2000) wrote that the literature on the effects of developing market-oriented cultures is inconsistent, with some studies suggesting that the new culture improves employee satisfaction and commitment and others indicating this is not the case.

However, researchers tend to agree that the success of any attempt at creating a market-oriented culture is contingent on employees who have to implement it. In nearly all cases, this is the front-line employees who are the primary link between an organization and its customers.

The authors also contend that developing a market-oriented culture should be concerned with the long-term generation of values, attitudes, and behaviours, but the underlying assumption of the market culture is continuing responsiveness to customer needs.

The dilemma for organizations is how they can craft short-term responses to "increasingly fickle" customer needs in a manner that does not conflict with long-term organizational objectives. Harris and Ogbonna concluded that this condition is "a contradiction yet to be resolved or fully understood".

Change, because it requires giving up what is known and routine for something new that may not be understood, is often met with resistance.

De Jager wrote that many managers perceive employees who resist change as a problem. He contends this short-sighted view that fundamentally misunderstands the causes of resistance and the potential benefits resistance can exert on an organization. De Jager wrote that businesses today acknowledge the need to change, but there is so much change that employees become confused and see themselves pushed in conflicting directions.

Management is wise to understand that resistance to change is a tool that can be used to guide an organization. "Another way of looking at resistance is as a gateway or filter. Resistance to change helps us select from all possible changes the one that is most appropriate to the current situation". Because change involves replacing old organizational routines and values with new ones, managers must be able to provide answers for employees to some fundamental questions:

- Why is the old status quo no longer sufficient?

- What will it cost to make the transition from the old to new ways of doing things? De Jager identified several likely costs: disruption of routines, training, temporary low morale, new hires, people leaving, and the emotional cost of destroying what was.
- Is the cost of change justified by the incremental benefits of the change proposed?
- Does the proposed change support and reinforce existing core values?

As the millennium approached, the newspaper industry faced imposing, concurrent challenges on several fronts: stagnant circulation and a slowly dwindling base of readers; a fragmenting mass modin market; new electronic media that are changing the way people access and use information; threats to traditional sources of advertising; and unpredictable but rising costs of production.

In the wake of a mid-1990s recession that saw significant cutbacks, layoffs, and downsizings, newsrooms were restructured and reorganized.

Hierarchical newsroom designs were flattened, and the beat system of coverage centered on social institutions was replaced by a team system that defined coverage areas by topics believed of greater interest to readers and consumers. What becomes apparent from the industry trade journals is that"change" became the guiding light of the industry in the late 1990s.

Feeling out of step with the social patterns and interests of the public, the industry questioned its news values and management has focused on changing the culture of the newsroom to include greater marketing awareness and knowledge. Editors are increasingly taking on marketing duties, working in cross-departmental teams with advertising, circulation, and marketing directors to create strategies to attract readers, often in specific demographic groups that advertisers are willing to pay to reach.

Rank-and-file journalists are expected to accept restructuring, redefined news values, and a greater sensitivity to marketing as part of a larger cultural change process that is redefining their jobs and norms as journalists. Organizational theory suggests that integrated organizations are more innovative and flexible and respond more quickly to opportunities and challenges.

The basis of power and decision making in integrated organizations shifts from being solely in the hands of management to a shared arrangement that empowers employees to use their knowledge and skills in team-based systems. Teams, and their individual members, respond to more decision-making power and autonomy by taking more responsibility for the quality of their work and becoming more productive.

Organizational change and development is understood as a process with several stages, including planning, executing, and monitoring the progress and results.

Because organizations have different values and goals, the study of OD has usually focused on one organization at a time, identifying the impact of site-specific variables on organizational development.

This approach, while making theory building more difficult, has, however, led to researchers identifying several variables that impact the success of OD efforts.

These variables include an organization having a clear mission, employees who understand the mission and organization's core values, effective organizational communication, employee participation in Grafting and implementing change initiatives, strong leadership, trust, flexibility, and mechanisms that monitor the progress of change initiatives and reward desired behaviour.

The effect of successful OD efforts should be empowered employees who, in self-directed work teams, are more motivated, productive, and responsible for their work. In theory, at least, successful OD efforts should in the long term improve employee morale.

However, change is also understood as a difficult and risky process. It requires employees (both management and rank-and-file) to embrace new values, to alter routines, and to think differently about their organizational roles and the nature of their work. It requires greater accountability from empowered rank-and-file and a new, less autocratic style from management. Accordingly, resistance to change should be expected, and in some cases is rational.

For management, successful OD includes understanding the reasons for resistance and having the flexibility to find ways of working through resistance. In short, the challenge of conceiving and leading change falls on management, while rank-and-file are expected to enact and embrace change initiatives that affect many of their conventions and values.

Management perceives it is initiating change in the best interests of the organization and industry, while rank-and-file ponder the reasons for change and are sensitive to how it is implemented. Organizational theory and change models provide conceptual guidelines that should help predict effective organizational development (OD) initiatives.

Given the vast amount of change in the newspaper industry and the relative dearth of research studying these OD initiatives, this study of top newsroom managers and rank-and-file journalists at newspapers leading industry change explores the following research questions and tests three hypotheses.

*RQ*l: What are the attitudes and opinions of management and rank-and-file journalists toward organizational change?

*RQ*2: How do management and rank-and-file perceive the change process in relation to organizational development theory?

*RQ*3: How do management and rank-and-file perceive organizational change in relation to the normative values of journalism and marketing?

*RQ*4: Have change efforts affected rank-and-file perceptions of news values and organizational structure?

*RQ*5: Have change efforts affected rank-and-file morale?

*RQ*6: Does organization size (measured by circulation) affect how rank-and-file perceive change?

*H*1: Management will perceive it has done significantly better at organizational development than rank-and-file.

*H*2: Morale among rank-and-file will be low.

H3: Rank-and-file perceptions of organizational development will predict morale.

METHODS

This study used two survey instruments: a 62-statement survey sent to a sample of rank-and-file at 17 newspapers that have been engaged in change initiatives and a 20-statement survey sent to a census of top newsroom managers at the same papers. The rank-and-file survey was designed to explore respondents' attitudes toward concepts important to all newspapers experimenting with change: news values, organizational structure, and morale.

The survey included statements that allowed measuring the degree to which the newsroom change process has adhered to organizational development theory. There were also statements asking rank-and-file to assess the relationship of change with journalistic and marketing goals.

The 20-statement management survey focused primarily on issues of organizational development, asking managers to assess the change process and their leadership of it. These 20 statements also appeared on the rank-and-file survey, allowing for a comparison between managers and rank-and-file on issues important to successful organization development. On both surveys, respondents were asked to record their level of agreement or disagreement to stimulus statements along a 5-point Likert-like intensity scale.

Choosing the Newspapers. The intent was to generate a large enough number of respondents from abroad enough sample of newspapers (in terms of size, geographic location, types of ownership, and experience with change) to have results that are generalizable to newspapers implementing change. To ensure the newspapers in the sample were among those most experienced in change initiatives, the 1997 ASNE Change Committee annual report was used to draw a purposive sample. These newspapers had top managers who were members of the 1997 Change Committee, or the newspapers' experiments with change were discussed in the committee's annual report.

The publisher or a top news executive of all 17 U.S. newspapers active on the committee was contacted by telephone. Only two Change Committee papers declined involvement in the study: Chattanooga (Tenn.) Times and Charlotte (N.C.) Observer.

It should be noted that the Columbia Missourian is staffed by students in the University of Missouri School of Journalism, and the rank-and-file from this newspaper - because they are not professional journalists - were not included in the sample.

Three newspapers were added to the study: Si. Louis Post-Dispatch; Kansas City Star; and The Los Angeles Times. The Post-Dispatch was chosen because its editor at the time, Cole Campbell, instituted sweeping changes focused on issues relevant to this study. The Kansas City Star was chosen because that paper was sold and restructured in the years immediately preceding the study, and its publisher, Arthur Brisbane, was the chair of the 1998 Change Committee.

The Los Angeles Times was chosen because of its self-proclaimed desire to set an industry example of how to restructure a news organization into cross-departmental teams that are more marketing conscious. The additions created a sample of 18 newspapers with a circulation range from about 5,000 (Columbia Missourian) to more than 1 million (The Los Angeles Times). The papers come from 14 states, representing every major geographic region of the nation. At the time of the survey, newspapers from 11 companies were in the sample, including 9 newspaper groups or chains and 2 family-owned papers. Thirteen of tho papers were owned by public companies (those that offer public stock), and 4 were private.

CREATING THE SAMPLE

Sixteen of the papers supplied the researcher with a list of newsroom employees. At the remaining paper, the San Jose Mercury News, a contact person worked with the researcher to identify top newsroom managers and draw a random sample of rank-and-file. To ensure a response from managers that would be large enough to allow for statistical comparison with rank-and-file data, a census of the top newsroom managers at each paper was included in the overall sample.

Each paper was asked to identify its top newsroom managers or those people at the rank of department head, section editor, or team leader and above. These managers were chosen because they are responsible for creating or implementing and overseeing newsroom policies and procedures. At several papers, there were as few as a half-dozen people at these ranks or higher, and at some of the larger papers, there were more than a dozen managers in these positions.

The rank-and-file sample was determined by newspaper size. The first consideration was to have enough responses from the smaller papers for statistical analysis by organizational size. Accordingly, all rank-and-file at the four smaller papers (less than 50,000 circulation) were included in the sample (n=137).

Overall, a sample was sought that would enable an approximate proportional representation of journalists for all three circulation strata. From the seven papers between 50,000 and 250,000 (the actual range is 71,000 to 156,000), a random sample of 1 of 3 newsroom employees was drawn from each newspaper (n=259); from the six papers with more than 250,000 circulation, 1 of 5 newsroom employees was randomly selected (n=313), except for The Los Angeles Times, where 1 of 10 employees was randomly selected (n=98).

A total of 989 surveys - 182 to top managers and 807 to rank-and-file - was mailed in May 1998. Following closely Dillman's Total Design Method (1978), a postcard was sent as a reminder to nonrespondents about 10 days after the first mailing; a complete survey packet was sent to nonrespondents about 3 weeks after the first mailing.

Of 807 surveys sent to rank-and-file, 457 were completed and returned, a response rate of 56.6%. The 182 surveys sent to top managers yielded 68 responses, or 3 7.3%. The instrument sent to management had 20 statements, mostly about organizational development, that were also on the rank-and-file survey. This approach allowed for a comparison of management and rank-and-file responses. The lower response rate for management can be partially explained by the instrument; beyond the 20-statement survey, management was asked to complete a Q study (not reported in this monograph). Comparative results are reported first, followed by rank-and-file data.

Management respondents' demographics:

- 26 women, 42 men;
- 1 African-American, 2 Asian-Americans, 2 Hispanics, 62 whites, and 1 indicated othor;
- Ages ranged from 26 to 59, with a mean of 44.5;
- Experience ranged from 3 to 38 years, with the mean 22.0 years.

Rank-and-filo respondents' demographics:

- 177 females, 274 males, and 6 did not respond;
- 25 African-Americans, 19 Asian-Americans, 9 Hispanics, 2 Native Americans, 382 whites, and 20 indicated other or did not respond;
- Ages ranged from 22 to 77, with the mean 41.98;
- Experience ranged from 1 to 60 years, with the mean 17.72 years;
- 272 indicated they had "no managerial duties," 181 said they had "some managerial duties," and 4 did not respond.

Variable Measures. Most of the 62 rank-and-file survey statements were written to probe change initiatives in relation to news values, organizational structure, organizational development, and morale.

The statements exploring news values incorporate ideas from trade journals about the changing nature of news, but also reflect norms articulated in the Libertarian and Social Responsibility theories of the press.

The statements that construct the organizational structure variable were taken from trade journal and organizational development literature.

The statements in the organizational development construct were all derived from the OD literature. Morale statements were written to explore both individual respondents' attitudes about their own morale and their perceptions of morale in the newsroom. Factor analysis of the rank-and-file data assisted construction of the four concepts: 14 statements measure news values; 12 statements measure organizational structure; 14 statements measure organizational development; 6 statements measure morale.

Statement responses - on a 5-point scale with 1 strongly agree, 5 strongly disagree, and 3 neutral - were coded so that a positive response indicated support for the concept (i.e., positive response indicated high morale). Conceptual quotients were created by calculating the mean response to the set of statements measuring the concepts. Accordingly, a quotient significantly below 3.0 (the assumed population mean on the 5-point scale) indicates positive agreement with the concept, and a quotient significantly above 3.0 indicates that respondents disagree with the concept (i.e., disagree with statements suggesting high morale).

COMPARISONS BETWEEN MANAGEMENT AND RANK-AND-FILE

ORGANIZATIONAL DEVELOPMENT

The literature indicates that cultural change is difficult, requiring management and rank-and-file to adapt to new values, structures, routines, and goals. However, management and rank-and-file have different roles in the change process. Management is responsible for conceiving, guiding, and monitoring change, while rank-and-file must execute management's vision and live with the new roles and values associated with change.

Management is expected to perceive OD initiatives more broadly, in concert with strategic organizational goals, and guide and assess the change process from a position of leadership and accountability. It is expected that management will perceive that its OD initiatives are rooted in sound strategies and practices, while rank-and-file will question the reasons for change and be sensitive to how it is implemented. This logic is the basis of the following hypothesis:

Hl: Management will perceive it has done significantly better at OD than rank-and-file.

A t test of independent samples was used to compare the OD quotients (mean value of the 14 statements in the construct) of management and rank-and-file. This hypothesis is supported. The data indicate that management believes OD initiatives have generally followed theoretical guidelines, as the OD quotient for management shows modest overall agreement with the statements (quotient is less than 3.0).

Conversely, the rank-and-file OD quotient shows general disagreement that change initiatives are in accordance with the parameters defined by OD theory.

Thus, there is not only a significant difference between the OD quotients, there is also a clear difference of attitudes: management perceives it has generally implemented change in accordance with OD, while rank-and-file think the process of change has not adhered to ideas and practices consistent with successful OD.

This finding is further reinforced by looking at the pattern of responses to the variable statements. Of the 14 OD statements, management agrees with 9 and ranl:-and-file agree with only 3.

T tests wore also used to compare individual statement means, and there are significant differences on 11 of the 14 statements. Because the OD variable is a broad measure of change, with survey statements addressing planning, training, commitment, leadership, communication, participation, and a system of rewards, the significant differences on so many OD aspects reflect both the intensity and broad-based nature of the differences between the groups.

Six of the statistically significant OD statements show a clear difference of attitudes, with management agreeing with the statement and rank-and-file disagreeing.

The two groups have differing opinions on some of the most basic aspects of change (means noted parenthetically). Management believes the newspaper's mission and core values are understood by newsroom employees (2.56), while rank-and-file are apparently unsure about their paper's mission and values (3.11). Management believes the staff has participated in drafting change (2.85), while rank-and-file disagree (3.20); and management says that it has asked for staff feedback about change (2.82), while rank-and-file apparently think management is not interested in feedback, or at least not interested enough to ask (3.35).

The importance of communication in the change process is also shown, as management agrees that change initiatives and the reasons for change have been continually communicated (2.88), while rank-and-file disagree (3.18).

Most telling about communication is the large difference of opinion concerning honesty. Management shows quite strong agreement that it has been open and honest with staff about the reasons for change (2.60), but rank-and-file exhibit equally strong disagreement (3.40). This.8 mean difference on honesty (on a 5-point scale) is the largest gap between the groups' responses to any of the 14 statements in the OD variable.

Even on the eight statements where the groups tend to agree, there are significant differences in their intensity of agreement on five statements. Although rank-and-file credit management for its strong leadership role (2.75) and unified commitment to change (2.82), management assesses its leadership role (2.26) and commitment (2.50) in significantly more optimistic terms.

In those areas where management is relatively self-critical, rank-and-file tend to be more critical. Management concedes it has not thought through the long-term implications of change (3.28), but rank-and-file take a harsher view (3.64); the scenario is similar concerning a system of rewards for work that meets the goals of change, with management disagreeing that such a system is in place (3.27), but rank-and-file disagreeing significantly more (3.59).

This trend might be best shown with management's relatively strong disagreement to the statement that change initiatives have helped build stronger trust between management and rank-and-file (3.72). Management's response is a candid assessment of an unpleasant reality and a subtle admission of a failure of change; yet, rank-and-file are significantly harsher in their assessment (4.03), with their strongest level of disagreement to any of the 14 statements. These differences underscore that even when management and rank-and-file find areas of common ground, they still tend to disagree.

Of the 14 OD statements, management has a stronger level of disagreement to only 2, and these 2 statements are among the 3 statements that do not have significant mean differences. Management disagrees that it has overestimated resistance to change (3.21), while rank-and-file are neutral (3.03); and managers disagree that the staff is open-minded toward change (3.32) marginally more than rank-and-file (3.14). Although not significant, taken together, the ideas that management perceives more resistance and less open-mindedness suggest that management believes their staffs are generally resistant to change initiatives.

This perception is likely to influence how managers approach leading change. Managers would be likely to view with more optimism the task of managing a staff that is open to new ideas and practices. Conversely, managers who perceive a resistant and inflexible staff are more likely to judge the task of leading change as more difficult.

Comparisons of Statements Not in the OD Variable. There were six statements appearing on both surveys that were not part of the OD variable. T tests were performed on the responses, and significant differences were found on four of the statements. Two of the significant statements show a clear difference of attitudes.

Management, consistent with other responses that show more optimism about change than rank-and-file, agrees that there has been a noticeable change in the newsroom culture that has improved the organization (2.76), while rank-and-file disagree quite strongly (3.58).

This large difference of opinion (.82 on a 5-point scale) underscores the different experiences and perceptions the two groups have about the impact of change on the newsroom culture.

But the pattern of management optimism is reversed when the groups are asked about an indicator of journalism quality. In this case, rank-and-file agree that newspapers arc doing a boiler job portraying a representative picture of society than in the past (2.61), while management is significantly more pessimistic, disagreeing with the statement (3.22). This finding could help explain why management sees a need to get closer to readers and redefine news to be more aligned with the lives of people in a changing and diverse marketplace.

Management and rank-and-file show similar attitudes toward two of the statements, and one of the responses is quite surprising.

The two groups both slightly disagree that "I look forward to when change is no longer a large part of work." Given the difficulty of change, especially rank-and-file's general frustration with the process, it seems logical that rank-and-file have had enough change, but this is not the case.

Rank-and-file actually disagree slightly more (3.15) to the statement than management (3.10). This finding supports an issue discussed earlier: management tends to perceive a culture of resistance to change; however, rank-and-file respond that they have accepted change as a part of work.

The increased profit pressure is acknowledged by the groups, with both agreeing strongly with the statement that there is more emphasis on profits than there used to be. Considering the extent of differences between the groups on most of the measures, it is quite revealing that the groups believe with approximate equal strength that there is an increasing emphasis on profit (management = 2.10; rank-and-file = 1.89). For both groups, their level of agreement was stronger with this statement than any of the 20 statements that appeared on both instruments.

Exploring the relationship between change and morale, both groups disagreed with the statement: "Morale in our newsroom appears to be getting better." However, consistent with statements that indicate management does not perceive the newsroom climate to be as bad as rank-and-file, there was a significant difference in the groups' level of disagreement. Management disagreed with the statement (3.28), but its disagreement was not nearly as strong as rank-and-file's (3.81).

RANK-AND-FILE RESULTS

Morale: Low morale among newspaper journalists has been an industry issue for more than a decade. OD research indicates that change initiatives tied to creating a different organizational culture can be threatening for employees because embodied in the new culture are new organizational values, work routines, job skills, and rewards. Based on this evidence, it was hypothesized:

H2: Morale among rank-and-file will be low (morale quotient significantly higher than 3.0).

The morale quotient is 3.32. A one-sample t test indicates the quotient mean is significantly higher than the assumed population mean.

This hypothesis is supported. Six statements comprise morale. T tests on each statement and the assumed population mean found that 5 of the 6 statements were statistically significant. Respondents agreed with only one statement indicating high morale: "I am committed to this newspaper's plans for change" (2.57).

Respondents were neutral to the notion that changes have given them more job skills (3.09), and they disagreed that changes have created more job autonomy (3.26). The remaining three statements constituting this concept make more general (non-first person) references to morale, and these had higher levels of disagreement.

Rank-and-file's relatively strong disagreement that changes have been implemented smoothly (3.58) supports theory that suggests change affecting jobs, skills, and values is difficult. This difficulty of embracing change draws more support from respondents' disagreement that there has been a positive change in the newsroom culture (3.58). However, most telling is the statement that is probably the purest measure of morale. Journalists show their highest level of disagreement to the idea that morale in our newsroom appears to be getting better (3.81).

NEWS VALUES

The 14 statements that construct this study's measure of news values probe how rank-and-file journalists perceive newsroom changes have impacted their news judgment and news content. The news values quotient is 3.23.

A one-sample t test indicates the quotient mean is significantly higher than the assumed population mean. Accordingly, rank-and-file have a negative attitude about changes in news values.

In general, respondents think they are doing what they can to preserve some traditional journalism values in an era when newspapers are more market driven. Responses to the individual statements shed some light on specific news value issues that shape respondents' attitudes (statement means noted parenthetically).

Journalists agree that newspapers are doing a better job portraying a representative picture of society than in the past (2.61), but they are neutral about whether papers are doing better at providing a truthful account of the day's events in a meaningful context than in the past (2.94).

The rank-and-file journalists do not believe that content decisions are based solely on journalism criteria, as they agree strongly that more gossip, trivia, and non-news features are used to fill the paper (2.38) and recent changes in design stress style over substance to the point that look and feel of the paper are more important to editors than the depth of the news (2.40). They have slight agreement that their newspaper has less breaking news than before change initiatives (2.88), and significant disagreement that changes in the industry have made papers more thoughtful and provocative (3.27). Journalists feel the impact of new methods and structures on their news values.

They agree focus groups, surveys, and community meetings are good methods to generate ideas for news coverage (2.82), but they acknowledge an impact of organizational integration, showing strong agreement that journalists working at papers that have eliminated divisions between news and business are more likely to engage in self-censorship when writing about issues important to advertisers (2.36). And they disagree that change has increased resources for practicing journalism (3.57) and led to more investigative reporting (3.46).

This point is underscored by journalists' agreement that an important issue is less likely to become news if it takes a great deal of time to uncover and report (2.66).

The respondents see journalism independence, a traditional benchmark of news values and credibility, as on the road to obsolescence.

Journalists agree that the opportunity for independent-minded publishers or editors to run their own newsrooms is coming to an end (2.30) and are neutral when asked whether the role models for today's managers are those editors and publishers who in the past told the truth when it was not popular or profitable to do so (2.93).

ORGANIZATIONAL STRUCTURE

The quotient for the 12 statements that construct this variable is 3.55, which a one-sample t test shows is significant to the assumed population mean. This finding suggests that journalists generally responded negatively to the impact of changing newsroom structures.

When viewed individually, the statement means indicate that journalists recognize that changes in structure (the most common being from beats to teams) have impacted their work, but seldom in ways theory would predict nor management would desire.

Journalists indicate modest (but significant) agreement that they work more closely with their colleagues than in the past (2.89), but they agree much more strongly that newsroom changes have too often meant attending meetings that cut into time spent on journalism (2.05).

Contrary to theory, rank-and-file don't see that restructuring the newsroom has flattened the hierarchy, disagreeing strongly that the number of layers of management has decreased (3.75).

This finding is reinforced by nearly equally strong agreement that newsroom restructuring seems to require more editors who send out memos about the new goals of restructuring (2.42). The journalists in this sample are still wary of the impact of cross-departmental teams, indicating strong disagreement that directors of advertising, circulation, and marketing should participate in news planning (4.26). Also, they do not see a connection between the team structure and better journalism, disagreeing that reorganization has helped the staff better understand readers (3.53) and that work teams have improved product quality (3.11).]

Moreover, the rank-and-file see media executives as having different values than they do, with executives more focused on market and strategy than on the experiences of their employees (1.78); respondents also disagree strongly that structural changes place more emphasis on nonprofit goals (organizational efficiency, the latest technology, product quality, and worker autonomy and creativity) than profit goals (3.87).

VARIABLES AFFECTING MORALE

Considering the vast amount of change being implemented at newspapers in the sample and the difficulties associated with OD in general, a particular interest of this research project was to measure the impact of change initiatives on morale. Toward this end, the variables constructed to measure the three concepts common to change efforts at newspapers - OD, news values, and organizational structure - were used as independent variables in a regression model to assess their relative impact on morale.

Because OD is a broad measure of change and OD initiatives impact an organization's structure and values, it was expected that the 4 variables (OD, news values, structure, and morale) would be highly correlated. This was indeed what occurred, as the correlations were all significant at the $p < .001$ level. A colinearity test for tolerance showed these correlations did not violate the assumptions of multiple regression. A multiple regression model was then built to test:

*H*3: Rank-and-file perceptions of organizational development will predict morale.

To control for the demographic variables of age, ethnicity, gender, experience, and duties, these variables were entered as a block into the regression model before the three independent variables. Experience, duties ("some managerial duties" or "no managerial duties"), and age were significant predictors in the block. Together, the demographic variables accounted for 5.77% of the variance.

H3 is supported. Organizational development, entered as the second block in the model, explained 45.8% of the variance after controlling for demographies. OD is clearly the strongest predictor of morale among all the independent variables. Accordingly, the data indicate that as rank-and-file's attitudes toward OD become more positive their morale increases; or, as rank-and-file's attitudes toward OD become more negative their morale decreases.

After all the independent variables were entered in the regression model, OD, structure, and news values are significant predictors of morale. However, after controlling for demographics, the explained variance each variable adds differs notably. OD explains 45.8% of the variance, organizational structure accounts for 7.8% of the variance and news values accounts for 2.0%.

What is interesting is that news values, so basic to journalists' jobs and how they perceive their roles, explains a relatively small amount of the variance.

Perhaps this is because in the midst of organizational changes that affect the most basic elements of work - schedules and routines - journalists continue to see the basic elements of news as information gathering, interviewing, writing, and editing.

It is logical that news values impact morale, but change initiatives that require training and re-ordering of work priorities, as well as newsroom restructuring, are tangible symbols of a new culture.

Because they are the most easily identified signs of change, they are the most likely targets for acceptance or resistance. Thus, it appears that changes most affecting morale are those OD and restructuring initiatives that management believes will eventually reconstitute news. News values are changing, but the results suggest that among the types of change, rank-and-file see changing news values as having a smaller impact on their morale.

After all the variables were entered in the model, duties was also shown to be a significant predictor of morale. A dichotomous variable (0 = no managerial duties, 1 = some managerial duties), the negative beta weight indicates an inverse relationship. In other words, journalists who have some managerial duties have significantly lower morale than those who have no managerial duties; or, those with no managerial duties have higher morale than those with some managerial duties. This result supports anecdotal evidence that change has been most difficult for low- and mid-level managers. These managers tend to get "squeezed" by change, expected to execute the change initiatives of top management while working most closely with non-managers.

Statements Not Part of Variables. The statements not part of variables also provide some useful insights. One of the research questions in this study was whether newsroom employees think the direction of change better fits the goals of journalism or marketing. As noted in the comparative results, of the 62 statements in the survey, rank-and-file's strongest agreement was with the statement: "There is more emphasis on maintaining or increasing the paper's profits than there used to be" (1.89).

There was also strong agreement that newsroom managers have become increasingly aware of the concerns of stockholders and capital investors (2.13). Respondents think this increased awareness or pressure created by financial performance does not need to be expanded, as there is significant disagreement to the statement that the newspaper industry needs a culture that requires greater marketing intelligence in the newsroom (3.26). Taken together, these statements indicate rank-and-file journalists believe newspapers are becoming more sensitive to marketing and this movement has gone far enough.

There is also a concern about the ethical issues and threats to journalism independence that removing the wall between the news and business may initiate. There is strong agreement that ethical committees are needed to draft guidelines for editorial staff participation in promotional events (2.27) and significant agreement that journalistic independence has helped establish newspapers as credible (2.59).

The journalists in this sample still use journalism excellence as the standard for quality, and they like competition. Even in the era of increased profit pressures, there is significant disagreement that most newspaper companies would trade Pulitzer Prizes for consistently high profits (3.36), and, in an apparent longing for days past, respondents show strong agreement that journalism has suffered in the era of one-newspaper towns (2.07).

There is additional evidence that rank-and-file do not perceive OD as progressing in accordance with theory. Rank-and-file disagree that management has done a good job preparing employees for change (3.38), and they disagree that management has done a good job measuring the results of change (3.63).

Respondents have even stronger beliefs that management is ego driven and inflexible. Rank-and-file agree that some managers have embraced formulas of change because they have invested so much money, time, and ego in them that they can't admit their lack of success (2.26).

And there is a similar strong agreement to the idea that managers who have found resistance to change have responded by saying in effect, "The train is leaving the station, you can get on or get off" (2.27).

Furthermore, journalists don't see change meeting its stated objectives, as they show strong agreement there is little evidence that common changes (i.e., redefining of news, newsroom restructuring, and use of emerging technologies) are attracting more readers and advertisers.

The data also lend support to the idea that news managers and the growing number of consultants employed in newsrooms misunderstand journalists' resistance to change. The journalists in this study do not see themselves as opposed to change; in fact, they show significant disagreement to the statement that they look forward to when change is no longer such a large part of work. But journalists tend to like to be left alone to do their jobs which runs counter to theory that predicts workers are happier when they collaborate and more productive in teams. The more than 450 rank-and-file in this sample significantly agree with the statement: "I am happier when I can work alone".

ANALYSIS BY CIRCULATION

Because organizational resources are determined in part by an organization's size and group dynamics can be impacted by group size, this study explored whether newspaper size (measured by circulation) impacted respondents' attitudes toward change. To test for differences by circulation, means for each variable were calculated by circulation size (4 small papers with circulations less than 50,000; 7 mid-size papers with circulations between 50,000 and 250,000 [actual range is 71,000 to 156,000]; and 6 large papers with circulations more than 250,000).

The data show that small newspapers are having more difficulty with change as it relates to two variables: OD and morale. A one-way analysis-of-variance test indicates that morale is significantly lower at small papers; also, small paper respondents indicate significantly higher disagreement that OD initiatives have been in accordance with theory. It is worth noting that the means for all four variables are higher for small papers.

These results also reveal no significant differences between mid-size and large papers. But perhaps more telling about this analysis is that there is not a positive attitude toward any of the variables at any size paper. In other words, even though some aspects of change are more difficult at small papers, these strata show that respondents do not believe change has gone well (or in accordance with theory) on any of the measures, regardless of newspaper size.

The challenge of change from the standpoint of management is getting rank-and-file to accept the core values that embody management's vision for a transformed newsroom culture.

The data provide strong evidence that management's OD initiatives are failing to win rank-and-file support - regardless of whether the initiatives are in concert with theory. What is surprising in these findings is the extent to which management and rank-and-file disagree and how often.

Of the 20 statements that appeared on both surveys, there are significant differences on 15 of them. Of these 15, the responses to 9 statements indicate clear differences of attitudes, with one group agreeing and the other disagreeing. Of the 14 statements that construct the OD variable, there are significant differences on responses to 11 statements.

Taken as a whole, the responses show that many important divisions exist between management and rank-and-file, and even when the groups can agree, they often disagree on their level of agreement. In many instances the gap between responses is so large that it is hard to understand the two groups are sharing the same experiences, and perhaps they are not.

The groups' roles in the change process differ. The sample of newsroom managers in this study is comprised of many of the nation's leading editors. Their involvement in the ASNE Change Committee reflects their interests beyond the walls of their newsrooms, and suggests they positioned themselves as leaders in an industry-wide effort to respond to the forces mandating change. The rank-and-file in this sample must adapt to management's vision by executing their jobs in accordance with the new procedures and goals of change. Despite these different roles, however, as part of the same organizations, management and rank-and-file should share similar values. Both groups are journalists.

Management's self-assessment may be a bit optimistic, but it is grounded in reality and is at times unflatteringly candid. Managers have a great deal invested in change initiatives, both in terms of organizational resources and their individual careers. A role of management is to "see the big picture," which suggests that management should be able to assess the process and progress of change within its overall strategic goals better than rank-and-file.

Thus, management's general optimism regarding change may be a reflection that the broader process is proceeding in the right direction, even if certain aspects tend to get off course. The data support this. Management gives itself high marks for leadership and generally following the prescriptions for change articulated in OD models and theory. Management views itself as trying to do what should be done to enable change to succeed.

Yet, as Kanter suggests, change requires a "leap of faith" to get people to embrace an organizational reality that is not yet known. And on this issue, the data show management to be quite honest, admitting the entire change formula has not been worked out. Even more candid, however, is management's admission that certain parts of the process that it can control have not been well-managed.

Management concedes that it has not adequately thought through the long-term implications of change, and it acknowledges there is not a system of rewards for work that meets the goals of change initiatives.

Accordingly, it is not surprising that management recognizes that its short-comings have contributed to a breakdown of trust with rank-and-file, while at the same time perceiving a cultural change that has improved the organization. This apparent contradiction must be perplexing and difficult for newsroom managers. There is some evidence in the data that managers are a bit frustrated, placing the "blame" for a lack of success on rank-and-file, who are perceived as close minded and resistant to change.

However, the results from the rank-and-file survey suggest it is not accurate to simply dismiss journalists as resistant to change. Rank-and-file indicate they accept change as a part of work and are personally committed to their paper's change efforts. They credit their managers for taking leadership roles and being committed to change. However, they question the factors motivating change and are able to distinguish between intentions and results. In brief, while management says it has articulated a vision, included employees in creating changes, been flexible, and sought feedback about the change process, rank-and-file respond that they are confused about the vision, fool loft out of the process, and perceive their managers as inflexible.

Rank-and-file also sense management's vulnerability and frustration in leading change, showing strong agreement that change is ego driven by inflexible managers who, refusing to recognize its lack of success, resort to authoritarian measures to counter pockets of resistance.

Rank-and-file's perception that management has failed at nearly every step of the process, combined with their sense that profit is increasingly important to newsroom managers, further explains the low level of trust rank-and-file express toward their managers. Numerous scholars cite trust as a prerequisite condition for successful OD initiatives. Thus, despite management's general optimism about an improving newsroom culture, the breakdown of trust that both management and rank-and-file acknowledge does not bode well for continuing efforts at change, as theory suggests and common sense reveals that people do not readily accept the ideas of those whom they do not trust.

Beyond the organizational development issues associated with change, rank-and-file's skepticism about change can be understood by an apparent lack of producing successful results. Change initiatives are not only failing to create more efficient, productive, and happier newsrooms, they are also falling short on their stated goals. Journalists don't perceive changes as attracting more readers and advertisers, or helping to produce better newspapers. Instead, rank-and-file connect change initiatives with fewer resources for journalism in a more market-driven culture and industry.

Kanter, Drucker, Bergquist, and many organizational scholars would suggest that "breaking down the wall" between the newsroom and other departments in the news organization is an important step toward creating the "integrated" and "innovative" organizational culture required to meet challenges swiftly and capitalize on opportunities in the postmodern business world.

The data in this study suggest that rank-and-file perceive the new, integrated culture as a threat to their values, most of which are rooted in journalism. Much of rank-and-file's resistance to change is related to a sense that the "journalism-based" culture of their newsrooms is being replaced with a culture that places less value on journalism norms.

In this way, there is a cultural "battle" unfolding in news organizations as they become more integrated. Harris, writing about the clash that occurs when an organization attempts to create a market-oriented culture, asserts that the market-oriented values that define the culture must come to dominate the existing cultures for the transformation to succeed.

This study indicates that this type of cultural struggle is being waged in newsrooms experimenting with change. When viewed in this regard, resistance to change can be understood as both rational and part of a cultural conflict.

However, if cultural change is achieved through a combination of macro (values and beliefs) and micro forces (the tangible things such as practices, policies, and procedures that define daily life in the organization), then management's attempt to change the newsroom culture by changing the organization's structure and work routines appears to be well-advised and well under way.

This study also opens for re-examination several theoretical assumptions. The idea that modern newspaper organizations are characterized by complex, hierarchical bureaucracies and specialized labour appears to be less accurate today than it was before "change" became an industry buzzword and organizational goal. Media corporations, no doubt large bureaucracies, can however be understood to be "disassembling the assembly line.

The goals of OD and change most often focus on creating flatter corporate flowcharts with the expectation that employees need to be more versatile and multiskilled. Clearly, this is the opposite of labour specialization. Furthermore, the empowerment assumptions of restructuring hierarchical organizations into flatter, team-based units have not materialized for the rank-and-file journalists in this sample.

Rank-and-file understand restructuring as a mechanism that affords them fewer resources to practice journalism, and, contrary to theory, rank-and-file perceive restructuring has created more layers of managers and a more "managed" newsroom. The journalists in this sample say that the team-based structure has not brought them more autonomy, nor has it provided more decision-making authority.

It is possible that the empowerment expected to result from restructured newsrooms is misconceived. A primary rationale for less hierarchical organizations is the team-based structure unleashes the knowledge and creativity of lower level employees. This view presupposes that management, under the hierarchical structure, has not previously afforded employees the power to effectively utilize these assets.

However, this assumption seems to neglect the nature of newspaper work, which has traditionally afforded rank-and-file a great deal of latitude, encouraging journalists to apply their knowledge and be creative. Long before empowerment became a management cliche, Gassaway's 1984 social construction work found that rank-and-file journalists and newspaper managers negotiate for power, with rank-and-file having considerable leverage, because as newsgatherers they control the initial flow of information.

Furthermore, journalism is one of the few occupations where employees at the bottom of the corporate ladder consider themselves professionals. Valuable newsroom employees have long been those who could work well on their own, digging for stories and building relationships with sources. Interviewing is a craft, writing and design are forms of self-expression, and editing is a skill built on an individual's grasp of language and professional values.

To require journalists to give up the individual nature of their work asks them to sacrifice some of the skills that have become a part of their professional identities. There is strong evidence in this study that journalists have not accepted the idea that team-based newsrooms empower them or better utilize their skills. This finding supports previous research and reinforces the idea that the organizational theory that managers are using to empower their employees and restructure their newsrooms could be misapplied, as it misunderstands the nature of newspaper journalism work.

The assumptions about the organizational role of management are changing, too. This study finds little support that newsroom managers are "technocrats" who value organizational and technical development more than the profit goals of their "capitalist" owners.

The data indicate it is more accurate, as Kanter and others suggest, to understand change as a process of integration, where the marketing goals of the traditional "business side" of the news organization have become more apparent to journalists and more valued by management throughout the organization (my italics).

Galbraith's "approved contradiction" concept - that innovative managers will focus on professional and organizational goals while returning just enough profit to keep their capitalist owners satisfied - is a core assumption of Demers'research on the corporate newspaper.

This study found little support for the existence of an approved contradiction; rather, managers and rank-and-file perceive change as both market and profit driven at the expense of organizational issues thought to be of prime concern to professional managers (product quality, technology, and employee development).

These findings suggest that modern news executives are no longer "technocrats" in the sense Galbraith defined them, but are closer to the "capitalists" who sought maximum financial return on their investments. The practice of offering newsroom managers incentives (salary bonuses or stock options) tied to the financial performance of the company is one way corporations subtly "disapprove" of the approved contradiction.

Limitations of the study: An obvious shortcoming of this survey method is that it can only provide a "snapshot" of attitudes at the time of the study. Change is an ongoing process, and the instruments used can only provide a one-time glimpso of the process.

As the change process unfolds in newsrooms across the country, it would be wise to continue to monitor change initiatives and journalists' attitudes toward them. Also, this study did not attempt to measure the amount of change orthe phases of the change process. Thus, while all the respondents have a commonality of change experiences, it is not clear if attitudes toward change differ based on the amount of change or stages in the change process.

There is also a chance to refine the instruments and measures of change used in this study. Organizational development research has generally focused on one organization at a time, using site-specific variables. By taking a different approach, there were very few established measures. Accordingly, the attempt here was to create "tools" from which scholars can begin to empirically assess change.

The findings in this study point to several theoretical areas that should prove fertile ground for exploration. This study adds to the small amount of research Thai suggests restructuring newsrooms into team-based systems does not "empower" journalists in the manner theory predicts. If team-based newsrooms are the future of the industry, then changing organizational relationships spawned by restructuring offer interesting opportunities for study.

Among some of the questions these changes suggest: Do team-based structures impact the ways journalists work with one another? Do teams impact the ways journalists develop relationships and interact with their sources? Do teams require and reward different personality traits? How does the resourceful journalist, the "gumshoe" who worked well alone, often producing front page stories in the beat system, perform in the team structure?

Do team-based newsrooms produce different content than the beat system does? And possibly most important to understanding the values that will drive the industry in the future are the questions of management influence and power. Do newsroom managers and editors see themselves as the innovative "technocrats" that theory presupposes? How much influence do newsroom managers have when it comes to setting the vision for change? To what extent do newsroom managers embrace the changes they are expected to lead? These questions, along with the need to develop better change-related measures over time (throughout the process of change], provide an abundance of directions for research.

This study surveyed a purposive sample of the nation's newspaper managers most experienced in industry-wide change initiatives; it also surveyed a much larger sample of rank-and-file from those same papers. The managers in this study have, in effect, used their newsrooms as laboratories to experiment with new and far-reaching change initiatives.

These changes have become - depending on whom you ask - new standards of excellence or points of controversy and resistance. Although the results from this purposive sample cannot be generalized to the entire industry, the relatively large sample gives a good indication of what change has meant to journalists at newspapers on the cutting edge of industry-wide change.

These findings should prove useful for the many news managers and editors who find their newsrooms embarking on or considering similar change initiatives. This study has also tested the key concepts of organizational development, making it one of only a few attempts to understand the complexities of newspaper industry change through the lens of organizational theory.

Given the size of the sample and the scope of the newspapers (circulations ranging from 5,000 to more than 1,000,000, including public, private, and family-owned papers that are located in every major geographic region of the country), this study represents one of the largest scale attempts to date to assess journalists' perceptions about change initiatives that are sweeping through newsrooms nationwide.

Management, despite some reservations about the market-driven nature of change, thinks it is doing reasonably well following the guidelines of organizational development in a manner consistent with creating a more outer-directed and reader-driven newsroom culture. In short, management believes it has "managed" the change process in general accordance with theory. Rank-and-file, on the other hand, feel more victims of change than participants in it. The gulf between management and rank-and-file experiences with change has facilitated a breakdown in trust that could seriously hamper ongoing change initiatives. Morale among rank-and-file is low, and data suggest it is getting worse.

The newspaper industry finds itself in the throes of a cultural revolution precipitated by internal and external forces. Yet, the industry remains highly profitable and has shown resiliency in the information age, remaining a respected and widely utilized source of news and information. The predictions of doom are far from materializing, but many of the challenges that served as catalysts for cultural change remain. The findings of this study suggest there is a struggle unfolding between the core values of two cultures - marketing and journalism - and rank-and-file perceive organizational development efforts are focused on creating a more dominant marketing culture, often at the expense of journalistic norms.

This study has extended previous change research by approaching the problem differently. Organizational research has seldom been conducted on more than one organization at a time, and its methods are usually qualitative. The constructs in this study held up quite well to tests of reliability and statistical analysis, showing the depth of common experiences of journalists at newspapers implementing change.

An important methodological finding of this study is that change can be studied at more than one newspaper at a time. Studies that go beyond site-specific variables are possible, which should encourage more research using larger, representative samples with the goal of testing and building theory.

Chapter 5

Conflicting Views from the Newsroom

10 years ago, the primary duties of reporters and producers at local television news affiliates were to fill the newscasts with live shots, packages, good writing, and plenty of video.

But in today's world of media convergence, TV news staffers are doing much more than"just TV." They are producing news content for multiple media outlets. In many cases, the companies they work for provide news to or own more than one television station in a media market (so-called Limited Marketing Agreements [LMAs] or Duopolies). Stations across the country also are increasingly partnering with radio stations and newspapers to cross-promote their product and share news content. And, according to a recent study by RTNDA, virtually all television stations are now providing news content for Web sites.

There are conflicting views about what it means to practice convergence. Experts, such as Andrew Nachison of the American Press Institute's Media Centre, define convergence as"the strategic, operational, product and cultural union of print, audio, video and interactive digital informational services and organizations". Much to the chagrin of critics, however, many media operations tout their convergence activities when they are simply practicing cooperation. According to Al Tompkins of the Poynter Institute, few media companies are truly converged in the sense that they actually share news content.

In recent years, scholars have examined various concepts of convergence from both print and broadcast perspectives. Most of the research, however, focuses the opinions of media managers--surveying news directors, general managers, and newspaper editors or the workplace realities of print journalists. To date, no published empirical studies have examined how convergence affects local television news workers whose job it is to write, report, and produce news content on a daily basis.

To fill that void, this study's authors surveyed reporters and producers across the country about convergent news practices in their newsrooms. Researchers chose to study staffers in small and medium TV markets because research shows news workers in these markets are more likely than those in larger markets to contribute to Web-based and other convergent activities. According to Papper, 20% of news staffers in larger markets are required to provide content for their station's Web site--this percentage more than doubles for staffers in smaller markets.

This study gives communications scholars a glimpse of convergence practices inside TV stations at a time when news staffs are shrinking and demands on news workers are increasing. The survey explored the specific activities news workers are tasked with as well as the perceived impact of convergence on their jobs and, ultimately, on the content they produce. The perceptions of these news workers were then compared to those of news managers (surveyed in previous research). Findings show significant differences in what these two groups think.

The research demonstrates that how well convergence works depends on whom you ask. Conflicting views from the newsroom are discussed in terms of the challenges that multimedia content production poses in the modern age of ownership consolidation and convergence. With TV news viewership in steady decline, and only 33% of Americans stating they believe local TV news is reliable and accurate, it is critical that news workers and managers grapple with these complicated issues and determine how best to provide quality news content (and enhance journalistic performance) in today's evolving media environment.

LITERATURE REVIEW

Because there are differing opinions about what convergence means, it can be difficult to determine to what extent it is being practiced in television newsrooms across America today. According to two recent studies, between 80 and 90% of local TV stations practice some form of convergence. Another finds more than 96% of local TV stations produce news content for the Web, a singular practice that many news managers define as convergence.

DEFINING CONVERGENCE

Does producing content for the Internet equal convergence? Some academicians and media professionals say yes, taking a broad view. The American Press Institute, for example, defines a convergent news relationship as a "partnership" or "collaboration" between print, broadcast, and online news outlets. Pavlik and McIntosh's perspective is broader still, describing convergence in the digital environment as the melding of the media, computing, and telecommunications. An earlier, and more narrow, definition states that convergence occurs only when print, online, and broadcast media merge into a single news operation.

In recent years, many scholars have studied convergence to better understand and explicate the phenomenon. Much of this research relies on the opinions and perspectives of news managers. Duhe et al., for example, surveyed news directors and general managers from 170 local television stations in the United States.

They found the majority of respondents believe convergence means sharing content within their own organization (such as Web sites), sharing content with other organizations, sharing staff, and promoting other media. They were less likely to define convergence in terms of integrated newsrooms or cross-integrated editorial systems. Generally, the authors discovered that television news managers defined convergence in terms that mirrored the way their station already practiced it.

This same survey gauged the opinions of news managers about the skills required for news workers to succeed in a converged media environment.

To be hired today (and be successful in the future), news directors agreed that reporters needed, first and foremost, the ability to write broadcast copy and use computers—including the Internet, e-mail, and word processing programs.

After that, and in order of importance, they needed the ability to:

- Adapt news copy for use by multiple media;
- Shoot and edit video;
- Work in an integrated media technology environment;
- Adapt visual news content for multiple media;
- Write for print;
- Shoot still photographs;
- Design graphics; and finally,
- *Design Web sites*: Although news managers indicated they need employees capable of doing this kind of work, 67% of respondents said their stations provided no training support to help employees develop the required skills.

In light of such findings, it is not surprising, perhaps, that other researchers have turned their scholarly attentions to journalism education.

In trade-related fields such as journalism, teachers and institutions of higher learning commonly assess industry standards in order to make curricular changes and train students to meet the demands of employers. In today's multimedia world, studying how best to teach convergence journalism is no exception.

Examining curricular concerns in the age of convergence has gained considerable cachet in the academy. As is the case with industry research, many studies published in recent years employ survey design. Typical of such research is a 2005 study by Kraeplin and Criado. The authors surveyed newspaper managers, television managers, and journalism teachers to find out what they thought about convergence training at the collegiate level.

The researchers found that industry executives and educators share many similar views about which specific skills should be taught—from basic writing and reporting skills, to knowledge of media law and ethics, to Internet researching skills.

NEWS ROUTINES AND TODAY'S JOURNALISTS

Despite all this research into convergence practices, skill sets, and the future of journalism education, very few researchers have studied today's working journalists—to assess the ways in which convergence is having an impact on the jobs they do or to ask their opinions about this multimedia trend.

Some media experts believe, with the proper training, news workers will adjust to their new duties with little difficulty. Others are concerned that convergence simply puts too many additional pressures on already overworked journalists. Stone, for example, thinks that "while some multimedia journalists can handle a variety of tasks efficiently and professionally, most will only deliver mediocre journalism". At present, little scientific evidence exists to support either view.

Researchers stand to gain substantial insights about convergence (and other critical issues and concerns in journalism) by examining news workers' daily routines. In fact, there exists a significant body of research to demonstrate the many ways in which daily practices in America's newsrooms have an impact on news content.

Through such studies it has been learned, for example, how news content is affected by entrenched social structures, daily deadlines, and resource allocation. To better understand workers' decisions, perceptions, and their role in the newsroom, Shoemaker and Reese urged researchers to examine the routines that go with news jobs.

To date, several scholars have examined convergence in relation to news routines and practices. Commonly, however, their studies have focused on individual cases in trend-setting multimedia operations. For example, through in-depth interviews and participant observation in three, high profile convergent newsrooms, Lawson-Borders unveiled several ways in which convergence and convergent technologies have had a profound effect on media content and newsroom culture.

She describes that impact in extremely broad terms, such as "communication," "commitment," and "competition." Her observations do not describe the daily, lived experience (or grounded reality) of news workers in these organizations—the specific struggles or challenges they face.

Although more detailed analyses exist (e.g., Singer), case studies like these, while insightful and useful, do not provide systematic, empirical evidence about convergence that can be generalized to the larger population of newsrooms currently practicing convergence nationwide. This study seeks to change that.

Without a doubt, pressure is growing on news workers to provide content to multiple media outlets—pressure that builds every day as media cross-ownership and consolidation expand across the country. Media organizations and news consumers are demanding information be made available through multiple media platforms.

To respond to those demands and succeed in their jobs, news workers must now craft content for their primary news outlet (for example, a television newscast) and produce additional versions of their stories for other media outlets, including the Internet and local radio. But in which specific ways and to what extent are such responsibilities having an impact on the jobs of today's local television journalists? The impact of convergence on news workers' daily routines and job perceptions is the focus of this study. Specifically, the following research questions were developed for the analysis:

RQ.sub.1: How do convergence-related tasks affect reporters' and producers' general news routines?

RQ.sub.2: How does media convergence affect reporters' and producers' perceptions of their jobs?

Previous research suggests market size might impact convergence activities. As noted earlier, Papper (2005) found top-50 television markets are more likely to dedicate staff to convergent content production. It could be assumed that news workers in larger media markets will feel more positive about convergence because they personally are required to devote less time to convergence-related tasks. Therefore, the authors posed the following hypothesis:

H.sub.1: As market size increases, reporters' and producers' perceptions of media convergence become more positive.

Finally, the authors were curious to find out how news workers' views about convergence compare to the opinions of news directors regarding the problems (or challenges) convergence poses in the newsroom. Therefore, one additional research question was posed:

RQ.sub.3: How do news workers' opinions about convergence compare to the opinions of news directors (as cited in previous research)?

To answer these questions, researchers conducted a nationwide survey of local television news reporters and producers. Because no sample frame exists for local television news workers, one was constructed for the study. This was a lengthy, three-step process. It took more than 6 months to develop the final sample frame and achieve an acceptable response rate.

The process began with a stratified random sample of small and medium television markets. The authors excluded top-50 media markets from the analysis because research shows news workers in these markets are less likely to personally perform convergence duties. Remaining media markets were divided into three subgroups based on Nielsen-defined DMAs: 51-100, 101-150, and 151-210. Twenty markets from each stratum were randomly selected.

Then, using a recent edition of the NATPE Guide to North American Media (NAPTE Guide to North American Media, 2004), NBC, ABC, CBS, and FOX affiliates within each market were identified. Only network affiliates were included because these stations are more likely to produce local news than are nonaffiliated stations.

Calls were made to each television station to procure a list of reporters and producers who worked in the newsroom on weekdays, contacting 238 television stations in 60 media markets across the United States. Of those, 185 were found to produce television newscasts. The names of 1618 producers and reporters were obtained and included in the original sample frame. Researchers mailed letters to each person requesting his or her participation in a Web-based survey. Postcard reminders were sent out 2 weeks later.

The initial response rate was lower than anticipated. A review of the data showed zero responses from workers in 14 different media markets. Authors theorized this might be because of the possibility that no convergent activities were taking place in these markets (so workers chose not to answer survey requests). Calls were made directly to the assignments desk at stations in these markets to determine whether that was, in fact, the case.

If no convergence was taking place, names of workers from those stations were removed from the original list. If convergence was taking place, researchers asked the stations' assignments editor (or in some cases, a news manager) to contact all reporters and producers and remind them about the survey deadline. The revised sample frame consisted of 1492 names.

Ultimately, 302 respondents participated in the study—a 20% response rate. This rate falls at the higher end of the 1-30% rates commonly achieved through Internet surveys in mass communication research. Authors address the response rate, issues regarding the sample's representativeness and generalizeability, and the advantages/disadvantages of Web-based surveys in greater detail in the Discussion section.

MEASURES

After logging onto the survey Web site, respondents were first given a definition of convergence and asked whether the station they worked for was involved in any convergent activities. For this study, convergence was broadly defined as "any kind of news partnership, alliance and/or collaboration with print, broadcast (TV or radio) or online news outlets. This includes your station's Web site."

If their station was not involved in any exchange of media content—meaning they, personally, did not participate in any convergent activity—they were automatically "skipped" to the end of the survey instrument to answer questions about themselves and the stations they worked for. If respondents' stations were involved in any kind of convergent activity, they continued on with the survey.

Although previous studies have assessed the opinions of news managers and journalism professors about the subject of convergence, this survey measures the opinions of reporters and producers. As such, it borrows from and adds to the work of previous researchers.

Using some elements of Papper's 2005 study and a list of convergent-related tasks employed by Tanner and Duhe, respondents made note of specific convergent activities that directly affected their daily news routines. In order to directly compare the responses of news workers with news managers, respondents were also asked to rate their station's overall experience with convergence.

Additionally, a battery of questions was included to ascertain how convergent activities affect news workers' own personal work habits as well as their perceptions about the habits of their peers. Researchers asked, for example, how much time they devoted to convergent activities per day, which specific challenges they faced in producing convergent content, how they would rate their personal experiences with media convergence, and whether they believed convergence activities interfered with the quality of their local television news content. To clarify, the researchers only measured perceptions about the impact of convergence on quality versus measuring the actual quality of content.

Finally, respondents provided pertinent station and demographic information. They were asked to identify their station's affiliate status (ABC, CBS, etc.), market size, how many hours of local news programming their station typically broadcast each weekday, and details about station ownership (such as whether their station was locally or group-owned and whether the station was part of an LMA or a Duopoly). Respondents were also asked to list their job title, gender, age, race/ethnicity, and category of income.

Online survey responses were first funneled directly into a Microsoft Excel spreadsheet. They were later uploaded into and analysed using the Statistical Package for Social Sciences (SPSS). Descriptive statistics were generated and chi-square analyses conducted on all categorical-level data.

Participating in the survey were 302 reporters and producers. Almost all respondents (97%) indicated their station practiced some form of convergence. Because this study deals specifically with news staffers who do participate in convergence, the 3% of respondents not practicing convergence (N = 10) were eliminated from the analysis.

Forty-five per cent of survey respondents worked in Nielson-defined DMAs sized 51-100; 24% were from markets 101-150 and 31% from 151-201. All of the stations produced news but the amount of news varied dramatically, ranging from 1/2 hour to 8 hours of local news programming per day. The average newsroom staff size was 30. The majority of respondents were reporters or anchor/reporters (60.6%). One quarter (24.1%) were producers or anchor/producers. Remaining respondents (15%) had "other" job titles, such as reporter/meteorologist or sports anchor/reporter.

Nearly 7 of 10 news workers (68%) said they now personally perform convergence-related tasks as part of their assigned duties. Most commonly, they produce content for their station's online product (61%). Less than one-quarter of respondents said they worked with another television station (21.6%) or radio station (19.5%). Fewer still worked on newspapers (7.5%) or magazines (.07%).

Clearly, when it comes to convergence, the Internet is the dominant medium with which local television reporters and producers are involved—100% of respondents (N = 292) said their station now had a Web site. More than half (55.1%)

indicated their stations had dedicated staff to their online convergence projects; 44.4% said no staff had been added. The rest were not sure.

Regarding the specific kind of work they do for their stations' Web sites, some of the most common tasks included writing summary stories (49.3%), physically posting content (47.9%), conducting question & answer sessions with viewers (32.5%), and providing previously unaired video and sound bites for the Web (21.6%).

Relatively few news workers said they provided Internet links through which viewers can find more information (15.4%), provided streaming video of stories (12.3%), posted still pictures (4.5%), created blogs (2.7%), or provided additional story facts or copy (2.4%). Not a single reporter or producer said he or she produced Internet-only stories.

Research Question 1 asked: How do convergence-related tasks affect reporters" and producers' general news routines? Of those news workers who report personally participating in convergence activities, almost three-quarters (72.1%) agreed or strongly agreed their workload was increasing because of it. Three-quarters (75.4%) indicated their coworkers' workload was also increasing.

When specifically asked how much time they spend on these tasks, most said they dedicated less than 30 minutes per day to convergence activities. However, nearly 14% of news workers said convergence work took more than an hour each day. Post hoc analysis found no significant correlation between market size and the amount of time employees spent on convergence work.

Research Question 2 asked: How does media convergence affect reporters' and producers' perceptions of their job? Much of what respondents had to say about their own work was generally positive. Among those doing convergent work, almost half (47.8%) agreed or strongly agreed that they "enjoyed working in other media." Of the other half, 36% were neutral on the subject and 16.3% said they did not enjoy it.

Although almost half of respondents reported that they personally enjoyed working with other media outlets, they could not say the same for their peers. When asked whether their coworkers enjoyed convergence work, only about one-quarter answered in the affirmative (25.4%).

Nearly one-third (30.3%) disagreed or strongly disagreed that their peers enjoyed the work. Post hoc analysis shows news workers were significantly more likely to think their peers disliked convergence work compared to themselves, although the association was relatively weak.

Regarding the impact of convergence on news quality, one-quarter of news workers agreed or strongly agreed that the quality of their own work (24.9%), as well as the work of their peers (24.2%), was suffering as a result of growing multimedia duties.

Because previous research shows stations in top-50 markets are more likely to dedicate staff to convergent content production, it was hypothesized that market size would affect the perceptions news workers have about convergence. Specifically, the authors expected to find: As market size increases, reporters' and producers' perceptions of media convergence become more positive. Results, although statistically significant, were in the opposite direction of what was expected. Reporters and producers in markets 51-100 were significantly more likely than their peers in smaller markets to have negative perceptions about certain aspects of media convergence, including feelings that:

- Their peers' workload was increasing;
- Multimedia activities were negatively affecting the quality of their peers' work;
- Their bosses were putting increasing pressure on them to provide convergence content to other media outlets.

The Cramer's V statistic suggests the strongest relationship is between the variables "market size" and "peers' workload increasing." The strength of association between the other two variables is relatively weaker, but the relationship is still statistically significant.

Despite these negative perceptions, the majority of reporters and producers (60.8%) perceived their television station's overall experience with convergence to be positive or very positive. No significant differences were found on this variable when market size was analysed.

Less than 10% said their station's experience had been negative (7.1%). When it came to their own personal experience with convergence, however, figures were slightly lower. Only 55.6% of news workers say they personally had a "positive" or "very positive" experience with convergence; 36.4% were neutral and nearly 8% (7.8%) said their personal experience was "negative" or "very negative."

Finally: How do news workers" opinions about convergence compare to the opinions of news directors? To compare the two groups, national survey data was culled from Duhe et al.'s 2004 study of news directors and general managers in the United States.

Both the current study and theirs asked respondents to rate their stations' overall experience with convergence. News workers were significantly less likely than their bosses to have a positive opinion about convergence:

As reflected in the Cramer's V statistic, the variables are moderately associated. Compared to their employees, news managers were far more pleased with their stations' experience with convergence. Not a single news manager reported having a negative experience.

Digging more deeply, significant differences were also discovered between the two groups regarding specific problems convergence might pose in the newsroom. However, before addressing the specific findings, a brief description of this method of analysis is called for. In both studies, researchers asked respondents to remark about a list of potential problems.

The questions, however, were asked somewhat differently. Duhe' et al. asked news managers to indicate (by checking or not checking a box) whether they felt a specific issue posed a problem in their newsroom—basically a "yes" or "no" response.

In this survey, respondents were given the same list but were asked to gauge (on a 5-point Likert scale) the extent to which the problem posed a challenge for them in their daily work routine—ranging from "no challenge" to "very challenging."

To compare the two studies, slight recoding was necessary. If the news worker said the issue was "no challenge" or "almost no challenge," the answer was recoded as "no." If respondent said the issue was "somewhat of a challenge," "challenging," or "very challenging," the response was recoded as "yes."

News managers and news workers had similar views about many of convergence's challenges. For example, the majority of managers and workers believed the pressure to increase content production was a challenge. The two groups also shared concerns about the lack of training, competition with partnering media (such as notifying each other of breaking news stories), and "losing their niche" (as broadcast television news providers). This analysis finds, however, news managers and news workers had significantly different views about the remaining three issues.

Reporters and producers were significantly more likely than news directors and general managers to believe decreasing quality, technological conflicts (such as computer software being incompatible for different media), and differing values or expectations when producing content for various media (such as print vs. broadcast culture) were at least somewhat a challenge in today's converged television newsrooms. The strength of association on these measures is somewhat weak regarding product quality and technology but moderate regarding differing values.

This study of medium and small market local TV news producers and reporters is the first of its kind. The random sample survey describes some of the ways in which convergence journalism affects news workers across America and the content they produce. Compared to previous research involving news managers, several results are notable.

PERSPECTIVES ON CONVERGENCE

- Differing opinions between managers and workers

regarding the impact of convergence on the newsroom are key findings of this study. Compared to news directors and general managers, reporters and producers are significantly more likely to feel that:

- Convergence negatively impacts the quality of the news;
- Technological hurdles hamper their efforts to produce convergent content;
- The values they hold about television news conflict with efforts to produce content for other media outlets.

Many news workers believe these issues pose substantial challenges in their daily news routines. News workers are also significantly less likely than their bosses to say their stations' overall experience with convergence has been a good one.

WORKLOAD AND QUALITY

Although the majority of news workers said their stations' forays into convergence have been positive, they did not characterize their own personal experiences in quite the same way. Less than half said they personally enjoyed convergence work and only one-quarter thought their coworkers enjoyed it.

Even though the majority of respondents spent, on average, less than 30 minutes per day producing convergence content, one-quarter of all news workers believed it interfered with the quality of their primary work. They also believed the work of their peers was suffering.

As one respondent wrote, "We spend too much time serving other masters. This reduces the quality and comprehensiveness of our own reporting." According to one reporter: "Convergence places a lot more responsibility on my shoulders.

I have far more work to do here than if my station did not practice convergence." Yet another worker believed convergence "makes it difficult to make deadlines and our staff is spread very thin."

Results demonstrate that a fair amount of discontent exists in the newsroom regarding convergence work. It is not surprising that news workers who spend the least amount of time on convergence work are the ones who are least bothered by (or concerned about) it. Compared to those who spend more than 30 minutes a day on convergence content, reporters and producers who spend less than 30 minutes per day are significantly less likely to believe that their multimedia duties interfere with quality of content that their station produces, the quality of work that they personally produce, and the quality of work that their coworkers produce.

They are also significantly less likely to believe that convergence poses at least somewhat of a challenge to their station's ability to maintain its niche in the market. In other words, the less time one spends producing convergence content, the better they feel about it. Conversely, those who dedicate more of their workday to convergence are more likely to be concerned about its effects on the news/journalistic product.

Because the average news worker spends less than 30 minutes per day on convergence, some readers might think that"concerned" news staffers are simply complainers--unhappy with their growing workload. As such, some might wonder whether their judgment about decreasing quality is biased. While that is certainly possible, it is also possible to interpret their opinions in another way. While 30 minutes per day may seem like a relatively short amount of time, to those who work in the television news industry, a half-hour represents something much different.

Only a decade ago, news producers and reporters commonly produced newscasts at 6 and 11 p.m. only--totaling an hour of news per day. According to this study, TV stations aired more than 4 hours, on average, of news per day. Coupled with shrinking budgets and staff sizes, news workers now have to produce more than ever before, with fewer resources. For some respondents, even spending 10 or 15 minutes on convergence is"lost" time--time that could be devoted to improving journalistic performance--following story leads, polishing writing, conducting research, and checking sources.

Perceptions and Market Size. Among all the news workers surveyed, reporters and producers in medium-sized markets appeared to have the most negative perceptions about the effects of convergence. Those in DMAs 51-100 were significantly more likely than their peers in smaller markets to feel pressure from management to produce convergent content. They were also significantly more likely to indicate that their peers' workload was increasing and that the quality of that work was suffering. These findings run contrary to the researchers' expectations.

Based on previous research, it was expected that workers in DMAs 51-100 would feel more positive about convergence than their peers in smaller markets because larger markets are more likely to dedicate staff to producing convergent content. This was not the case among the stations/markets studied. Results showed no relationship between convergence staffing and market size. Results did show, however, that producers and reporters in DMAs 51-100 were responsible for producing significantly more hours of news per day than workers in smaller markets.

Perhaps higher negative feelings towards convergence in medium markets stem directly from the lack of additional resources and increased pressure to produce more news in markets known to be more competitive. This assumption is reflected in open-ended statements from several respondents. When asked about what they would tell their bosses about convergence, for example, numerous respondents from these markets said things such as"more manpower is needed,""we are maxed out," and"unless more staff is added to handle the additional workload, overall quality of all products will be reduced."

Despite these concerns, it is unlikely their bosses can (or will) do much to change current conditions. Competition is growing, cost-cutting measures are being instituted throughout the industry, and pressure is mounting to produce new and different kinds of content to attract fragmenting audiences. Whether they like it or not, most managers and news workers understand convergence is here to stay.

Open-ended responses show news workers realise the increasingly important part convergence plays in their employer's strategic plans to gain exposure, audience, and advertising revenue. As one respondent put it:"At first it's a real challenge, but you learn quickly to adjust to the market. If you don't, your newsroom ends up at a loss."

Another worker said:"I understand the reasons behind convergence, but I'm not a fan." But some other workers are fans and say it draws necessary attention to the station:"Our newsroom is heavily invested in terms of time and talent with convergence--it seems to work very well. It gives us a bigger presence and ability to reach new viewers.... We are always looking for new ways to get our product out there."

CONVERGENCE DUTIES IN DETAIL

In addition to gauging news workers' perspectives about convergence, another central goal of this study was to describe the specific kinds of convergence tasks staffers were performing. Results indicate that, in local television newsrooms today, nearly 70% of the reporters and producers now personally perform tasks for media other than their own TV stations. Typically, that meant generating content for their station's Web site, followed by another TV station, then radio. A full 100% of respondents said their station now had an online presence. Only about half of those stations, however, had added staff to help with computer-based content.

Most convergent-related activities that reporters and producers were tasked with involved re-purposing content for a Web site. Such jobs include summarizing and then posting stories that have already run on their newscasts. In addition, many news workers said they had taken part in online question and answer sessions with viewers. Generally, however, little or no new information was being produced for the audience.

Very few respondents said they provided still pictures, added additional facts, or posted links for stories on the Web.

Not a single person said he or she created an Internet-only story. In one interesting finding, less than 22% of respondents reported providing unaired video or sound bites for their station's Web site and only 12% provided streaming video of selected stories--surprising because video is so readily available at TV stations.

Almost none of their duties involve what some experts would call"true convergence"--such as a TV reporter working with a local newspaper reporter and writing and producing an investigative piece for both media. These results are in line with previous studies that suggest television stations are not necessarily practicing innovative and new forms of convergence journalism or requiring their newsroom employees to truly report for multiple media.

RESPONSE RATES, ONLINE DESIGN, AND SAMPLE FRAME

Finally, some of the biggest insights gleaned from this study did not involve specific survey responses. Instead, they involve the process of developing the study's sample frame, the authors' choice of survey method, and the process of achieving an acceptable response rate. All three could be viewed as limitations by readers and, as such, are worthy of further consideration.

RESPONSE RATE AND ONLINE SURVEY DESIGN

Only 20% of news workers who received a request to participate in this study actually filled out a survey. While response rates on broadcast news surveys vary widely in peer-reviewed media journals, ranging from 20% to approximately 50%, response rates are notoriously lower for Internet surveys. According to Wimmer & Dominick (2006), rates typically range between 1% and 30%. By current standards, then, the response rate to this survey is reasonably good.

Still, there is cause to wonder whether the results can be generalized to the larger population of newsrooms practicing convergence nationwide and whether the choice of a Web-based survey was the best approach. The authors believe the answer is yes on both accounts. Besides being cheaper, easier, and more cost-effective, Internet research has several advantages specific to the study of television news workers.

Because they are busy professionals, frequently out in the field, working on deadline, working unusual shifts, and working in different time zones, reporters and producers are notoriously difficult to reach—making them a perfect population for an Internet survey approach versus a phone survey.

Generally, the current authors believed news workers would be more likely to fill out a survey if they could do it on their own schedule and proceed at their own pace.

Additionally, because news workers spend hours in front of computers as part of their daily routine, it was assumed a Web survey would not deter them from participating (as might be the case with members of the general public). Finally, there is no guarantee that response rates would be higher if they had received the survey by mail. In fact, with survey fatigue rising among news workers, it is possible response rates achieved through this survey method were higher than would be reached through other means.

As for the representativeness of the sample, according to Wimmer and Dominick (2006), there is no way for researchers to determine if an Internet sample is representative of the population from which the sample was selected. While there is no way to guarantee that this sample is representative of all reporters and producers in small and medium markets across America, there is evidence to suggest the results are generalizable.

The most compelling evidence involves the demographics of survey respondents. When gender, race, age, job title, and market size are taken into consideration, the makeup of the survey respondents fits roughly within the parameters of the population at large. Even though the response rate is relatively low at 20%, there is nothing to suggest a larger sample would be any more representative of the population.

Sample Frame. Finally, the difficulty locating potential research subjects and building the sample frame bear further consideration. Many previous researchers have studied convergence by assessing the perspectives of news managers. This makes a great deal of sense given that managers' names and station affiliations are readily available through organizations such as the Radio-Television News Directors Association (RTNDA) and the National Association of Television Programme Executives (NATPE).

No such lists exist, however, for news workers. For this study, constructing the sample frame was laborious and time-consuming. Individual stations were called numerous times and managers were asked (in some cases, begged) to provide the names of reporters and producers. The process took several months and, in some cases, proved to be problematic. Many news managers were simply unwilling or unable to provide such information.

Producers' names were especially difficult to obtain because, unlike reporters, they work largely behind the scenes. Their names and faces are not publicly displayed on the station's newscasts or Web site and for some reason the stations feel these news workers deserve anonymity.

Media ownership issues further complicated development of the sample frame. Early on, students who called to obtain the names of reporters and producers discovered many duplicate names between stations in the same market. For example, they found the same reporters worked for WWXX and WWYY but the two stations did not share producers.

Confusion quickly set in. It became increasingly difficult to determine who worked for which station and how best to cull the sample frame (so that duplicate survey requests were not sent out to potential respondents). Researchers made several follow-up calls to clarify and correctly amend the list.

Even during those calls, in some cases, employees were unable to describe whether they worked for a duopoly (where the same company owned both stations) or as part of an LMA (where one company hires another to produce its news). Such matters make developing a quality sample frame tricky, a complication that will only increase as consolidation takes hold in more media markets. Ultimately, data revealed 40% of respondents worked for a duopoly.

Whether studying convergence or any other media topic, these problems have direct bearing on communications research.

A review of the past 10 years of several peer-reviewed journalism and mass communications journals revealed few, if any, studies of local television news that surveyed staffers. The authors believe the dearth of literature related to the daily routines of working journalists, especially in television, could be related to factors such as those described above.

In years to come, one would expect it to become increasingly difficult to construct quality sample frames and gather national survey data.

Although news managers' expectations and viewpoints are important, for a more complete understanding of the news process, it is critical that communications scholars examine the news staffers and their workplace realities. These workers can have a significant impact on what information is ultimately disseminated to the public.

These findings should raise red flags for news managers, media scholars, and critics. At the very least, they should generate at least some concern and conversation in newsrooms (and classrooms) across the country. Perhaps most important are the implications for news managers. News directors and general managers believe convergence is working well at their respective stations. But they are not the ones producing content for newscasts on a daily basis.

These days, news directors frequently become bogged down in budget and staffing decisions, finding less time to focus on editorial content. Convergence might provide ways for stations to brand themselves in the marketplace, create a competitive edge, and enhance revenue streams, but keeping an eye on the financial potential of convergence at the expense of editorial impact might spell more trouble for an already struggling industry.

If the quality of news content suffers further because of convergence, local TV news viewership might continue its steady and well-documented decline. The research also has implications for journalism educators.

Nearly half of the news workers surveyed in this study believed additional training would increase their job performance. Research shows, however, 67.3% of newsrooms in America offer no such support.

It is troubling that the industry for which these reporters and producers work is generally failing to provide them with the help they need to improve.

It presents an opportunity, however, for journalism programs to step in and fill the void—providing future journalists with the skills they need to compete and excel in the modern workplace. Some of those specific skills were outlined in this study and could be translated into curricula in various ways.

Then, there are implications for media scholars. This study has laid the groundwork for a number of future research possibilities. Because the opinions of news workers should not be overlooked in broadcast news research, scholars should explore the best manner in which to reach and examine this rarely studied population.

Relating specifically to the topic of convergence, the differences between TV news managers and news staffers concerning their perceptions of media convergence needs further exploration. It would also be profitable to assess the workplace behaviours and perceptions of print journalists and compare it to the experiences of broadcast workers.

Efforts to analyse actual content quality as it correlates with convergence could also be profitable. In this study, only perceptions about quality were gauged. Future research should attempt to quantify what "quality" news content looks like, content-analyse media messages produced in convergence versus non-converged newsrooms, and compare the two. Such a method would demonstrate the actual effect of convergence on quality (vs. perception alone).

Though the current study focused specifically on local television news workers' perceptions of convergence, it is evident that the entire media industry is experiencing seismic changes. No matter the focus, it is critical that scholars continue to examine the phenomenon of media convergence and its impact on news workers. This is especially necessary as the news and information industries, and their methods for delivering content in an ever-shifting technological world, continue to evolve.

Chapter 6

Interpreting Nonverbal Behaviour

According to Gumperz, our ability to communicate with others depends on 'shared interpretive conventions'. To make sense of talk between people, communicators must have language-based and socio-cultural knowledge that allows them to use information in and around an utterance to help choose from an array of meanings that could be given to that utterance. This convention-based view of communicative practice becomes complicated when applied to the use and understanding of nonverbal cues, however, because not all nonverbal behaviours require interpretive processes.

Nonetheless, many nonverbal cues that occur in communicative contexts are, like language, open to a range of meaning attributions and necessitate communicators understanding the set of interpretations that may he attached to the cues through contextualized and conventionalized practice.

One way to think about conventional interpretive practices is with the idea of framing. Frames are definitions for communicative events that guide our subjective involvement. According to Gumperz, frames 'enable us to distinguish among permissible interpretive options... [and the] typifications reflected in... interpretive frames derived from previous interactive experience are the foundations of the practical reasoning processes on which we rely in the conduct of our affairs'.

Thus, a way to make sense of the meanings given to communicative acts—and to understand the larger conventions within which the meanings are embedded—is to assess the underlying frames that support certain meanings for potentially ambiguous cues.

Although many interpersonal communication researchers understand the importance of framing as a means by which people make sense of specific interpersonal behaviours, events, and relationships, media theorists have thus far discussed framing much more expansively. According to Entman,'the concept of [media] framing... offers a way to describe the power of a communicating text'. Specifically, to frame is to select some aspects of a perceived reality and make them more salient in a communicating text, in such a way as to promote a particular problem definition, causal interpretation, moral evaluation, and/or treatment recommendation for the items described.

For media framing theorists, the results of framing--or choosing certain things to talk about and particular ways to talk about them within texts--is the creation or reinforcement of what is or should be salient to an audience, how that audience should evaluate the thing being framed, and, possibly, a move to get the audience to undertake some action related to what has been framed. Although texts (e.g., news coverage) are embedded in a set of institutional practices that may constrain them, they can also work to construct a reality for those who attend to those texts.

In this way, news media are seen as active participants in a larger social drama, promoting particular performances and not others. One way to look further into the frames used in meanings given to nonverbal behaviour is located in media discourse about nonverbal cues. Jaworski and Galasinski referred to the particular set of flames that encompass media talk about communication as metapragmatics. They argued that such metapragmatic flaming is a useful way to view the textual presentation of nonverbal cues:

The relative indeterminacy and immediacy of non-verbal behaviour (e.g., facial expressions and gestures) accounts for the great ease with which the media, as well as the social actors in non-institutional, face-to-face contexts can and do use metapragmatic manipulation of non-verbal behaviour...

It is often the verbal accounts of non-verbal behaviour that we rely on in disambiguating and/or imposing preferred interpretations on the non-verbal medium.

The authors used this argument to investigate several British newspapers' coverage of Clinton's nonverbal communication during his grand jury testimony regarding his relationship with Monica Lewinski. They found, among other things, tremendous variety in the interpretations of (or meaning given to) Clinton's nonverbal behaviours by different newspapers, and these presentations of the behaviours largely mirrored the political orientation of the sources.

Viewing the representation of, or metapragmatics for, nonverbal communication in media texts is helpful for a number of reasons. First, examining the meanings given to nonverbal cues by the media shows potential ways in which audiences are likely to think about the communicative ability of the cues. In searching for evidence of frames in media discourse, interpersonal scholars may also find evidence of conventionalized flames reflecting everyday understandings of what nonverbal cues may mean.

Second, investigating potentially diverse media coverage of a nonverbal event allows us to think more about the choice making behind how we use nonverbal behaviours. Although the list of possible meanings given to nonverbal cues is numerous, media discussions--particularly those that may be affected by politics and perspective--provide a largely untapped resource for increasing awareness of the repertoire of conventionalized meanings for nonverbal cues.

The primary aim of this study, however, is not to use the discourse to find evidence of political perspective, as was the case for Jaworski and Galasinski, although such a goal is laudable (and, although, discussion of political views occurs in our data). Nor are we concerned primarily with looking at the media texts as representations of culture. Rather, we are interested more generally with broadening the database from which we can learn about nonverbal cues by discerning the general flames, and within these, the meanings, given to nonverbal cues.

Specifically, we argue that an understanding of flaming can help link the processes involved in both interpersonal and media-based interpretations of nonverbal cues. Such a goal is consistent with calls to integrate better the interpersonal and mass communication literatures and to reach across communication subdisciplines more generally. A flaming perspective, particularly the well-developed one used by many media scholars, also provides an opportunity to reveal conventionalized'organizing principles' within which specific meanings for nonverbal cues may be understood.

Given the importance of media for socializing people into the use of nonverbal behaviour, specifically enactments of emotional expression, and the limited discussion attempting to capture the myriad media messages that may be attributed to nonverbal action, these goals seem an important step in understanding more fully the nature of interpreting nonverbal actions.

In this study, we use metapragmatic discourse about the 1993 handshake (and other nonverbal cues surrounding the handshake) between Yitzhak Rabin and Yasser Arafat that was'guided by' Bill Clinton to assess the frames (and within those frames, the meanings) given to the nonverbal cues that occurred in and around this event. Specifically, we analyse English-language Israeli and Palestinian press coverage, and translations of Israeli Hebrew and Palestinian Arabic coverage, to assess the interpretive frames given to this oft-described'historic' nonverbal event. We do so with two purposes:

- To provide evidence of conventionalized media frames for nonverbal interaction behaviour;
- To assess some meanings for nonverbal cues that occur within these frames. Doing so, however, requires greater awareness (and framing) of the event itself and the cultural and political climates in which the media accounts are embedded.

THE EVENT

The handshake between Rabin and Arafat took place

before a long-lasting backdrop of violence between Israelis and Palestinians (CNN, 2003).

The unrest between the two peoples had become normative since the founding of the Israeli state in 1948 and, whereas a substantial peace movement existed within Israel at the time of the handshake, most Israelis and Palestinians did not have much hope for a peaceful end to the complex conflict.

The issues at stake were never as clear-cut as the Western media portrayed. The basic foundation of the conflict found its feet on one small and coveted piece of land split by outside European interests between two peoples.

For the most part, Israelis saw their return to Israel as a return to their historic Jewish homeland, a place of safety that was thought especially necessary following the Holocaust. And, for the most part, Arab countries saw the Israelis' arrival as another wave of colonization.

Following several wars waged and lost by Arab countries against Israel, Palestinians began their own uprising on the ground in the form of the first Intifadah. It was within this climate prior to September 1993 that, in hopes of achieving peace, Israeli Prime Minister Yitzhak Rabin and Palestinian Liberation Organization leader Yasser Arafat agreed to a series of unprecedented secret negotiations conducted under the auspices of Norwegian negotiators.

The talks were to culminate and make their public debut in the form of a signing ceremony on the White House lawn. Discussion arose immediately in newspapers, television, and radio about the nature and content of the upcoming ceremony.

The handshake itself generated a flood of discussion in various nations' media that has continued to the present time. At the end of 1999, the handshake was still present enough in media consciousness to make Time Magazine's list of 100 events of the 20th century we shouldn't ignore.'

The handshake itself occurred on a stage created for the event, and flags and other ceremonial decor accompanied the stage setting. The three primary participants, Clinton, Rabin, and Arafat, walked out from the White House together (with Clinton in between the other two). In descriptions of the event in the US media, once on stage, Clinton used his arms to pull the two other men toward one another.

The end result was a handshake and other concurrent nonverbal cues, caught in still and moving photographs, which created an enduring image of the event.

The public ceremony captured on film preceded the primary purpose of the meeting: the signing of the Declaration of Principles on Interim Self-Government Arrangements.

In this declaration, the Israeli government recognized the legitimacy of the Palestinian Liberation Organization, and the PLO agreed to Israel's right to exist. Rabin and Arafat jointly received the Nobel Peace Prize in 1994 for these efforts.

But peace did not reign (CNN, 2003). In 1995, reportedly in response to Rabin's peace efforts, an Israeli assassinated Rabin. Israeli leadership shifted to the right politically, and currently another'sworn enemy' of Arafat, Ariel Sharon, is in power. Palestinian leadership also shifted, though Arafat continued as the official leader of the PLO until his recent death in November 2004.

Palestinians currently wage a second, more violent and deadly Intifadah, and Israel has commenced building a wall between Israel and the Palestinian Territories.

Still, the Israeli and Palestinian governments negotiate off and on with talks that are based on the Oslo Accords, set into motion by Rabin and Arafat's handshake. Coverage of the handshake, and the subsequent events related to it, thus continues within Israeli and Palestinian media.

ISRAELI AND PALESTINIAN MEDIA

Although our focus is not on comparison of these two media groups, some understanding of their role in their larger cultures is important for revealing frames and meanings that emerge across their discourse. Like all national/cultural groups, Israeli and Palestinian communication is likely to reflect the values, characteristics, and tensions within the larger societies.

In their review of Israeli-Jews' and Palestinians' interactional communication practices, for example, Ellis and Maoz (2002) asserted that these two cultures 'have each emerged from the special circumstances of its history', and their communicative practices reflect these unique histories.

Little research has focused thus far on Palestinian media specifically, but Arab media generally have been examined in some depth. Specifically, El Affendi argued that a weak economic base, Arab nationalism, the development of a politicized Islam, and cultural norms all affected the development of Arab media.

As well, most Arab journalists are particularly likely to work toward the preservation of Arab culture. In addition, Amin (2002) argued that, in general, Arab governments and internal (media-based) values both limit freedom of the press. Importantly, freedom of the press may be limited because of concerns with libel and slander, consistent with the cultural values of harmony and the importance of personal reputation.

Israeli media are, on the other hand, defined as multivoiced, reflecting a range of ideological 'camps' that are consistent with ideological divisions within the larger nation. In particular, newspapers have been characterized as reflecting the 'variety of opinions within the public at large' and often present quite different interpretations for the same event. Overall, Israeli coverage tends to be quite direct and confrontational.

Despite these differences in history and style, the media in both cultures are concerned greatly with politics. Bloch (2000) contended that Israelis are particularly interested in 'issues of the public domain', and the Israeli media are considered 'the central arena for deliberation'.

More specifically, First (2002) described Israeli media as 'naturally preoccupied with the Arab-Israeli conflict'. Likewise, Amin (2002) described the media as playing 'an important role' in the Arab world, and El Affendi asserts that the Arab media have particularly close ties to politics and political movements. It is within this full cultural context that our analyses are drawn.

Assuming that using various media texts allows for greater access to conventionalized frames for nonverbal behaviour, the present study looks across a range of Israeli and Palestinian media sources for the primary interpretative structures (i.e., frames) apparent in the metapragmatic discourse surrounding the handshake.

We also wanted to identify particular meanings given to the handshake and other related nonverbal cues. Based on these goals, we ask, across our collection of media texts, what are the most notable frames and meanings provided for nonverbal communication surrounding this event? We used the following methods to help assess this research question.

The first step in our project included collecting a corpus of data from which to find general frames and specific meanings apparent in discourse surrounding the handshake and its related behaviours. Because of language limitations, we limited our search for the present study to English language and already translated to English Israeli and Palestinian media that originated from within Israel or the Palestinian territories; we note the constraints of this choice in our discussion section.

English-language Israeli press is relatively plentiful, but English-language Palestinian press and translated-to-English Israeli and Palestinian press are neither plentiful nor easily accessible. Data, therefore, were gathered using a variety of search engines and methods. The search engines that we used were Lexis-Nexis, the Index to the Foreign Broadcast Information Service (FBIS), and the World News Connection. For Lexis-Nexis, we used the search terms 'Arafat' and 'Rabin' and 'handshake' on full texts.

FBIS, which only existed through 1996, is a limited search engine, so we did our searches more broadly, using the terms 'Arafat' and 'Rabin.' We did two searches of World News Connection, a successor to the daily reports from FBIS that provided translations of non-US print and broadcast media: an open search using 'Rabin,' 'Arafat,' 'handshake' not combined; then a Boolean search using 'Rabin,' 'Arafat,' and 'hand*.' In addition, we searched the Palestinian Report

Online directly, using search terms 'Arafat' and 'Rabin' and 'handshake' on full text.

MEDIA SOURCES

The media sources that provided the data derived from the above search engines represented a range of outlets. Israeli media were more accessible and, therefore, formed the majority of our data.

The data comprised articles that were a majority news stories and a minority opinion pieces and letters to the editor. Letters to the editor and opinion pieces, though often not authored by media professionals, were included in our study based on the understanding that their publication in the press, as well as their editing by journalism professionals, consist of media choices of how to represent an event.

All our media searches garnered multiple publications that we then narrowed down to articles that addressed the handshake in some substance, ranging from describing the handshake with at least one adjective to in-depth description of the handshake.

Articles that mentioned the handshake but did not apply any description or attribute any meaning to the handshake were discarded and not included in the study.

Lexis-Nexis archived the Jerusalem Post, an Israeli English-language daily newspaper, and the Jerusalem Report, an Israeli English-language magazine published biweekly in Jerusalem.

Each was available archived from before the handshake until the present. Lexis-Nexis also recently picked up Ha'aretz, the Israeli Hebrew-language daily that is the paper of record and that recently started to publish an English version. The earliest Ha'aretz story found was dated July 16, 1999. The Jerusalem Post provided the most articles (n = 126).

The Jerusalem Report provided the second largest amount of articles (n = 35). Ha'aretz provided fewer (n = 3). Lexis-Nexis archived no Palestinian press. FBIS directed us to US government translations of news, providing four articles from between September 9, 1993 and December 31, 1993: two from Israel's Qol Yisra'el radio news programme, one from Israel Television Network, one from Yedi'ot Aharonot, an Israeli daily newspaper; and, again, none from Palestinian media. Searches of the World News Collection unearthed 11 Palestinian articles and 3 Israeli articles, with the earliest dating February 13, 1999.

Palestinian outlets providing articles were print and internet versions of Jerusalem's Al-Quds (n = 5), the largest circulation Palestinian newspaper and an independent outlet that supported the peace process and the Palestinian Authority, and print and internet versions of Ramallah's Al-Ayyam (n = 6), an independent newspaper supportive of the Palestinian Authority.

Israeli outlets were limited to Ma'ariv (n = 3), Israel's second largest circulation Hebrew-language daily newspaper. Five stories were culled from a search of the Palestinian Report Online, an English-language publication billed as Palestine's only independent news digest, the earliest dating June 28, 1996.

ANALYTICAL PROCEDURES

The above searches resulted in 187 texts for analysis: 171 from Israeli coverage, and 16 from Palestinian/Arab coverage. The group of articles was divided into two content-balanced halves, with one half going to each researcher.

The researchers each reduced the content of their halves to handshake-relevant sections of the articles and then combined the cut-down versions.

Although there are a number of methods used to analyse data for framing studies, we chose to use a grounded approach. Given that no previous research provided likely frames identifiable in our data, we followed Strauss and Corbin's reasoning that the best approach was to create an interplay between ourselves and the data, allowing for the emergence and subsequent modification of concepts in our data.

To do so, we used Strauss and Corbin's three steps:

- Examination of the data to develop an initial classification scheme (i.e., open-coding);

- A return to the data after the initial classifications were defined and named in order to assess their fit with the data (i.e., asking questions);
- Choosing from amongst the many classifications those that appeared most salient or relevant to the analysis (i.e., trimming).

For step one, both researchers read the full set of texts separately and made notes about possible frames (i.e., general ways to talk about the handshake and other cues) that appeared to be apparent in the data as well as specific meanings (i.e., interpretations of the cues). We then compared our open codes. We identified seven possible frames and termed these, initially, motivations, symbols/metaphors, change agents/transformative, denials of importance or meaning, choreographed, political/oppositional, and emotion producing.

The list of specific meanings was more extensive and included the following: dependency, trust, personal characterizations, emotional expressions, peace/end of hostilities, change in role, contact, legitimacy/recognition, breaking a taboo, time marker, empty of meaning/symbolism/ value, pledge/promise/agreement, political exigency, resignation, hope, attempts to humanize, betrayal, creating a dialogue, reluctance/hesitance, violence, distaste, exuberance, curse, invoking, irreversibility of process, mental transformation, change in relationship, wishing to be somewhere else, good will, honour, vision, betrayal, and reciprocity/understanding.

For step two, the first author returned to the data to see if the initial frames defined the data well, could be described adequately as frames, and were inclusive enough to represent the data. From this assessment of fit, it seemed, for example, that certain frames (e.g., 'political' and 'emotion-provoking') were better seen as important to discuss across the data rather than as framing devices.

The first author also looked at the data in comparison to the list of meanings created in the first round to see whether there were others that were not included previously, there was too much overlap between any of the meanings, and if there were enough data to suggest that such meanings were salient in the texts.

At the third step, the first and second author discussed the data in terms of these criteria and worked to'trim' the categorization process to those frames and meanings that were most identifiable within the data corpus.

The second author then returned to the full data set to assess her view of the frames and meanings that emerged after step two. With some minor modifications, the second author confirmed the strength of the frames and meanings identified by the first author. It is the results of this third step that we discuss in our analysis.

Although what counts as a'frame' may itself be subject to interpretation and dependent on the researchers' goals, we determined that frames in these data were large level conceptualizations of what functions the nonverbal cues served in this interaction.

These larger frames did not appear to dictate a particular meaning. Instead, they can be seen as a sort of'meta-level meaning,' within which more particular interpretations fit. Our final exploration of the data reflected two primary, although not mutually exclusive, frames. We call these selected frames representations and transformations. Within each frame, we identified specific meanings that cluster in and characterize the frame.

REPRESENTATIONS

One overarching frame that we saw in these data involved the conceptualization of nonverbal cues as a'stand in' for a larger process, issue, or state. This type of frame worked to conceptualize nonverbal cues as representative of something intangible/ abstract and based in the larger event or context in which the behaviours occurred. The most notable referents (i.e., specific meanings) for the nonverbal cues framed as representations were peace/hope/optimism, authority/legitimacy, agreement/promise, violence, betrayal, anguish, and dislike.

In one account, for example, Arafat's handshake represented peace:'We want to tell President Bush again that President Yasir Arafat is a symbol of national liberation and a freedom fighter, and that he still extends his hand for a fair peace, a peace that Israel rejects'. Another asserted,'the handshake... meant simply peace, no more intifada, no more Israeli soldiers in the streets'.

Relatedly, Leah Rabin, Yitzhak Rabin's widow, was quoted as saying that'[t]he handshake (of Yitzhak Rabin) two years ago with Yasser Arafat symbolized hope', and another noted that the handshake could be viewed as a representation of optimism for conflict resolution,'the historic handshake... has since come to symbolize the inherent solubility of all international conflicts'.

In addition to peace, hope, and optimism, some of the metapragmatic discourse we reviewed talked about the handshake in terms of its function for representing legitimacy of the process and those involved in it. For one author, for example, the recognition of Yasser Arafat and the PLO as'the two legitimate representatives of the Palestinian people... [was] confirmed by the late Israeli Prime Minister Yitzhaq Rabin in his historic handshake'.

For another,'[i]t was Rabin's handshake that lent the Oslo accords the widespread legitimacy in Israel and throughout the world'. Relatedly, and consistent with previous view of the functions of handshakes, the handshake was seen as an acknowledgement of the handshakers' agreement and a promise to move forward.

Although much of the media coverage of the handshake, especially that which occurred soon after the handshake, was positive, other descriptions of the handshake (and the hand itself) as representational were not as positively toned; the discourse provides very different meanings than those we just discussed.

The hands, for example, were often discussed as'bloodstained,' and the discourse using this metaphorical approach appeared to see the hands doing the shaking as representative of violence. For instance, one source noted,'[t]he hands of [the Democratic Front for the Liberation of Palestine's Secretary General] Hawatimah are stained with Jewish blood.' Another made a similar claim about Arafat's hand:'To the writers of this column who stood on the White House lawn that September day in 1993 and watched an Israeli prime minister shake the bloodstained hand of Yasser Arafat, the atmosphere seemed funereal'.

Other more negative interpretations were offered in these texts. One meaning, betrayal, can be seen in the following:'Many Israeli Jews saw his handshake with Arafat as an act of betrayal'. For another, betrayal as a meaning was countered with others' reactions:'[W]hen the peace accords were signed and the historic handshake on the White House lawn took place, my sons and daughters were pleased, hopeful, excited. I was sick to my stomach. How could Rabin do it?

Arafat was a terrorist, the enemy, the murderer of small children'. In a less direct way, an additional source revealed an interpretation of the handshake as betrayal by stating,'[t]he handshake says:'Terror wins.''Eventually, terrorists get what they want.''Murdering innocent Israeli men, women and children is the best way to negotiate a deal'. Such texts reflect the attitudes of the media sources about the handshake and the process it represented. They also present real differences in view about the nature of the peace process within Israeli and Palestinian communities.

In addition to representations of abstract ideas and processes surrounding the participants, additional coverage reflecting a representational frame, and involving an evaluative component to such frames, centered on attitudes and emotions of the participants as the particular meanings represented.

Many of the texts focusing on this type of representation included discussion of an array of nonverbal behaviours that occurred alongside the handshake and worked to conceptualize it. One of these particular attitude-meanings was anguish. Focusing largely on kinesic cues, a reporter noted that'Rabin looked miserable and as if he wanted to get out of there... Rabin looked very tight, tense, and self-protected, he stood with his hands hugging himself, rocking back and forth.

This is a form of self-protection--autistic children do this a lot'. This interpretation was'confirmed' in a text quoting Shimon Perez:'After [Rabin] did shake his hand--following a lot of pressure from Clinton--he turned to me [Perez] and whispered:"It's your turn. I went through hell, now you go too"'. Other texts provided interpretations regarding attitudes toward others, particularly a representation of dislike.

Dislike as a meaning was apparent in the following:'Rabin's body language showed more than a thousand witnesses that he found Arafat repellent'; and'Rabin did not hop into bed with Arafat overnight. It took years before he could bring himself to shake Arafat's hand--and we all remember the look on his face when he eventually did'. Interestingly, Arafat's behaviours were interpreted typically as more ebullient.

Overall, the discourse we identified as consistent with a representational frame talked directly or indirectly about one or more nonverbal cues as'stand ins' for some larger, value-laden, abstract concept. This general frame for the handshake and related nonverbal cues shows an interpretation that nonverbal cues can act as representatives of, or conduits for, a more abstract issue or process. The range of the specific meanings was enormous.

Sometimes these representations--whether positively or negatively toned--were conceptualized as very strategic or orchestrated. For instance, one source talked about how a future handshake ceremony could'send a signal to rejectionists in the Middle East that they will not be allowed to thwart Middle East peace efforts'.

Another article, quoting Shimon Peres, reflected that the behaviours may have been strategic for the participants themselves. It explained,'Yesterday, he [Rabin] must have been imagining how he was going to be able to shake Yasser Arafat's hand... his wife Leah so aptly put it yesterday, he was going to have to'swallow it' and extend his hand'.

Whereas other behaviours were described as representative in some more natural or accidental way, other cues were representational of a strategic process. This form of orchestrated representation occurred most commonly for Clinton's role in the interaction.

Within this larger way of framing the representational function of nonverbal behaviour, there was a cluster of specific abstract concepts (i.e., meanings) represented by the handshake and related cues. These included the behaviours as representing (i.e., standing in for) peace, hope, optimism, legitimacy, agreement/acceptance, violence, betrayal, and emotions or attitudes.

Typically, only one of these meanings was offered within a particular text. The diversity of meanings, especially when representing very different affective responses, reflects the ways in which the media may provide evidence of contested meanings (i.e., showing that one interpretation may be better than another).

Perhaps the best evidence of contestation occurred, however, in those texts that provided'antirepresentative' framing, stating, often explicitly, that the behaviour did not have a particular meaning.

Despite the denial of meaning, the nature of the frame centered on the capacity of nonverbal cues to stand for (or not represent) a particular, often abstract, referent. Thus, the frame remained the same even if the individual interpretations within it did not.

TRANSFORMATIONS

Our first theme portrayed the handshake and its related behaviours as reflections of something that is. The second frame apparent in this discourse focused on the potential of nonverbal cues to bring about some state or process that did not yet exist. That is, a primary meaning given to the handshake and related cues was as actions or events portrayed as either:

- Having the power to change situations, things, and people from one way of being to another,

- Marking a point of change. What was transformed or changed included many of the meanings identified in the first frame: the legitimacy of the process and the people involved and the potential of the peace process.

But the framing oriented an understanding of these nonverbal cues as functioning primarily to bring about, rather than just represent, a new reality. As noted, some of the discourse using a transformation frame talked about the same specific meanings that we identified in the representation frame.

For example, the handshake was described, not only a representation of peace, but also as having agency in bringing about peace. This type of transformation discourse took a number of forms.

As one writer stated, 'referring to the historic White House handshake... Clinton said: "As we have seen before at this house... what first seems unlikely, even impossible, can actually become reality when the will for peace is strong."'

Likewise, 'Veteran Israeli peace campaigner Abie Nathan said yesterday that after 20 years and a handshake... he was closing the Voice of Peace radio station... "I believe the ship did its job—there's peace now"'.

Another transformation meaning, recalling the representational meaning of legitimacy, asserted that the handshake brought about legitimacy: 'the successes of the peace process, highlighted by the Arafat-Rabin handshake... clearly pushed the peace groups into a prominent position, in many ways vindicating their previous calls for negotiating with the Palestinians'.

Economic 'legitimacy' was also displayed as brought about by the handshake: 'The Big Six firms were petrified by the prospect of angering their clients and member firms in the Arab world. The "historic handshake"... changed all that, so much so that in the course of a single year—1994—each of the Big Six took on board Israeli firms, thereby triggering a series of mergers and a general shakeout in the Israeli profession'.

Not all of the peace-related transformation meanings were as optimistic, however, nor did they reflect transformations of only those meanings discussed in our first frame. An additional specific interpretation, for example, was that the handshake reversed a process and/or brought about trauma/trouble. One text, for example, noted that what 'Rabin did on the White House lawn, with that handshake and with that agreement which he signed... catapulted us 46 years back, to 1947'.

Another stated, 'for seven long years since that hesitant Rabin-Arafat handshake at the Whitehouse, we have been tearing ourselves apart over this peace process... we have dug ourselves deeper into our own mindsets, rejected other viewpoints with ever greater force, justified our own intolerance'.

In one more text, 'recognition of the PLO and the traumatic handshake between Rabin and Ararat set off a crisis of confidence which injured, first of all, those Diaspora Jews who are the closest to the State'. Summing up this view, the event was described in one text as 'the jarring handshake that changed Middle East history forever'.

In some cases, the trauma was the result of what was labeled a curse originating in the handshake: 'It seems that... Arafat's handshake brings with it a terrible curse'. Likewise, one reporter stated that '[e]ver since... Rabin shook the hand of war criminal Yasser Arafat... the Jewish-Zionist state has started going downhill with every increasing momentum'.

For another, '[t]he price of that handshake with Arafat can be seen, in retrospect, as a bloody disaster. It killed 200 Israelis and wrecked the lives of hundreds of others. It embittered the entire land of Israel and led to the shameful act of a young Jew assassinating his prime minister'.

In this last quote, the application of the handshake as a curse bringing about negative outcomes was associated specifically with Rabin's murder: The handshake was discussed as the event that prompted the assassinator's actions. This view of the handshake was mirrored elsewhere. For one writer, 'It was a handshake that also led to Rabin's assassination by Yigal Amir, leading to a new era in the way Israelis relate to one another'.

Also referencing the tie between the handshake and Rabin's assassination, one article included this quote from Perez: 'We cannot go on hearing about the Oslo criminals all the time. Yitzhaq and I were criminals? We are traitors? Rabin has already paid for it with his life, and still it goes on'.

Even when it was not portrayed as starting another process, the handshake was discussed as, at least a time marker, an event around which change could be chronicled. One reported noted, for example, 'more Israelis, almost 100, have been killed by terrorists in Israel since the fateful handshake'. Most commonly, the handshake was referenced as the event for which the media could mark 'before' and 'after' periods. Likewise, 'Egypt, with which Israel has been at peace since 1979, wasn't interested in selling the gas it has in abundance... until after the 1993 Rabin-Arafat handshake'.

Although many of the specific applications of a transformation function suggested that the handshake led to or marked a move toward other (hopeful or horrific) events, other discourse portrayed individuals as transformed through their relationship with the handshake. Much of this discourse was toned positively.

For example, one writer noted that '[a]fter the famous 1993 handshake... Clinton came to view Rabin as a 20th-century figure of Churchillian proportions, someone whose visage could be chiseled into Mount Rushmore granite'. For another writer, 'the switch from Arafat the terrorist to Arafat the statesman was... rapid and unexpected'.

These individual transformations often included gaining more dependency and trust in the other, a meaning revealed in the first frame but more notable here because of the emphasis on transformation. For example, 'Clinton's image of leading... Rabin over to shake hands with... Arafat... is alive in the international memory until now. Therefore, it seems natural for the Palestinians to turn to the United States and to ask it to present a flagrant and open initiative for halting the deterioration in the peace process'.

These texts also reflected, tied likewise to a specific meaning best seen in the representation theme, a new legitimacy to an individual, organization, or nation. For instance, one text included the following: the handshake 'catapulted the PLO from the status of terrorist organization in the eyes of Israel and the United States to the governor of a Palestinian proto-state'.

Another article noted, 'the Rabin-Arafat handshake has overnight made Israel a "normal part" of the region'. In a later story, this report was made: 'the handshake [has]... succeeded in breaking down a good part of the international hostility to Israel'.

An overarching frame we saw in these media accounts of the handshakes dealt overtly with the handshake as an agent of change: The handshake's primary function in this subset of texts was as a creator of transformation or as a time marker that worked to show the point at which things changed.

In some cases, the particular transformation overlapped with our first theme, but rather than representing the meaning itself (e.g., existing legitimacy), these discourse presentations focused on the cue as bringing about that condition (i.e., through the enactment of the handshake, legitimacy was achieved).

These transformation meanings were not always positive in nature (nor always accurate in terms of where the peace process went in the future).

In addition, and just as in the case of the representational theme, denials of transformation existed: As one source noted, '"the only one in military uniform, next to everyone else's suits and ties, was Yasser Arafat. He hasn't put them in mothballs yet, and this is a statement that the armed battle, the terrorism, are not over yet"'.

Others admitted some change, but did so with qualifications: 'The attitude toward Israel in the United Nations has changed—but not fundamentally—since the historic handshake'. Overall, however, most of these texts framed nonverbal actions like the handshake as an agent of change or as a time marker. As if to sum it up, one journalist noted, 'The handshake changed the rules of the game'.

Our goal in this study was to argue that the media provide frames, through their metapragmatic discourse, that reveal different meanings for the same nonverbal cues. Some interaction scholars have argued already for an incorporation of framing principles in interpersonal scholarship; but framing, as a theoretical and methodological concept, has been used more commonly by media scholars.

We thus extend the argument by asserting that a frame analysis of media texts on what can be defined as 'interpersonal' or interactional behaviours can help cross over disciplinary divides to help scholars understand more fully what meanings may be given to nonverbal cues and how framing may work as part of this process.

To help make our case, we chose a range of media texts from Israeli and Palestinian news agencies, not to represent those groups and their cultures, but to show what some of these frames and meanings may be. We found two predominant, overarching functions or structures (i.e., frames) when looking across this body of discourse and labeled these representations and transformations. Within each of these, more specific meanings clustered. Indeed, we believe that the frames work as structuring devices to organize the large set of particular interpretations (e.g., the specific meanings) seen within these data.

Representations, or portraying the nonverbal cues as 'stand ins' or conduits of some larger abstract concept, for example, included a number of specific referents or meanings. Extending previous representation meanings given to handshakes, for example, we found that, at least within the particular political context we investigated, handshakes were portrayed as representations of peace, hope, optimism, legitimacy, agreement, violence, and betrayal.

Each of these used the handshake as an embodiment of a more abstract principle. More fully consistent with existing research, facial expressions and kinesic cues co-occurring with the handshake were discussed as representations of emotions or attitudes, personality (for an interesting discussion of handshakes representing personality), including sentiments about one's partner, topic of conversation, or events. In some cases, the discourse we reviewed portrayed these meanings as brought about or revealed strategically (i.e., orchestrated by the parties involved).

Transformation meanings are rarer in previous scholarship on the meanings or functions of nonverbal cues. Whereas nonverbal behaviours are talked about as having a conversation management function, often organizing and bringing about certain language forms, and their appearance in the media may create images of what occurs in 'reality', scholars have not talked as fully about nonverbal cues as markers for larger social or personal changes. And yet, such interpretations made up an important frame within the discourse we analysed. Future work would do well to find evidence of such transformative interpretations for other nonverbal behaviours, occurring in other communicative contexts.

In addition to revealing overarching frames and, within the frames, specific meanings provided in the media texts we examined, the data also show the strong emotional responses that may develop naturally from or are attached to nonverbal cues in this context. As noted, in our discussion of analytic procedures, we first saw the evaluative tone of many of the texts to be a particular frame: evaluations or political representations.

We came to believe, however, that emotional tone could occur across frames. There were many instances in which the evaluation of the writer or the person whom she or he quoted was apparent. For example, one reporter stated the following: It was 'with much disgust and queasiness we even got to that handshake in Washington'; and as another cited earlier in the paper: 'I was sick to my stomach.'

Reflecting a different emotional response, however, other stories read like the following: 'The picture that left an indelible mark and swayed the hearts of hundreds of thousands of Israelis and Palestinians was the Rabin-Arafat handshake'. This form of positive reaction was common in the US media coverage of the event.

Certainly, the fact that the handshake occurred as a ceremonial correlate of the signing of the accords and a commitment to beginning peace talks confounds the potential characterization of—and emotional reaction to—the handshake itself. This confound between events occurred in the transformation frame particularly.

That is, it can be argued that it was the peace accords and not the handshake that was the actual change agent or time marker.

Our view of these data, however, suggests that the visual and personal nature of the handshake, and the cues surrounding it, appeared to allow the media discourse to portray the behaviours themselves as responsible, at least in part, for the transformation. It was the nonverbal action itself that was talked about as an important change agent (e.g., '[I]t is precisely such gestures, spontaneous or negotiated, that may be necessary to bring the peace process to a successful conclusion').

Despite the diverse evaluations of the process embedded in the different media framings, one thing was consistent among most of the texts. A closer look shows the saliency and potency that comes along with the meanings presented for the behaviours or cues. Just as Manusov and Bixler (2003) revealed in their assessment of US media coverage of these behaviours, we found abundant evidence that the handshake and its accompanying behaviours were viewed as very powerful in terms of what meanings they can carry, what they can bring about, as well as the evaluative reactions people had to them.

Whereas the political and public context in which these cues occurred influenced the potential saliency of the behaviours, we argue that the nature of the behaviours—particularly their capacity to be given diverse and contestable meanings—means that the power of nonverbal cues may be likewise found in everyday action. Certainly, however, this argument requires empirical validation.

It is important to emphasize that the discourse we studied here does not provide a full account of all of the meanings given to the handshake and its related cues nor of the larger issues and processes in which the behaviours were embedded. Given some constraints in conducting this study, we were unable to access or interpret texts that were not originally in or already translated to English. In particular, we were unable to access much Palestinian coverage, and the majority of our Israeli data were from Israeli English-language newspapers. Thus, we can in no way compare the coverage from the two cultures nor argue that what we have is representative of either culture.

Our aim, however, was much simpler: We wanted to begin to catalog some of the overarching frames and particular meanings given to nonverbal cues within media coverage. We were still able to do this because of the rich, albeit incomplete, array of metapragmatic discussions we found. Our analysis helps reveal the potential for nonverbal cues to be given a variety of meanings and for the media to be concerned with and provide information regarding the way that nonverbal events ought to be construed.

'Because these symbols [including gestures] "acquire a sentimental significance symbolizing the common feelings about the movement, their use serves as a constant reining and re-enforcement"' of what we hold to be important and how we feel about the things the cues represent. This argument is by necessity an important one for both mass and interpersonal communication scholars. Interpersonal scholars would do well to examine media coverage of an array of interaction activities to learn more about how the processes of importance to them are framed by others.

Chapter 7

Media Ethnography in Virtual Space

The interpretive turn in audience studies has grown in two decades from an exploratory foray into many vibrant areas of theory and empirical research. While such issues as the locus of sense-making and how media practices lead to the reproduction of social structure are still debated, the arguments and methods for studying media interpretation are now well known.

Recently, forms of distributed "audience" activity have emerged with networked digital media to confront interpretive analysts with new versions of old issues about the study of mediated communication. The most widely used of these systems is the global "network of networks," the Internet, whose growth in the 1990s was fueled by several developments: the rapid upgrading of the infrastructure to allow high-capacity data traffic; introduction of the hypertext-based World Wide Web and search tools; the growth of access providers; fiercely competitive pricing of high-performance computers and modems; and the emergence of a consumer desire for access to an abundance of electronic texts.

The Internet's decentralized structure provides its users with the ability to receive, create, and send information in many forms, including electronic mail, Usenet news groups, Listserv mailing lists, simulation spaces, and World Wide Web sites. Most of these are in the public domain and foster a concept of the Internet as home to many virtual communities of interest.

Private companies have also rushed to colonize the Web with multimedia versions of their products and services. For example, television stations and networks have launched Web sites in order to promote their programming and other services and to invite viewer response. Some of these ventures, such as NBC and Microsoft's MSNBC, create original content for the medium. Familiar genres are also crossing over to the Web, as exhibited in the "cybersoaps" that have gone into production since 1995.

Usage of media Web sites is now measured by Nielsen Media Research's PC Meter service in terms of page requests, minutes per request, and total minutes of usage for each household. For some events, the number of page "hits" approximates what might be considered a mass audience in the traditional sense. Industry observers now wait to see whether new products such as video-streaming, "push" technology, and Web/TV units will widen Internet access beyond its current 20-25% share of U.S. telephone homes.

Despite these efforts at making computer usage compatible with television viewing, computer-mediated communication (CMC) is very different from other forms of attendance. In contrast to the reception of a fixed content schedule, CMC is transient, widely distributed, multi-modal, and allows for a high degree of end-user manipulation of content.

Except for workplace monitoring of employees' Internet usage, there are few codes of conduct governing consumption. Locality of source is also largely irrelevant in the sprawling Internet—a condition that offers new possibilities for civic life, shared learning, and intercultural contact free of geographic limits, but that also opens spaces for explicit sexual content, hate speech, rumor propagation, alcohol advertisements aimed at children, and other problematic material.

The Internet encompasses an array of settings in which symbolic culture is performed and in which participants mean to express something coherent. The global, yet perceptibly intimate, nature of these settings and the social affiliations they spawn has attracted interest from interpretive analysts.

Certainly the culture of networked computing is a prime example of the challenges that a mobile world economy poses to ethnographers, who are far more accustomed to single-site studies of a community or a stable subjectivity. This chapter assesses some of the conditions, strategies, and limits in conducting ethnography in the virtual spaces created by computer networks.

Several key issues of CMC and methodology are discussed, including community, social presence, and the social strategies and technical utilities for studying Internet communication. Our intent is to suggest a set of possibilities for research in a new cultural arena, not to preclude any that we do not consider here.

AT THE INTERFACE OF CMC AND ETHNOGRAPHY

Interpretive social science starts with the hermeneutic axiom that human beings act on the basis of collective (cultural) understandings that are continually negotiated through linguistic and other symbolic practices.

These cultural understandings are neither mentalistic entities nor a correspondence of physical reality. As Taylor points out, "The meanings and norms implicit in... practices are not just in the minds of the actors but are out there in the practices themselves, practices which cannot be conceived as a set of individual actions, but which are essentially modes of social relation, of mutual action."

Cultural understandings are the semiotic products of people acting in a common spatio-temporal frame, with the meanings themselves (manifested as encoded texts of some sort) embedded as objects of attention in each successive frame. The social actors we refer to as "audiences" signify the meanings of media texts and technologies within the purposes and routines of their social milieu.

As with any other social practice, media use emerges out of a dialectic of personal agency and social constraint. We choose when and how to act, but only in relation to the historically "possible" or "acceptable" ranges of conduct that we believe constitute the world we live in. That is, we affirm community-formed notions of what can count as a choice every time we choose.

Yet every choice is authored in a particular way, enacts some degree of free play due to the resources uniquely available at any time, and can be read differently by those who participate, all of which work to change incrementally the parameters of what is possible or acceptable.

An analysis of a family's VCR use, for example, may show that the practices for using the device are always in flux, and that each family member "knows" the VCR in a different way. The family member, however, can only know the VCR in the context of what has already been said and signified about the VCR in his or her social worlds.

Thus interpretive analysts study the dynamic processes of mediated communication as they occur in social relationships: dyads, groups, families, subcultures, organizations, and communities. The questions they ask are mostly about the pragmatics, ethics, and politics of using media: What is going on here?... How do they do it? How does it change over time? How do they evaluate what they do? What does it mean to them? How do they interpret what it means to others?... What is the relation of us to them, of self to other?

Ethnography has become a preferred strategy for engaging these questions. Since meanings are embodied in practice, and meanings are what the researcher wants to recover, the researcher must participate in some way in the practice under study.

Elaborating further, Rosen writes that ethnography is:

Based upon achieving a conscious and systematic interpretation of the culture system operating for those the ethnographer observes to those who may eventually take in the ethnographer's end product, perhaps a film or video, a journal article, a conference presentation, or most commonly, a book.

Persistent and sensitive attention to the stories, conversations, rituals, and routines of living enables the ethnographer to grasp the realities held by "native" members.

The knowledge claims produced from fieldwork are always partial, local, and contingent on the researcher's own ability to read discourse and discern its significance.

Their value lies in the disciplined access an analyst has given us into the way some other human collective has lived, spoken, and acted.

From a critical perspective, the close study of media experience can also specify the local effects of unequal allocation of resources and rights and the processes of moral valuation.

The present state of interpretive media studies, however, rarely achieves the goal of a contextual understanding of social action.

Operating under the rubric of "qualitative" research, media analysts often employ the methods of interviewing or document analysis as the major or total thrust of a project.

As such they elicit a special kind of discourse (e.g., interview talk) which is then used as evidence of the (unobserved) action (e.g., television viewing) in order to develop interpretations of the action (e.g., family viewing rules). Besides the obvious risk of taking someone's talk as an adequate description of how they behave, this approach also risks treating the interviewee as a vehicle in which ideological positions are vocalized with little regard for context, social exigency, or personal history.

In virtual space, most behaviour is inscribed as visible discourse only. Context and personal history either accrue over time as the researcher becomes more familiar with threads of orthographic text, or must be sought in non-CMC sectors of the participants' life world.

Thus the worlds that CMC ethnographers investigate are simulacra of an indexical kind (there really are bodies out there behind keyboards), in which a high degree of self-referentiality in the text to ongoing and past events helps to build the sense of a continuous, living project.

Ethnography presumes a culture system from which people derive collective resources, interpretive strategies, and sense of identity. As mentioned earlier, CMC user activity—

especially when there is evidence of regular patronage, social bonding, or communal action—is often called a community, albeit prefixed with "virtual" or "cyberspace." Since virtual spaces often function as running conversations among many actors, and since it takes a measure of unselfish effort to sustain these conversations, the use of a community concept to indicate this social form seems fitting. A more refined explanation comes from Smith:

Virtual communities produce a variety of collective goods. They allow people of like interests to come together with little cost, help them exchange ideas and coordinate their activities, and provide the kind of identification and feeling of membership found in face-to-face interaction.

In the process they face familiar problems of defection, free-riding and other forms of disruptive behaviour although in new and sometimes very unexpected ways. The novelty of the medium means that the rules and practices that lead to a successful virtual community are not yet well known or set fast in a codified formal system.

The term "virtual community" not only has metaphoric resonance, it describes how users engage in networked relationships and account for the moral order of their activity. For example, Correll's study of the Lesbian Cafe—a computer bulletin board system (BBS) that serves lesbian users by utilizing a "bar fantasy"—found the patrons moving about in the bar's "physical" features (a fireplace, a hot tub, a bean bag chair, etc.), ordering beverages, making new friends, visiting old ones, celebrating special events (like a Super Bowl party), flirting with each other, and learning about news of importance to lesbians.

The regulars were able to recognize the inappropriate behaviour of "newbies" (newcomers to the Cafe) and impose corrective sanctions.

Conversely, "bashers," who sometimes disrupted the cafe's atmosphere by making anti-lesbian comments, were met with defensive strategies by the patrons, who believed that their virtual community had been strengthened and unified as a result of these encounters with offenders.

The Lesbian Cafe is one instance of a counter-hegemonic movement in which socially or politically marginalized groups find expressive space on the Internet in which to locate like-minded others, speak freely, and forge solidarity. Such groups must often exert themselves in boundary maintenance work (social marking, policing, sanctioning), due to both the permeability of their spaces and the fact that external agents often control some of the key technical, economic, and legal resources on which their spaces depend.

A virtual community is founded intentionally by people who share a set of similar interests, often revolving around certain texts or tropes imported from non-CMC venues, such as soap operas and their characters, the television series X-Men and Star Trek, and even the concept of "cyberspace" itself. Much of the argumentation may turn on the issues, events, histories, and other details surrounding these valorized, meaning-charged objects. In doing this, virtual communities are not very different from the "interpretive communities" of media use, in which individual competency stems from experience in the social traditions for using a text or genre.

What is obviously different about most virtual communities based in popular culture is that the users usually bring with them to the Internet a long history of engaging the text (or genre) in another medium.

Thus social networks of fans are able to extend their meaning constructions through an overlap of face-to-face and virtual action centered on a multi-formatted popular culture referent. Audience agency may take on different forms than is the case in mass media, as fans exchange on-line comments with production executives and creative artists, and even collaborate with them in shaping the text on which the community is based.

A more salient difference lies in the special circumstance of belonging to a virtual community. A virtual community is what might be termed a "dedicated use," requiring initiative, attentional focus, knowledge of a site's collective memory, acculturation to the social and technical protocols of electronic communication, and user characteristics that are broadly, but specifically identified to the other users.

As Smith points out, if these intentional communities are to succeed beyond short-term goals, they must "[be] capable of directing individual action towards the construction and maintenance of goods that could not be created by individuals acting in isolation." In her study of a soap opera news group's interpretive norms, for example, Baym found politeness and other helping behaviours, as well as humour, insight, and personality construction, to be key CMC performance skills.

Providing a communal service, especially when reward to the self is not expected, is also central to CMC community-building. Lindlof et al. found that Webmasters of X-Men sites often intended their graphics; text archives, page links, and other material to be a service to all X-Men fans, and expected the same of other site managers.

Similarly, sharing privileged information enhances the status or efficacy of the community membership. Examples of this are Winter and Huff's study of Systers, a women-only electronic mail group that circulates information of special value to female computing professionals, and Harrington and Bielby's finding that different kinds of gossip on soap opera BBS's are tied to different levels of perceived status.

Aspects of virtual community that remain ambiguous for the media ethnographer tend to be those that depart decisively from the conditions of face-to-face. The ethnographer must contend in some way with the distinctions between the active players and those who take on a more passive stance, and the difference these make in defining community. The prevalence of "lurkers" (individuals who do not contribute to a discussion) raises the issue of the social costs of free-ridership, or the extent to which non-involvement riding on the efforts of others detracts from or dissipates the well-being of the community.

As contrasted with traditional media audiences, in which practically everyone lurks (in relation to content providers, not the local reception situation), the lurker's presence does not materially deprive the active users of a resource, but their psychological effect on others and the loss of their potential contributions may diminish the conversation at times.

Some benefits may be realized from the ability of users to monitor a discourse invisibly, such as to publicize (or contest) a community's ideas in secondary or off-line conversations; however, it would require a very sensitive strategy to detect this level of influence. To the extent that ethnographers also function as "lurkers" sometimes, a further dilemma is introduced over the possible necessity of noninvolvement.

Finally, a note on method appended by Phillips to his case study of the rhetoric of a Usenet news group conflict instills caution about what one can infer about virtual community phenomena. Phillips reports that the amount of text used in his study—"over 22 days I saved 326 articles with 49 different subject lines"—was only a small percentage of the total posted during that period.

Moreover, the exclusive focus on Usenet text meant the omission of "an inestimable amount of e-mail, phone calls, and face-to-face interaction that groups members engaged in outside of the newsgroup itself". Phillips' situation is emblematic of a larger problem faced by most interpretive analysts of CMC: justifying a claim about community process or structure based on a thread of discourse, albeit an interesting one, pulled from an exceedingly large and complex volume of both on-line (mostly public) and off-line (mostly private) communication.

While the ethnographer of embodied social life builds explanations from his or her reflexive participation in multiple forms of action, the CMC researcher's analysis often depends on non-interactive contact with a limited body of text. This quandary may leave unresolved the dimensions and properties of the "community" being studied, as well as the salience of the thread itself to the identity and concerns of the broader membership.

SOCIAL PRESENCE

An important consideration in doing ethnographic

research in the study of new electronic media is the social presence attributes of the technology itself.

Short, Williams, and Christie were apparently the first researchers to conceptualize the construct they called social presence, which they defined as being a quality of the communications medium itself. As they elaborated, social presence "varies between different media... affects the nature of the interaction... and interacts with the purpose of the interaction to influence the medium chosen by the individual who wishes to communicate".

Media perceived as high in social presence are generally judged (on Semantic Differential Scales) by users as warm, personal, sensitive, and, sociable; those low in social presence as cold, impersonal, insensitive, and unsociable.

Chief among the reasons for differentiating media in their degree of social presence is the medium's ability to restrict stimulus-conveying information. More specifically, media that are less able to convey nonverbal elements are more likely to be judged as being low in social presence.

In another sense, social presence is the degree to which a medium is perceived as conveying the "presence" of the communicating participants; it is dependent not only on the words involved in the communication but on the full range of verbal and nonverbal cues, and the communication context.

Thus CMC technologies typically would be judged lower in social presence than face-to-face communication (FTF) because of the lower bandwidth of information conveyed by the former (vis-a-vis verbal and nonverbal messages).

This notion of the bandwidth of the medium is closely related to media richness, a construct developed by Daft and Lengel. Rice describes the term as the:

Extent to which media are able to bridge different frames of reference, make issues less ambiguous, or provide opportunities for learning in a given time interval, based on the medium's capacity for immediate feedback, the number of cues and senses involved, personalization, and language variety. The essential underlying element in both of these notions is that a good match between the medium's characteristics (high in social presence or media richness) and the intent of the communication activity (getting to know someone, strategic decision making) should lead to higher performance and satisfaction.

The importance of all of this to ethnographic research is, how can one adequately do participatory research with media that are judged low in social presence or media richness?

Stated another way, how will the ethnographic researcher be able to make adequate sense out of communication that restricts important cues such as nonverbal behaviours? in their study of e-mail in organizations, Garton and Wellman have discussed the consequences of e-mail's exclusion of nonverbal cues: E-mail does not supply nonverbal interactional cues to group members, such as eye contact, gestures, nodding approval, frowning, or hesitating before replying.

There are no contextual cues, either: Participants cannot use seating arrangements to identify coalitions and cleavages, or choose meeting sites to identify the importance of sponsorship of meetings. Because e-mail users typically are identified by name only, people are not constantly reminded of the social roles cues others have beyond the narrow confines of the task group.

Users may not be aware of another group member's gender, race, expertise, or organizational position. One approach to this dilemma is to take account of the ways participants do compensate at times for the restricted bandwidth of the medium by providing clarifying cues in their messages.

Social role cues can be transmitted in e-mail (either implicitly or explicitly) by adding status information to their "signatures," by their writing style, or by forwarding communications to (or from) important persons.

Baym also found the standard components of Usenet posts for a soap opera news group—e.g., "from" line, "subject" line, "organization" line (site of message's origin), and the quotation system, in addition to signatures—to provide subtle contextualizing cues about the sender's interests and status.

Other examples of clarifying cues are:

- Emotions used to pictorialize emotional states (e.g., the computer "smiley face" ":-)"),
- Meta-messages included to communicate physical states (e.g., using " " to designate jocularity),
- Acronyms used to designate degree of emotion (e.g., "FOTFL" to represent "failing on the floor laughing," or a greater degree of merriment beyond a mere smile or grin).'

As Walther, Anderson, and Park noted in their meta-analysis of computer mediated interaction, the interpersonal effects expected to accrue rapidly in face-to-face interactions can (and do) occur in CIVIC, but these interpersonal cues require extended time interactions. That is, interactional, contextual, and social cues that provide immediate feedback in FTF communication have to be stated explicitly in CIVIC and require more time to develop. Deep knowledge of an organizational culture may also enhance the participants' hermeneutic ability to embellish an e-mail with meaning.

Of course, social cues do more than merely clarify or boost informational richness in FTF or CMC encounters; they also mark a person's identity (e.g., gender, age, ethnic, class, sexual, cultural, occupational, etc.) as being of a certain moral or political character. Gender norms, for example, are a powerful means of designating the inappropriate or disvalued behaviours of men and women in specific contexts and vary widely from ideologically dominant expressions to the communication contexts and media of subaltern groups.

Thus, women ethnographers learn very quickly how their bodies—not only skin colour and body shape, but also aspects of clothing, adornment, hair style, and facial, gestural, and speech styles—affect the way they are perceived in the field, and the roles and motives attributed to them.

Embodiment in all of its forms is not a condition that can be controlled independently or somehow neutralized. Rather, it is through the ethnographic body performing with other cultural members that one learns the schemes of cultural valuation. Practical problems of "fitting in" are of a piece with issues of acculturation which are enormously important to understanding the scene being studied.

In CMC environments, where perceptions of identity derive almost totally from what and how one writes, the notion of representational reality collapses and the ambiguity of action becomes foregrounded. Multiple identities are tried on, and specific traits or behaviours may be expressed more boldly in the widespread use of aliases, aptonyms, and role-playing domains in which players build characters for themselves. By detaching self-expression from the politics of the body, CMC liberates its users from certain kinds of discriminatory practice and promotes a low-risk, often playful, exploration of skill sets.

Certainly, the texts one writes may unwittingly leak signs of personal identity which could be attributed by readers to the author's embodied self. As long as there are other users supervising the actors and the threads of their discourse, standards of plausibility, coherence, and trustworthiness will still apply to the textual contributions. Ultimately, the CMC ethnographer should be prepared to confront the ambiguity of identity performance as a central fact of virtual life, worthy of study on its own terms.

Concerns about testing the informational richness, or the authenticity, of virtual action against criteria of embodied action may be much less important to the project of ethnography than issues of how computing worlds are socially constructed, what recognizably human purposes they serve, and how they relate to a range of other "possibility spaces."

Reduced social presence also affects the way in which researchers enter virtual scenes. Interaction management seems to function similarly in FTF and CMC in the opening and closing phases of encounters, but in CMC the choice of names and the use of attention-getting strategies are critical decisions.

The risks of field entry may be lessened by learning the norms of such strategies in advance. Thus the "outsider" designation one usually expects in the first stages of an FTF project may be less of a problem in entering a virtual space once the right level of competence has been gained via observation.

On the other hand, veteran members often do not suffer novices gladly, and the ethnographer may need to ask for the cooperation of the group (or its influential members) in order to be heard, or to engage them in directed queries or tasks. Researchers face subtle differences in the social makeup and interactional preferences of virtual scenes, which may require them to devise different strategies for entry and field positioning than in FTF situations.

SOCIAL STRATEGIES

Matters of self-presentation and scope of action are critical to the relations built among researchers, the virtual "places" populating the Internet, and the cultural membership. Correll, for example, was able to convey the location, look, and meanings of the "furniture" of the Lesbian Cafe mostly from her observations of electronic postings, but also from interviews. Compared to Leal's analysis of the relation of TV sets to the domestic material culture in working-class Brazilian homes, the mise-en-scene of the Cafe is not nearly as dense, tactile, and sensuous.

Despite this possibly unfair comparison, "the sense of a common reality [in the Lesbian Cafe] was used by patrons much like physical settings are used by co-present conversationalists—as a source of mutually relevant topics". Like the dialogue one hears in a radio play, conversationalists in the Lesbian Cafe must include many more references in their ordinary talk to objects, the current status of the objects, and the presence or absence of people in and around those objects in order to maintain orientation and sustain a convincing sense of as-if reality. The lean exposition Correll offers would likely be unacceptable in other forms of ethnographic work, but it turns out to be the one that matters to the women who "drink" and socialize there.

Media ethnographers begin their on-line presence in a variety of ways. One mode used by some is that of the unknown, unobtrusive observer. Over a three-year period, Harrington and Bielby collected and printed messages posted on two soap opera BBS's by subscribers to two commercial on-line computer services. They do not report interactions of any kind between themselves and the posters.

Presumably, the computer services were not notified of the initiation of the research activity, nor were the BBS system operators. Interestingly, while the authors appear unconcerned about their own lurker posture, they note the suspicion held by many of the BBS users that their conversations were being overheard by "industry insiders". Scodari also relies on transcripts of fan BBS discourse in interpreting critical reactions to changes in the soap, Another World, although she aligns her own interests much more closely with the fans she quotes than Harrington and Bielby.

Open participation characterizes the approach of several other studies and more closely resembles normative field practice. Baym started as an unabashed soap fan and news group contributor and found it easy to continue openly as an analyst of the group:

My position in the [rec.arts.arts.soaps, or r.a.t.s., newsgroup] is that of a participant at least as much as a researcher. As a long-time fan of soap operas, I was thrilled to discover this group. It was only after I had been reading daily and participating regularly for a year that I began to write about it. As the work has evolved, I have shared its progress with the group members and found them exceedingly supportive and helpful. They have acted as research participants as well as subjects and have treated me more as an ambassador than a researcher.

The confidence each party had in the other paved the way for Baym to obtain other forms of data besides the news group's messages, especially electronic mail correspondence with several participants and responses to open-ended questions she posted to r.a.t.s. Similarly, Correll's membership in the Lesbian Cafe, and the approval she got from the bar's founder, assisted her in posting queries and interviewing several of the patrons both by e-mail and in person.

Some researchers actually run the facilities that enable computer users to "find" the research project. In an early study, Myers operated a university BBS for two months and set up a number of networked research tools in order to investigate the perceived social context of CMC: on-line surveys, a focus group, and a role-playing game.

More recently, Lindlof et al. launched a Web home page for X-Men fans that offered graphic content (thus participating in the X-Men array of more than 60 Internet locations), links to other X-Men sites, a survey to capture data, and a solicitation for dialogues with on-line X-Men users and page producers.

Like the Baym and Correll studies, the research purpose was stated openly in order to invite cooperation; however, its sudden appearance and the research team's initial contacts with users were sometimes met with suspicion, critique (of their knowledge of X-Men), and humorous skepticism.

It became clear that the World Wide Web page of hypertext URLS's (Uniform Resource Locator) that linked to other pages related to the X-Men topic constituted the study's "gatekeeper" in the traditional sense of enabling an initial contact.

The study also hints at the possibilities of participatory design in which ethnographers may act as the interpreters of diverse voices, usage interests, and aesthetic tastes in the design of networked systems.

A final strategy for consideration moves the researcher physically alongside the user in order to "read" his or her real-time decision making and styles of engagement.

The user's dyadic interplay with a computer forms a focal interest, but included in this arena would be the material context of computing (e.g., its location in a room, the CD-ROM's on hand), the institutional culture (e.g., considering open viewing of sex sites as sexual harassment), interpersonal resources or constraints (e.g., informal rules for sharing URL's), and the specific reality of what it means to "do computing" that these signify for users. Models for this approach exist in the literature on social television viewing and family computer usage. However, since Internet usage is typically a solitary venture, the more promising route would seem to lie in some version of the "shopping with consumers" protocol from the field of consumer behaviour.

Accompanying users on their way through the kinetic pathways of virtual space and eliciting talk on a wide range of subjects, either retrospectively or on-the-spot, enables the researcher to understand the more embodied dimensions of CMC. In effect, the researcher shadows the user's on-site computing. The advantages of the approach are its close proximity to the user and setting, and the ability to comprehend computing performance as an activity that has a rich, localized back stage—that is, as more than lines of type scrolling down a screen.

In ethnographies of embodied social scenes, the researcher must continually negotiate with the culture membership and convince them of the value of the study and the reasonableness of the person doing the research. It is not unusual for ethnographers to have to adjust their persona somewhat differently as they pass through a scene, or disclose different versions of the project, since the members of a group often relate asymmetrically or even conflictively to each other.

CMC ethnographies, as we have shown, also involve some degree of negotiation when anonymous observation is not the method of access. Virtual spaces offer a limited window in which to explain one's purpose, and electronic text is not the most suitable medium for engaging in a sensitive interaction.

Trust tends to be a heightened concern where entry and exit and unbridled information disclosure are easily accomplished. Mistakes, once made, can have disastrous results, and be very hard to rectify. Institutional principles for informed consent are now being formulated for research on the World Wide Web, but it will take longer for ethnographers themselves to develop a consensus around protocols for responsible virtual space entry and ways to insure the fair treatment of those they study without compromising very seriously the conduct of inquiry.

TECHNICAL UTILITIES

In this section, we discuss the use of technical utilities for accomplishing research tasks. Some computer systems allow asynchronous communication interactions to be studied either by saving the individual messages, or archiving all postings for later perusal. Most of these have been around for some time. The ones we discuss here are electronic mail, news groups over Usenet, and list servers.

Electronic mail is asynchronous (users generally are not communicating in realtime), quick (in terms of transmission and reply), text-based, and configured for dyadic or multiple connections (can be sent one-to-one, one-to-many, or many-to-many). Moreover, e-mail can be stored and manipulated. As Garton and Wellman noted in a recent review:

E-mail can be stored in external memory for future retrieval, searching, editing, and forwarding to others. People can edit their own or other's messages to change their meaning. The historical record of interaction may be used for surveillance of individual and group interactions, to review past decisions (as Oliver North belatedly learned), and to bring new members up to date.

What makes this modality particularly suitable for ethnographic research are its personal-contact and archival functions. For example, in his 9-month participant-observation study of "Zytech," a computer systems firm, Workman utilized e-mail in the following ways:

- Being placed on the company's various distribution lists, which on a daily basis delivered internal documents, minutes of meetings, meeting agendas, and announcements;
- Scheduling interviews;
- Accessing hundreds of BBS's, including Zytech correspondence going back several years;
- Communicating with informants, including follow-ups to FTF interviews.

Though the staggered progress of e-mail interviewing does not promote the same qualities of rapport or spontaneity as personal interviews, it does permit a more elastic time frame for both interviewer and participant to think carefully about the meanings of questions and replies.

In another organizational study, special software was used to automatically save the headers (but not the message content) of all departmental e-mail to a designated file whenever a user read or transmitted a message, yielding a nonreactive means of learning who communicates with whom, when, and about what.

For ethnographic purposes, the value of this procedure lies in its capacity to augment such methods as interviews or on-site observation.

However, the ability to retrieve and store this information without the users' permission (or below their conscious awareness, even when permission is granted) carries the potential for ethical abuse at worst, and suspicion on the part of participants at best.

Usenet is a protocol that describes how groups of messages can be stored on and sent between computers, many of which lay outside of the Internet.

In actuality, Usenet forms a "virtual forum" for the electronic community that is divided into a plethora of news groups dedicated to varied areas of interest. News group articles are read and written through programs called newsreaders that keep track of articles that have been read, allow users to edit what has been read, and enable readers to reply to previously posted messages in the aforementioned study, Baym reported her participant-observation of a news group made up of soap opera aficionados.

Even though some Usenet sites can archive messages off-line, Baym herself saved the messages posted on the r.a.t.s group while she was an active member.

Even working with a medium often described as low in social presence or media richness, she was able to develop a "thick" description of the personalities of this community based on features of their postings:

- Signature files (files automatically attached to postings containing identifying information about the sender),

- Humour in the messages,
- Self-disclosure,
- Comments made about personal lives.

By capitalizing on the features of Usenet news groups, variations of focus group interviewing become possible. During a two-month period of operating a public BBS, Myers set up a computer-mediated focus group "to determine what motivated frequent and active BBS use". As an alternative to a simple discussion, a focus group consisting of a theoretically interesting set of users could work on a virtual task.

MacGregor and Morrison describe an editing-group protocol in which groups of people were given the opportunity to re-edit existing news reports (including video footage) in order to produce a more "ideal" version, thereby enabling them to understand viewers' journalistic values more concretely.

It is not difficult to see how this task could be adapted to computer news groups and the multimedia capabilities of high-end work stations, although techniques for training and monitoring the users in their editing-group activities would need to be developed.

Listserv groups (managed by listserver software) are similar to news groups in that they are discussion groups, but they operate in a completely different way by using the Internet e-mail system to exchange messages. Once a person subscribes to a Listserv group (or Listproc group, as they are called on networks other than the early Bitnet), their name is added to a mailing list that receives postings from everyone else subscribed to the list.

Many listservers offer features that allow users to search and retrieve files that are archived, and search the archives using keyword searches. Thus, anyone from a remote site can access archived messages for study from the host computer.

This capability raises interesting ethical issues: How does one receive consent to study the stored communications of users of a particular listserver? Is open access to a person's communications implied in the use of this service? Are the archived files considered the property of the individual subscribers, or are they "owned" in some form of fiduciary relationship by the listserv operator? Because the Internet has developed so rapidly, many such legal and ethical questions have yet to be resolved.

The CMC technologies mentioned above have been in place for a while and are generally well known to most researchers. Most of the communication from these sources is asynchronous, i.e., it is archived for later review and becomes an excellent database.

However some of the newer systems allow for the actual observation of synchronous, or real-time, communication behaviour. It is to these we now turn.

Some of the more recent real-time technologies are:

- Internet Relay Chat (IRC) systems, or"chat lines";
- The entire gamut of multiple-user technologies, e.g., MUDs (Multiple User Domains, formerly known as Multiple User Dungeons), MOOs (MUD Object-Oriented), and MUSHes (Multi-User Shared Hallucination);
- Groupware,
- Desktop videoconferencing over the Internet. All of these systems operate synchronously and as such more approximate face-to-face communication.

Internet Relay Chat (IRC) is a multi-user synchronous communication capability available worldwide to users with Internet accessibility.

These real time"chat lines" provide for mutithreaded conversations from more than two users in something very similar to an"electronic cocktail party". In these"chat rooms" users are able to don bogus"personas" (false identities) and communicate with interactants from all over the globe. These chat lines are very popular on commercial services like America Online and are now available through various web browsers (e.g., students can "chat" with the president of a university via its Web site).

One step up from IRC is a whole family of computer programs that allow more than just written conversation in real time. These are multi-user programs that, in addition to providing text, allow the additional depiction of a physical environment.

Multiple User programs are designed to offer a pseudo-physical dimension via its object orientation. In MOOs, for examples, individuals"virtually" move through"rooms," interact with virtual"objects" such as chairs, doors, and the like, and have virtual conversations with others. As Reid has remarked, in MUDs,"text replaces gesture and has even become gesture itself".

A third, more recent technology is found in a generation of software called "groupware." Unlike MUDs, MOOs, MUSHes, MUCKs, and the like that are used more for entertainment and amusement, groupware is being developed mainly for business and professional uses.

Most of the newer groupware programs use Web-based technology and allow not only for sharing e-mail but for conducting synchronous multiuser conferencing.

The promise for ethnographers in this technology lies in the"common thread" that runs through all these programs--i.e.,"the construction of shared memory" and recording of group discussions.

In essence, groupware allows for observing the"virtual office," i.e., electronic mail, conferencing, scheduling, shared documents, electronic"whiteboards," and so on, and recording these interactions. All of this can function in real time or be archived for later study.

Appearing now on the horizon is the capability to use the desktop computer for real time videoconferencing. Using fairly inexpensive video cameras attached to desktop computers, and software such as CU-SeeMe technology, mediated FTF interactions are now available for study.

As soon as compression capabilities for full-motion video are perfected, these dispersed FTF interactions, mediated by the computer, can be recorded and used in data analysis.

When considering all these new technologies, the type of research done may have to be dictated by the characteristics of the medium. That is, for asynchronous media, the type of research conducted would be more akin to that for studying other forms of written communication, while synchronous media enable types of research more equivalent to naturalistic observation--i.e., observing the unfolding of communicative events in real time.

It was inevitable that interpretive analysts would turn their attention to the profusion of common culture now moving through the Internet. Forms of ethnographic inquiry are being applied to many of the events that occur in virtual space, although questions remain about how well these approaches engage CMC phenomena.

One such question is the appropriateness of"community" as a conceptual device. The conventional idea of community as a stable locus for the practice of ritual, custom, and moral obligation applies to cyberspace groups, albeit in the context of a shifting sense of commitment.

When members can easily come and go, when many"members" do not even post, and when identities cannot be verified beyond the current situation, the power of a community ethos may be weakened considerably. The structural properties of the Internet also raise questions about how far a user community extends. For example, can any array of Web sites found by a search term be considered a"community," and if not, what criteria do we use for including a site in the community set?

Finally, what is the relationship of computer-mediated action to local social networks? It has been suggested, for example, that the growing reliance on computer technology for communicating with distant others may undermine the vitality of public life in so-called real communities or play a role in their economic and social fragmentation. Answers to these and other important issues about virtual community await further and more inventive empirical studies.

If there is one theme that runs through the differences between FTF (embodied) and CIVIC (virtual) ethnography, it is the problem of participation. CIVIC ethnography moves us into questions of what it means to engage in and explain"experience" without being co-present with others. Screen-life is a social sphere of its own with vocabularies, motives, and expectations that increasingly re-interpret the meanings of off-screen-life (e.g., mail becoming known as"snail mail").

Objectifications of life in the screen world are also a part of that world. Computer users do act as textual performers and analysts, and knowingly comment on the skills of other text-makers.

The use of symbolic codes like"FOTFL" and the real-time deployment of a character in a MUD are operations that create the affect of participation for users, and it would be unusual for ethnographers; not to consider their situated usage.

However, the sites of semiotic action in CMC are not the texts, but the persons who produce them. The text-threads from a Usenet news group or a stack of e-mail messages exnominate the moments in which they were created and read, and the influences of local institutions on their users' action are seldom seen in the messages themselves. In the years ahead, ethnographers will be struggling with basic questions of what it means to"participate" in simulated worlds as well as with developing tactical ways to participate as researchers.

Closely related to the problem of participation are issues of trust and ethical conduct to which we have alluded at various points in this chapter. These issues assume even more importance than usual in research practice due to the greater potential for engaging in covert surveillance of CIVIC social life and the still-unsettled distinctions between"public" and"private" behaviour across the range of cyberspace contexts.

The problem of the stable identifiability of persons who post in Usenet news groups, respond by e-mail, or visit a Web site may also confound the principle of informed consent as a precondition for engaging a human subject's participation. Generally, there is little debate about the need to provide as much disclosure as possible about research procedures to those who are asked to participate, and to shelter them from the possible harmful consequences of participation and subsequent publication.

However, as King notes, extremely wide ranges of"group accessibility" and"perceived privacy" exist on the Internet. The highest accessibility characterizes those public BBS groups that are unmoderated and unregulated, while the least accessible community is"a private, closed e-mail group where the subscription address is not published and there are enforced requirements to join".

Perceived privacy varies in terms of both the sensitivity of the information (in which, for example, a substance abuse support group would seek a very high level of privacy) and the need to disseminate information to the widest possible client group (the National Communication Association's CRTNET would seek a low measure of privacy).

Yet a great many Internet conversations can in fact be monitored with relative ease, which complicates the understanding of what is permissible to study and whether observation is truly"covert" if no barriers are erected to keep one from observing. Of course, it probably does matter to many virtual groups whether it is a naive visitor who is stopping briefly at their fora, or a person whose goal is to cast a long-term, analytic eye on their activities and publish the result.

The conventional view holds that any research of on-line participants should"strive to obtain some degree of informed consent whenever possible.... Most importantly, researchers should negotiate their entry into electronic communities, beginning with the `owner' of the discussion, if one exists".

Preserving the dignity and empowerment of the persons being studied, even if their"real" identities and locations are unknown, demands that the researcher take steps to explain all of the elements of the study that may bear on their decision to participate voluntarily. Taking a different view, Jones argues that the highly elusive, evanescent presence and essentially unknowable identity of most of the subjects in cylberspace obviates the need in most cases for pursuing consent formally:"If the research does not involve identifiable subjects, there is no risk to subjects, and therefore the protection of these rights and interests no longer applies".

Jones goes on to argue that the strict application of conventional human subject protections would be especially detrimental to the study of cyberspace, which exists as an arena in which individuals can enjoy the freedom of withholding, revealing, and even fabricating information about themselves.

Somewhere between these positions is King, who states that"the perceived level of privacy with which most members of cyberspace forums post notes is the level that researchers are obligated to protect".

At the stage of publication, she advocates the removal from messages of all headers, signatures, references to the name and type of the group (e-mail, Usenet news group, etc.), and references to any person's name or pseudo-name. It may be that the evolving use of networked systems will alter the customs and arguments for what constitutes"privacy" and"autonomy," in turn informing the ethical practice of ethnography.

Finally, the implications of computer networks for the construction of the research text are of great importance. One can adapt the same hypermedia programming tools used in other scholarly efforts to the production of ethnographies that would in turn be fully compatible with the World Wide Web's system architecture. An example of such an effort is the Survivors of the Shoah Visual History Foundation, which has set out to videotape oral histories of all living Holocaust survivors and digitize them in hypermedia format along with maps, documents, photos, and written texts of the interviews.

The files, perhaps numbering 150,000 by the end of the decade, will be fully cross-referenced and accessible for on-line searches by key words. Similarly, ethnographies of CMC culture can be envisioned which would provide the discursive threads that underpin an analysis, along with field notes, full-text interviews, generations of Web page design, graphic material, and URL's to the ethnographic sites themselves and related research projects. Presumably the author would also be"available" in a rather immediate sense to readers via the research text's Web site or e-mail.

What distinguishes an archive a reader can navigate at will from a research text is that the latter usually embodies arguments, claims, and evidence in a style conventionalized within the discipline. While readers have always had non-linear access to a text, it is the linear narrative designed by the author that academic communities recognize as the only one subject to critique.

The capabilities of hypermedia threaten this formulation of the research product and the concept of authorial control that stands behind it. If readings of an ethnography are neither the ones an author intended nor the ones deemed important or legitimate by a discipline, then its use-value becomes as widely distributed among communities of practical interest as the Internet itself. The move to modular, multi-threaded (but not necessarily plotless) research texts not only reduces the researcher's story to the stature of one among a potentially limitless number, it also accelerates the epistemological decentering of inquiry that began with the challenge to objectivist ethnography nearly twenty years ago.

Chapter 8

Factors in News Photo Use

The 1991 Pulitzer for spot news photography went to freelancer Gregory Marinovich, who documented the murder of an accused Zulu spy by African National Congress sympathizers in Soweto, South Africa. Marinovich tried, and failed, to stop the violence. Of 57 *Associated Press* newspapers surveyed, 24 ran either a photo of the victim being burned alive or an equally disturbing stabbing. This analysis reports that most editors who played the photos aggressively were also careful to place them in a substantive news context. Although reader reactions varied, the study also suggests that important, albeit violent, photos are more likely to be accepted by readers if they are presented thoughtfully and with context.

On September 15, 1990, freelance photographer Gregory Marinovich documented the killing, by a mob of African National Congress supporters, of a man they believed to be a Zulu spy. The photos, although they would eventually win a 1991 Pulitzer Prize and an array of other awards, presented tough decisions for editors.

Marinovich and Associated Press (AP) reporter Tom Cohen spotted the man being led from a Soweto, South Africa, train-station platform by a group armed with machetes and crude spears. As Marinovich and Cohen continued to watch, the man was stoned, bludgeoned, stabbed, and, ultimately, doused with gasoline and set afire.

The pictures that cleared the AP photo wire later that day were riveting. But their importance lies not so much in the dramatic episode they captured as in their insistence that we confront an ugly reality we might otherwise never see. In newsrooms, they challenged editors to step beyond constraints of everyday sensitivity. AP policy is to "transmit what we think is the right thing," said Tom Stathis, AP's senior photo editor for North America. "What a newspaper does with its decision. Graphic violence just for violence's sake with no context—we don't move that".

As the series was transmitted, Stathis recalls, several member editors called AP to question "the photographer's ability, or lack of ability, to stop the situation." In response, an advisory went out on the photo wire, explaining that Marinovich had tried to intervene and then, when told to stop taking pictures, had said he would stop shooting when the mob stopped its attack.

This is a study of how editors seek to reconcile their ethical duties as journalists with the sensitivities of their audiences and, specifically, of how the editors of 57 North American newspapers used the Marinovich photographs. Particular attention was paid to the news context—the combination of stories and cutline information—in which the graphics ran.

A great range of ethical theories figured in editors' choices. On one hand, the decision not to run the most shocking photos was attributed to proscriptive guidelines such as traditional "breakfast" and "dead body" tests. Others cited a more affirmative ethic, saying the pictures offered an invaluable insight into inhumanity that outweighed whatever offense to taste they might also carry.

The most substantive treatment of the Soweto story came from editors who chose the most dramatic photos and ran them assertively and thoughtfully. Instead of condescending to readers, they were accountable to readers' intelligence. Thus, by taking responsibility for thoroughly contextualizing the story, these editors effectively diminished the photos' violative or sensationalistic potential.

Although this was not a study of reader reaction, there are indications readers sense the difference between photos run for shock value and shocking photos run to tell an important story. Quietly, readers provide ethical leadership here, reminding us they are willing to take on difficult subjects that are addressed decently and honestly.

On a limited range of stories, fairly firm policies guide editors through the ethical quagmire of the news day: Identities of sex-crime victims and most juveniles are protected; dead-body shots are used with great restraint; victims aren't identified until families have been notified. Suggestive sexuality is out; so is most profanity. But there is no consensus on questions of degree: How much blood or pain is too much? Is the moment of death less objectionable than its aftermath? Most often these questions are submitted to a simple utilitarian balancing: If the photograph violates principles of compassion or taste, does its social or news value outweigh the other values it violates? Editors can shift this balance by adequate contextualization.

CONSIDERATION OF COMPASSION

Concerns of compassion focus on victimization and privacy; those of taste on violence, dignity, and decency. But compassion and taste do not translate easily into guidelines. Nor is "taste" easily defined. Perhaps the most useful distinction comes from Gormley:

If a reader knows the person pictured in a very dramatic photograph, he may find it offensive. That's a sin against compassion. If he is offended whether he knows the person or not, the sin is probably one against good taste.

The need for compassion generally arises in relation to the sanctity of grief, privacy of victims, and impact on survivors and friends. Further, the distinction between "people we know" and others helps shape a commonly cited distance test. "The closer to home an event occurs, the more likely readers are to be upset over the use of graphic news photographs". Although Lester reported that reader protests do not seem to relate to race or gender, others argue for distance measures by psychology and geography.

CONSIDERATION OF TASTE

Taste covers more than the slapstick and bizarre. The

reality prized by journalists—photos of gore, death, violence, and grief—may also offend readers' sense of good taste.

The most frequently applied taste test comes at the breakfast table. Some editors apply different values to morning and evening papers. Others treat offensive material more carefully when young readers are involved. A common breakfast test component is a ban on dead bodies or the moment of death.

There are suggestions, however, that death by immolation, as in the Soweto series, "may somehow be more 'sanitized' than a bloody death". Issues of taste may often hinge more on aesthetics than ethics, entering the ethical domain only when journalists withhold important stories from a squeamish public or bow to what McCulloch calls readers' "right not to know certain things".

CONSIDERATIONS OF NEWS VALUE

As editors weigh the harm photos can do to the people involved or to community sensitivities, they also consider news value.

Pennsylvania State Treasurer R. Budd Dwyer's public suicide in January 1987 yielded perhaps the most concentrated study to date of different editors' responses to difficult photo choices. Other subjects have included photos of a boy impaled by the jaw on a picket fence; a picketing hotel worker run over by a strike-breaker's car; and the aftermath of a Bakersfield, CA drowning.

Fairly consistently, these photographs offered contorted images, some verging on grotesque, triggering objections based on taste or aesthetics. More significantly for ethics, most also possessed debatable news value, and because they were shot in the United States, raised primary issues of dignity and privacy, both for subjects and survivors.

There have been few recent opportunities for systematic study of photos that, like Soweto, offer strong news values, and because they occurred abroad, raise few concerns of compassion. Here, reader squeamishness becomes the primary issue, recalling controversies surrounding Malcolm W.

Browne's photos of the self-immolation of a Vietnamese monk and Eddie Adams' series on the street execution of a suspected Viet Cong officer.

CONSIDERATIONS OF A PHOTOGRAPHER'S ROLE

Compassion, taste, and news value are subject- or reader-oriented questions. Photographer's role issues centre in the newsgathering operation itself. Here, journalists become a part of their own story. Editors must be alert to the ethical dilemmas photographers face in the field: Has being photographed deepened the victims' trauma? Might the photographer have intervened to prevent the tragedy rather than record it? Did the camera incite or distort the event?

Incitement and intervention issues were extensively debated after J. Ross Baughman donned the uniform of the mercenary Grey Scouts to document mistreatment of black prisoners in Rhodesia. Again, in Dacca, Bangladesh, photographers Horst Faas and Michel Laurent were criticized for recording the torture and murder of suspected Pakistani sympathizers.

CONSIDERATIONS OF EDITORIAL CONTENT

Editors are responsible not only for probing the authenticity and ethical integrity of pictures but for providing the frame within which readers see them. Readers respond to how photos and stories are com bined. A front-page picture with only a cursory cutline may seem disrespectful; colour can seem to add gratuitous drama to a sensitive image. "Even the most explicit story on a subject normally deemed offensive can be used in a newspaper or newscast if written in considered, responsible language and displayed appropriately".

Part of the worry here is prudential. Editors don't want to get in trouble with readers, who already suspect that sensational photos are chosen to sell newspapers by appealing to morbid tastes. Beyond prudential considerations, however, should lie the more profound ethical duty to communicate effectively and responsibly. The question should not be *whether* to run an important but sensitive photo, or where to hide it, but how to position it to tell its story most profoundly.

This study is based on content analysis of the September 16 and 17, 1990 editions of 57 U.S. and Canadian AP newspapers. Three readers tabulated which, if any, of the six AP Marinovich photos were used and where they were placed in the newspaper. The photographs were recorded as Lead, Harass, Beat/Stone, Drag, Stab; and Burn. The team also recorded what copy completed the package.

A basic story about South Africa's government crackdown on black-on-black violence, recorded as Iron Fist, was provided by several services. AP's version (recorded as AP) included one sentence saying AP staffers had witnessed an unarmed black being stoned, stabbed, and then burned to death at the Soweto train station.

The insertion of this sentence (recorded as Incident) in stories by other services, or deletion from the AP version, was also noted. AP subscribers also received Cohen's eyewitness account of the murder, recorded as Attack. Finally, AP explained Marinovich's attempt to intervene in a photo advisory tabulated as Photog.

A 5 for Copy reflects use of separate items on the crackdown, the Soweto attack, and Marinovich's attempt to intervene.

A score of.50 reflects use of only the AP crackdown story, deleting reference to the attack. Finally, telephone interviews with editors at 28 papers explored reasons for running, or not running, the photos; positioning and play; the selection of accompanying copy; and any formal or informal guidelines that might govern use of such material. Additional questions explored the decision process, previous coverage of South African troubles, and reader reaction.

Decisions on what to do with the photos varied across the country, with no apparent relationship to whether papers were large or small, Northern or Southern, tabloid or broadsheet, or conservative or aggressive in their journalism. If any pattern emerges, it may be that newspapers in competitive markets like Denver, Minneapolis-St. Paul, and

New York were more likely to go with the harsh graphics. In Chicago and Houston, however, both dailies took a conservative approach.

Only in Los Angeles—where the *Times* ran the burning in colour above the front-page fold and the *Daily News* ran a Mandela file mug—did competing papers take markedly different approaches. Although a dozen editors acknowledged that "breakfast test" considerations frequently arise during photo deliberations, 6 of the 12 said such tests rarely govern final decisions. Several newspapers routinely subject all dead-body photos to extra screening, but editors at only three papers said such shots are consistently rejected.

An important difference emerged among papers that used the strongest Marinovich images: the burning or the stabbing. Most papers that chose aggressive placement used accompanying stories to explain the significance and relevance of the photos. In contrast, papers that played the burning as a single-photo package on an inside page, were stingy with accompanying copy.

PHOTO CHOICES

Of 57 newspapers surveyed, 24 ran either the burning or stabbing. Seventeen avoided the most violent photos, running instead the victim being led away from the railroad station, dragged down the street, or pelted with stones. Sixteen ran none of the series.

The burning photo ranked first with 22 uses; Lead, the mildest shot of all, was second, with 17 uses. With only 10 uses, the stabbing stood at the other extreme from Burn; several editors said they specifically rejected it as too extreme. "It showed violence and animalistic hatred," said Roman Lyskowski, graphics editor for the Miami Herald.

Former Oakland Tribune Vice President Leroy Aarons, chairman of the Pulitzer spot news nominating panel, said he also would have chosen the burning but not the stabbing. Jeff Jarvis, Sunday editor at the New York Daily News, rejected both but found the burning less shocking: "I remember immolation pictures from the Vietnam era. That's not as unusual an image as that knife sticking right out of the skull."

The *St. Paul Pioneer Press,* however, chose the stabbing for frontpage colour. "I look at the moment that the photo freezes on film," said News Editor Joe Sevick. "Rarely do you see a photo where a knife is about to go into somebody."

Burn was also the consensus choice for front pages. Of nine papers that used Marinovich photos on Page A1, eight used the burning and one, the *Pioneer Press,* the stabbing.

Fifteen newspapers chose series of from two to five shots. After Burn, used in all 15 series, Lead was next most popular, with 11 uses. Mildest of the group, the shot advanced the story while relieving the tension of the stronger graphics. Next in series use, despite its overall unpopularity, was Stab, with 9 uses. Significantly, Stab was used only twice as a stand-alone photo, with editors apparently deciding it was too strong to be used without the context set by other images.

PAPER-BY-PAPER DECISIONS

When the Soweto series cleared on Saturday, *Miami Herald* editors sent Burn to Executive Editor Janet Chusmir's home for her approval. At her direction, the immolation picture ran on the front page, but below the fold and in black and white.

The detail revealed in colour reproduction, Lyskowski and Chusmir agreed, was too graphic. At the *Los Angeles Times* and *Dallas Morning News,* however, the shot ran above the front-page fold—and in colour.

New York City's four major dailies all ran photo stories. The *Post,* with no Sunday edition, assembled a Monday package combining the dragging, stabbing, and burning photos with second-day reaction to the government crackdown. The *Times* and *Newsday* both chose the burning. The *Daily News* ran only the stoning.

Chicago dailies were more conservative: The *Sun Times* (careful of its reputation, one editor said, because it is a tabloid and "we used to be owned by Rupert Murdoch") chose the mild Lead. The *Tribune* used none of the Soweto photos.

THE BREAKFAST, DEAD BODY, AND OTHER TESTS

Editors who ran none of the Marinovich photos or chose the less intense shots offered similar explanations. "Too strong, too grisly, too gruesome, even for an inside page" was the verdict at the *Sacramento Bee,* which ran none of the Soweto photos. "While we don't shrink from running certain body pictures," Sacramento Bee ombudsman Art Nauman said, "this was beyond the bounds of acceptability to our readers."

Several editors deferred to the "breakfast test." "The question is, 'Which of those photos would help tell the story without ruining everyone's breakfast?'" said Rod Deckert, managing editor of the *Albuquerque Journal.* One editor said his paper tends to de-emphasize disturbing material in the Sunday paper, which parents often read with their children.

But even many editors who rejected the more brutal pictures said they find the breakfast test irrelevant. "If you're putting out a paper in New York and don't have something that's going to cause some discomfort over breakfast, then you're probably not putting out the full paper you should," said Jarvis. "I don't think the breakfast test works for the '90s."

Several editors apply distance tests. At the *Portland Oregonian,* which used both stabbing and burning, Photo Director Serge McCabe said body photos from inside the Oregonian circulation area are less likely to be used, in deference to victims' families. Similar policies were reported at *Long Island's Newsday*. But at the *Albuquerque Journal,* Deckert said, a violent photo is unlikely to run unless it is local and has a "more immediate impact on our readership."

Overall, few papers reported firm policies governing violent photos. "We thought we had all these rules: You don't run pictures of snakes and toilets and bodies," said Steve Small, *St. Petersburg Times* photo director. "We discovered that the only rule we have is that we don't have a rule."

COPY CHOICES

Among papers that used the more graphic Marinovich photos, a pronounced difference emerged between those that ran the photos on the front page or in groups and those that ran the burning as a single photo on an inside page. Editors at the 19 papers that chose aggressive play placed the photos in a thorough news context, often as part of a two- or three-story package that backgrounded the South African situation, described the train-station attack itself, and—in four cases-explained Marinovich's attempt to intervene. At the handful of papers in the second group, the difference was marked.

Two ran only a brief description of the train-station incident in copy, plus a reference in the cutline. The remaining two—the *New York Times* and *Denver Post*—omitted any reference to the Soweto attack in the accompanying story. The *Post* cutline simply read: "Violence continues: A boy runs away as an ANC supporter clubs a Zulu foe who was beaten, stabbed, and set ablaze."

With scores of 3.33 and 2.66 for the top two groups. The lowest score for copy relevance, 1.38, went to the four papers that ran "burn" on an inside page.

Although 41 papers used at least one of the Marinovich photos, only 4—the *Charlotte Observer, Akron Beacon-Journal, Rocky Mountain News* and *USA Today*—told the story of Marinovich's attempt to halt the attack.

At most papers, news editors said they could not recall an advisory about Marinovich; several speculated it may not have made the trip from the Saturday-staffed photo department to the news desk. Only two editors remembered seeing the advisory and not using it, choosing to avoid focusing, one said, "on the news media as news maker."

THE NEWS CONTEXT

Among collateral considerations at many news desks was the coverage of earlier South African troubles. Within the week preceding the Soweto incident, the *Longmont (CO) Daily Times*-Call had run other beating and killing photographs from South Africa, weekend editor Rod Gerlach said. The Soweto photos were "just too, too much." *Seattle Times* photo editor Dean Rutz ran none of the photos. Catching the violence on film was "extraordinary," he said. "But it's been described in print and shown in the past."

Another view came from the Denver Post: "The world is turning its back," said Sunday Editor Isabel Spencer. Even if the only photo available had been the stabbing, which Spencer had rejected as too tough, she said, "I would not have much listened to anybody.... I would have run that one."

The *Los Angeles Times* backs off from high-impact photos only if the news context is weak, as in the Budd Dwyer suicide, Assistant Managing Editor Terry Schwadron said. In his view, the Soweto photos were directly on the point of the larger story.

At one paper, angry readers accused editors of racial insensitivity, suggesting the photos would not have run had the victim been white.

Others alleged a "racist plot" to show black-on-black violence. But with only three exceptions, editors said race did not figure in their considerations. One editor, who identified himself as white, said the fact that both attackers and victim were black deprived the series of clarity: "You don't have a sense of one side against another. You don't have a sense of right or wrong."

Two African-American editors, however, argued for aggressive use of the photos. Both work in communities with significant black populations. "I think black readers should be more informed about this," one said. "Across the board, black Americans don't realise what's going on with black-on-black violence."

THE DECISION-MAKING PROCESS

At several newspapers, photo editors said they often don't even suggest graphic violence for editors' consideration. The Soweto photos, however, generally made it at least to the news desk for decision. There, they were sometimes killed abruptly. "The editors at that point said no," one picture editor reported. "They would not take the heat."

Duty editors inclined to run the more challenging photos frequently moved the discussion up. The *Albany Times Union, Boulder Daily Camera, Dallas Morning News, Miami Herald,* and *Minneapolis Star-Tribune* were among the papers consulting top editors by telephone, or bringing them in from home, before going ahead.

Rocky Mountain News Managing Editor Mike Madigan approved running the Soweto photos, but credits the entire newsroom with helping shape the coverage.

The resulting package included stories on both the attack and the government crack-down, an editor's note on Marinovich's intervention, and three photos: Lead, Stab, and Burn. The only open page was deep in the paper, but a Page 3 box referred readers to the story while warning that the photos were "horrific and disturbing".

READER REACTION

Several editors said they avoided the more graphic Soweto photos simply to avoid reader outcry, essentially a marketing consideration. Others chose to run the pictures, but struggled to shape a context that would not only be acceptable to readers but would allow readers to experience the full significance of the story.

Here the desire to avoid reader rejection was more ethical than prudential: Editors wanted to avoid provoking a controversy that would distract readers from the story. "Just one word or the other can make a terrific difference in whether the public starts screaming 'sensationalize, sensationalize,' or takes it as a thoughtful, important piece of work, which is what we were after," Madigan said.

No papers reported systematic efforts to log reader reaction. Anecdotal evidence, however, suggests that positioning, photo choice, and copy selection worked together to shape reader response. The *Rocky Mountain News* reported no reader complaints; the *Albany Times Union,* with the central four photos down the left margin of the front page, was flooded by phone calls and subscription cancellations.

Front page placement was an obvious factor, but the adequacy of cutline information and accompanying copy also appears significant. The three papers perceiving the most reader unrest—the *TimesUnion, Dallas Morning News,* and *Los Angeles Times*—all ran Marinovich photos on their front pages, the *News* and *Times* printed the burning in colour. But each paper also ran the front-page photos with only cutline accompaniment, referring readers inside to the stories that placed the images in context.

The *St. Paul Pioneer Press* alone ran the chilling stabbing, in colour, on its front page. The photo was accompanied on page 1, however, by Cohen Attack and the *New York Times* Iron Fist stories. Reader's Representative Wayne Hassell, whose phone "normally rang off the hook" when readers objected to a story, recalls no significant reaction to the Soweto photo.

DISCUSSION

Few, if any, written policies govern photo selection, but there is an active folklore on what unwritten rules may be at work. Newspapers fall into two camps: a minority that will not use graphic violence and a majority that will at least talk about it.

In the first group, photo editors weed out photos that violate whatever they believe the prevailing sensitivity tests to be, with deadbody photos the most frequently rejected category. Some editors support such policies; others have reluctantly concluded that it is a waste of time to submit graphic photos for higher editors' consideration. Only a few continue to test the system, urging exceptions for shots that make strong statements.

We found no mainstream dailies that intentionally seek shocking art, but at a majority of the papers surveyed, dramatic photos are given a serious hearing.

At 42% of the papers studied (24 of 57), advocates of running either the stabbing or the burning successfully argued that the significance of the shots outweighed other considerations. Another 30% used milder shots from the series; 28% ran none at all.

An equally wide variation appeared in editors' efforts to place the powerful images in context. Some gave the photos such slim copy support that the rarity of the shots seemed more important than their human and political significance.

Others assembled carefully constructed packages that could provoke and inform, while sharing with readers some of the human dilemma the photographer faced at the scene.

This quest for context, for the line of moderation, has two aspects. First, there is a need for substantive content. Do the photo and copy work together to add to the reader's understanding of the event or issue? Second, there is a need for appropriate presentation.

Are the images treated respectfully? Will colour enhance or sensationalize the image? Is page 1 placement justified by the merits of the story, not just by the drama of the image? Journalists are increasingly being asked to account for their ethical conduct in the field: Responsible editors need to probe questions of incitement and intervention: Did the camera help provoke the event?

Might, or should, the photographer have intervened to save a life? Thoughtful communication with readers includes sharing the details and dilemmas of newsgathering. Over time, the circumstances under which Eddie Adams shot his dramatic street execution and the moral decisions Malcolm Browne made when summoned to the self-immolation of a Vietnamese monk have become critical to both stories.

The most disappointing single aspect of newspapers' treatment of the Soweto photos is that only four of the surveyed papers provided answers to legitimate ethical questions about the role Marinovich might have played in stopping—or intensifying—the attack.

Caution in assessing what level of violence readers will tolerate is justified. But it is heartening to hear editors speak of their responsibility to present unpleasant facts and pictures, to unveil cruelty and injustice in the world. "We have to use some of these photos sometimes or else nothing ever changes," the *Oregonian*'s McCabe said, noting that the war in Vietnam started drawing to an end only after "those images started coming in and [readers] realized what was going on."

There is a corresponding awareness among editors that reader benefit is enhanced if material is presented thoughtfully and with consideration. There are strong suggestions here, although the evidence is preliminary, that reader acceptance of shocking images is directly related to the adequacy of accompanying copy.

Both the *Rocky Mountain News* and the *St. Paul Pioneer Press*—which chose the most dramatic Marinovich photos, then supported them thoughtfully with accompanying copy—communicated effectively with readers without their message being distorted by cries of sensationalism.

News context is critical to dramatic photos. Merely running a powerful image, without sharing what one knows of its significance, is the essence of exploitation. Editors who cared about the Soweto story took care to tell it well.

Video journalism or videojournalism is a form of broadcast journalism, where the production of video content in which the journalist shoots, edits and often presents his or her own material.

A predecessor to video journalism first appeared in the 1960s in the USA, when reporters had to write and shoot their own stories.

Michael Rosenblum compared the introduction of video cameras to the invention of the portable camera in the 1930s: film spools of plastic made photography independent from heavy plates and tripods, and digital video technology liberates TV from heavy cameras, artificial light and studios in much the same manner. Video journalism makes it possible to document any event while it is still occurring.

In the early 1990s, the news channel New York 1 was the first to hire only video journalists. In the mid-1990s, the first German private stations followed the example of NY1, and in 1994, the regional channel Bayerischer Rundfunk became the first public broadcasting station to follow suit and hire a number of video journalists.

In 2001 the BBC started to switch to video journalism in all its regional offices. As of June 2005 the BBC has more than 600 of its staff trained as video journalists. Other broadcasting entities who now use video journalism include Voice of America and Video News International. It also seems to be becoming more widespread among newspapers, with the

Washington Post alone employing six video journalists. The Press Association (UK) is behind a training programme which "converts" regional journalists into video journalists, more than 100 as of March 2007.

In Australia, several commercial networks employ Video Journalists. They include WIN News, Golden West Network (GWN) and Network Ten. Increasing popularity in online news has seen Video Journalists employed by Fairfax, News Limited and The West Australian Newspaper Holdings to produce video content for their news websites.

In Canada, the Canadian Broadcasting Corporation made a widespread move into hiring video journalists (or retraining existing reporters or camera people to do multiple jobs) in the late 1990's.

In most cases, they were assigned to local newsrooms to do daily news, just as full crews had before. Primarily, it was a cost-saving measure.

Within a few years, however, it was clear that this rarely produced good results because of short deadlines and the assumption that VJ's could work the same way and on the same stories. The effort was scaled back.

The exception turned out to be video journalists who work more as independent documentary film-makers, using their mobility and easier access to do stories that don't have short deadlines.

One example of this is award-winning video journalist Sasa Petricic, who works for CBC's flagship daily newscast, The National, and reports solo from around the world.

PROS AND CONS

Growth in video journalism coincides with changes in video technology and falling costs. As quality cameras and editing systems have become smaller and available at a fraction of their previous prices, the single operator method has spread.

Some argue that video journalists can to get closer to the story, avoiding the impersonality that may come with larger crewing. In addition, the dramatically lower costs have made possible the birth of many cinéma vérité-style documentary films and series.

Others see this method of production as a dilution of skills and quality driven by TV management cost cutting incentives. There is a move towards finding independent distribution for freelance video journalists.

One of the issues is copyright, which can be difficult to obtain when broadcasters and agencies insist on full ownership of the footage. The other difficulty can be trying to find distribution beyond established contacts.

Increasingly, online companies such as Beamups are giving VJs the opportunity to keep ownership of their stories and find global distribution. News design is the process of arranging material on a newspaper page, according to editorial and graphical guidelines and goals.

Main editorial goals include the ordering of news stories by order of importance, while graphical considerations include readability and balanced, unobtrusive incorporation of advertising. News design incorporates principles of graphic design and is taught as part of journalism training in schools and colleges. Overlapping and related terms include layout, makeup (formerly paste up) and pagination.

The era of modern newspapers begins in the mid-nineteenth century, with the Industrial Revolution, and increased capacities for printing and distribution. Over time, improvements in printing technology, graphical design, and editorial standards have led to changes and improvements in the look and readability of newspapers.

Nineteenth-century newspapers were often densely packed with type, often arranged vertically, with multiple headlines for each article. A number of the same technological limitations persisted until the advent of digital typesetting and pagination in late 20th century.

"USA Today" was a leader in design changes, and was largely responsible for adding tools such as colour and infographics to newspapers' design vocabulary. These changes are partly intended to help readers "navigate", to scan and see priorities.

Some of these changes included:

- Fewer articles per page.
- Modules, or squaring off of articles and packages of related materials. Modules avoid what is known as "doglegs" or inverted-"L" shapes.
- More standardized column widths.
- More standardized fonts.
- More "art" —nontext elements, usually photos, but often including advertising or outline (or shaded) boxes for featured stories.
- More white space, known as "air". An area with too little white space is called "tight", and too much white space is called "loose".
- Colour.

PROCESS

Designers typically use desktop publishing software to arrange the elements on the pages directly. In the past, before digital pre-press pagination, designers used precise "lay out dummies" to direct the exact layout of elements for each page.

A complete layout dummy was required for designating proper column widths by which a typesetter would set type, and arrange columns of text. Layout also required the calculation of lengths of copy (text in "column inches"), for any chosen width.

Much of the variance and incoherence of early newspapers was due to the fact that last minute corrections were exclusively handled by typesetters.

With photographic printing process, typesetting gave way to paste-up, whereby columns of type were printed by machines (phototypesetters) on high-resolution film for paste-up on photographed final prints. These prints in turn were "shot to negative" with a large format production camera — directly to steel-emulsion photographic plates.

Though paste-up put an end to cumbersome typesetting, this still required planned layouts and set column widths. Photographic plates are (still) wrapped on printing drums to directly apply ink to newsprint (paper).

In the mid 1990s, the paste-up process gave way to the direct to plate process, where computer-paginated files were optically transmitted directly to the photographic plate.

Replacing several in-between steps in newspaper production, direct to plate pagination allowed for much more flexibility and precision than before.

DESIGN OPTIONS

Designers choose photo sizes and headline sizes (both the size of the letters and how much space the headline will take). They may decide what articles will go on which pages, and where on the page, alone or in consultation with editors. They may choose typefaces for special pages, but newspapers usually have a design style that determines most routine uses.

NOTABLE NEWS DESIGNERS

Notable in the field include Roger Black, Phil Autelitano, Bill Ostendorf, Richard Curtis, Mario Garcia, Tim Harrower, Lucie Lacava, Tony Majeri, Monica Moses, Deborah Withey, Alan Jacobson and Ron Reason.

Some other newspapers influential to the expanded role of design in the newsroom include the Detroit Free Press, the San Jose Mercury News, The Guardian, and the Virginian-Pilot. Edmund Arnold, who recently died, is widely credited as the father of modern newspaper design.

Photojournalism is a particular form of journalism (the collecting, editing, and presenting of news material for publication or broadcast) that creates images in order to tell a news story.

It is now usually understood to refer only to still images, but in some cases the term also refers to video used in broadcast journalism. Photojournalism is distinguished from other close branches of photography (such as documentary photography, street photography or celebrity photography) by the qualities of:

- *Timeliness*: The images have meaning in the context of a recently published record of events.
- *Objectivity*: The situation implied by the images is a

fair and accurate representation of the events they depict in both content and tone.

- *Narrative*: The images combine with other news elements to make facts relatable to the viewer or reader on a cultural level.

Like a writer, a photojournalist is a reporter but he or she must often make decisions instantly and carry photographic equipment, often while exposed to significant obstacles (physical danger, weather, crowds).

The practice of illustrating news stories with photographs was made possible by printing and photography innovations that occurred between 1880 and 1897.

While newsworthy events were photographed as early as the 1850s, printing presses could only publish from engravings until the 1880s. Early news photographs required that photos be re-interpreted by an engraver before they could be published.

The first photojournalist was Carol Szathmari (Rumanian painter, lithographer and photographer)who did pictures in the Crimean War (between Russia and Turkey, 1853 to 1856).

His albums were sent to European royals houses. Just a few of his photographs survived. William Simpson of the *Illustrated London News* and Roger Fenton were published as engravings.

Similarly, the American Civil War photographs of Mathew Brady were engraved before publication in *Harper's Weekly*.

Because the public craved more realistic representations of news stories, it was common for newsworthy photographs to be exhibited in galleries or to be copied photographically in limited numbers.

On March 4, 1880, *The Daily Graphic* (New York) published the first halftone (rather than engraved) reproduction of a news photograph. Further innovations followed.

In 1887, flash powder was invented, enabling journalists such as Jacob Riis to photograph informal subjects indoors, which led to the landmark work *How the Other Half Lives*. By

1897, it became possible to reproduce halftone photographs on printing presses running at full speed.

Despite these innovations, limitations remained, and many of the sensational newspaper and magazine stories in the period from 1897 to 1927 were illustrated with engravings.

In 1921, the wirephoto made it possible to transmit pictures almost as quickly as news itself could travel. However, it was not until development of the commercial 35mm Leica camera in 1925, and the first flash bulbs between 1927 and 1930 that all the elements were in place for a "golden age" of photojournalism.

In the "golden age" of photojournalism (1930s–1950s), some magazines (*Picture Post* (London), *Paris Match* (Paris), *Arbeiter-Illustrierte-Zeitung* (Berlin), *Berliner Illustrierte Zeitung* (Berlin), *Life* (USA), *Look* (USA), *Sports Illustrated* (USA)) and newspapers (*The Daily Mirror* (London), *The New York Daily News* (New York) built their huge readerships and reputations largely on their use of photography, and photographers such as Robert Capa, Alfred Eisenstaedt, Margaret Bourke-White and W. Eugene Smith became well-known names.

Henri Cartier-Bresson is held by some to be the father of modern photojournalism, although this appellation has been applied to various other photographers, such as Erich Salomon, whose candid pictures of political figures were novel in the 1930s

Soldier Tony Vaccaro is also recognized as one of the pre-eminent photographers of World War II. His images taken with the modest Argus C3 captured horrific moments in war, similar to Capa's soldier being shot. Capa himself was on Omaha Beach on D-Day and captured pivotal images of the conflict on that occasion.

Vaccaro is also known for having developed his own images in soldier's helmets, and using chemicals found in the ruins of a camera store in 1944.

Until the 1980s, most large newspapers were printed with turn-of-the-century "letterpress" technology using easily smudged oil-based ink, off-white, low-quality "newsprint" paper, and coarse engraving screens.

While letterpresses produced legible text, the photoengraving dots that formed pictures often bled or smeared and became fuzzy and indistinct. In this way, even when newspapers used photographs well — a good crop, a respectable size — murky reproduction often left readers re-reading the caption to see what the photo was all about.

The *Wall Street Journal* adopted stippled hedcuts in 1979 to publish portraits and avoid the limitations of letterpress printing.

Not until the 1980s had a majority of newspapers switched to "offset" presses that reproduce photos with fidelity on better, whiter paper.

By contrast *Life*, one of America's most popular weekly magazines from 1936 through the early 1970s, was filled with photographs reproduced beautifully on oversize 11×14-inch pages, using fine engraving screens, high-quality inks, and glossy paper. *Life* often published a United Press International (UPI) or Associated Press (AP) photo that had been first reproduced in newspapers, but the quality magazine version appeared to be a different photo altogether.

In large part because their pictures were clear enough to be appreciated, and because their name always appeared with their work, magazine photographers achieved near-celebrity status. *Life* became a standard by which the public judged photography, and many of today's photo books celebrate "photojournalism" as if it had been the exclusive province of near-celebrity magazine photographers.

The Best of Life (1973), for example, opens with a two-page (1960) group shot of 39 justly famous *Life* photographers. But 300 pages later, photo credits reveal that scores of the photos among *Life's* "best" were taken by anonymous UPI and AP photographers.

Thus even during the golden age, because of printing limitations and the UPI and AP syndication systems, many newspaper photographers labored in relative obscurity.

FARM SECURITY ADMINISTRATION

From 1935 to 1942, the Farm Security Administration and

its predecessor the Resettlement Administration were part of Franklin Roosevelt's New Deal, and were designed to address agricultural problems and rural poverty associated with the Great Depression.

A special photographic section, headed by Mark Arnold, was intended merely to provide public relations for its programs, but instead produced what some consider one of the greatest collections of documentary photographs ever created in the U.S. Whether this effort can be called "photojournalism" is debatable, since the FSA photographers had more time and resources to create their work than most photojournalists usually have.

ACCEPTANCE BY THE ART WORLD

Since the late 1970s, photojournalism and documentary photography have increasingly been accorded a place in art galleries alongside fine art photography. Luc Delahaye, VII Photo Agency are among many who regularly exhibit in galleries.

PROFESSIONAL ORGANIZATIONS

The Danish Union of Press Photographers (Pressefotografforbundet) was the first national organization for newspaper photographers in the world. It was founded in 1912 in Copenhagen, Denmark by six press photographers. Today it has over 800 members.

The National Press Photographers Association (NPPA) was founded in 1946 in the U.S., and has about 10,000 members. Others around the world include the British Press Photographers Association (BPPA) founded in 1984, then relaunched in 2003, and now has around 450 members. Hong Kong Press Photographers Association (1989), Northern Ireland Press Photographers Association (2000), Pressfotografernas Klubb (Sweden, 1930), and PK — Pressefotografenes Klubb (Norway).

News organisations and journalism schools run many different awards for photojournalists. Since 1968, Pulitzer Prizes have been awarded for the following categories of photojournalism: 'Feature Photography', 'Spot News Photography'. Other awards are World Press Photo, Best of Photojournalism, and Pictures of the Year as well as the UK based The Press Photographer's Year.

ETHICAL AND LEGAL CONSIDERATIONS

Photojournalism works within the same ethical approaches to objectivity that are applied by other journalists. What to shoot, how to frame and how to edit are constant considerations.

Often, ethical conflicts can be mitigated or enhanced by the actions of a sub-editor or picture editor, who takes control of the images once they have been delivered to the news organization. The photojournalist often has no control as to how images are ultimately used.

The emergence of digital photography offers whole new realms of opportunity for the manipulation, reproduction, and transmission of images. It has inevitably complicated many of the ethical issues involved. The U.S. National Press Photographers Association, and other professional organizations, maintain codes of ethics to specify approaches to these issues.

Major ethical issues are often inscribed with more or less success into law. Laws regarding photography can vary significantly from nation to nation. The legal situation is further complicated when one considers that photojournalism made in one country will often be published in many other countries.

THE IMPACT OF NEW TECHNOLOGIES

Smaller, lighter cameras greatly enhanced the role of the photojournalist. Since the 1960s, motor drives, electronic flash, auto-focus, better lenses and other camera enhancements have made picture taking easier. New digital cameras free photojournalists from the limitation of film roll length, as thousands of images can be stored on a single memory card.

Content remains the most important element of photojournalism, but the ability to extend deadlines with rapid gathering and editing of images has brought significant changes. As recently as 15 years ago, nearly 30 minutes were needed to scan and transmit a single colour photograph from a remote location to a news office for printing.

Now, equipped with a digital camera, a mobile phone and a laptop computer, a photojournalist can send a high-quality image in minutes, even seconds after an event occurs. Camera phones and portable satellite links increasingly allow for the mobile transmission of images from almost any point on the earth.

There is some concern by news photographers that the profession of photojournalism as it is known today could change to such a degree that it is unrecognizable as image-capturing technology naturally progresses. Citizen journalism and the increase in user contribution and submission of amateur photos to news sites is becoming more widespread.

As early as the Crimean War in the mid-19th century, photographers were using the novel technology of the box camera to record images of British soldiers in the field.

However, the widespread use of cameras as a way of reporting news did not come until the advent of smaller, more portable cameras that used the enlargeable film negative to record images.

The introduction of the 35 mm Leica camera in the 1930's made it possible for photographers to move with the action, taking shots of events as they were unfolding.

The age of the citizen journalist and the attainment of news photos from amateur bystanders have contributed to the art of photojournalism.

Paul Levinson attributes this shift to the Kodak camera, one of the first cheap and accessible photo technologies that "put a piece of visual reality into every person's potential grasp."

The empowered news audience with the advent of the Internet sparked the creation of blogs, podcasts and online news, independent of the traditional outlets, and "for the first time in our history, the news increasingly is produced by companies outside journalism".

Broadcast journalism is the field of news and journals which are "broadcast", that is, published by electrical methods, instead of the older methods, such as printed newspapers and posters.

Broadcast methods include radio (via air, cable, and Internet), television (via air, cable, and Internet), and, especially recently, the Internet generally. Such media disperse pictures (static and moving), visual text, and/or sounds. Scripts for speaking to be broadcast tend to be written differently than text to be read by the public.

For instance, the former is generally less complex and more conversational. Radio and television are designed to be seen and heard sooner and more often than is a daily or weekly newspaper. Broadcast "stories" (articles) can be written in "packages", "readers", "voice overs", and "sound on tape". A "package" is an edited set of video clips for a news story and is common on television. It is narrated typically by a reporter.

It is a story with audio, video, graphics and video effects. The anchor usually reads a "lead in" (introduction) before the package is aired and may conclude the story with additional information, called a tag.

A "reader" is an article read without accompanying video or sound. Sometimes an "over the shoulder graphic" is added.

A voice over, or VO, is a video article narrated by the anchor. Sound on tape, or SOT, is sound and/or video, usually recorded in the field. It is usually an interview or "soundbite".

Radio was the first medium for broadcast journalism. Many of the first radio stations were co-operative community ventures not making a profit. Later, advertising to pay for programs was pioneered in radio.

Later, television displaced radio and newspapers as the main news sources for most of the public in industrialized countries. Some of the programming on radio is locally produced; some is broadcast by a network, by syndication, etc. The "talent" (professional voices) talk to the audience, including reading the news. People tune in to hear engaging personalities, music, and information that they want. In radio news, stories include speech "sound bites", the recorded sounds of events themselves, and the anchor or host.

The radio industry has undergone a radical consolidation of ownership, with fewer companies owning the thousands of stations. Large media conglomerates such as Clear Channel Communications own most of the stations in the United States. That has resulted in more "niche" formats and the sharing of resources within clusters of stations, de-emphasizing local news and information.

There has been concern over whether that concentration of power serves the public. The opposition says that the range of political views expressed and supported is greatly narrowed and that local concerns are neglected, including local emergencies, for which communication is critical. Automation has resulted in many stations broadcasting for many hours a day with no one on the station premises.

Television (TV) news is considered by many to be the most influential medium for journalism. For most of the American public, local and national TV newscasts are the primary news sources.

Not only the numbers of viewers, but the effect on each viewer is considered more persuasive, as described by Marshall McLuhan ("the medium is the message" in his book *Understanding Media*).

Television is dominated by attractive visuals (including beauty, action, and shock), with short sound bites and fast "cuts" (changes of camera view). Television journalism viewership has become fragmented, with all-news cable channels such as CNN starting in 1980 and Fox News Channel and MSNBC in the 1990s.

LOCAL TELEVISION

The industry divides television into local markets. Such markets are defined by viewing area and are ranked by the number of viewers. New broadcast journalists generally start in the smaller markets (fewer viewers) and move up to larger stations after gaining experience. The larger stations usually have more resources and better pay.

United States stations typically broadcast local news 3 or 4 times a day: around 4:30, 5 or 6 am, 11, 11:30 am or noon, 5 and/or 6 pm, and 10 and/or 11 at night. Most of their nightly local newscasts are 30 minutes and include sports and weather.

Anchors are shown sitting at a desk in a studio. They read teleprompters. Reporters frequently tell their stories in live shots outside the studio where the news is occurring. Morning shows include more "soft" news and feature pieces, while the evening news emphasizes "hard" news.

NEWS JOBS

Anchors (formerly "anchormen"), serve as masters of ceremonies and are usually shown facing the camera in a studio while reading unseen teleprompters. They are often in pairs (co-anchors) side by side, often alternating their reading.

Meteorologists describe and forecast weather and show "graphics" (maps, charts, and pictures). Any of those people can become the most recognizable faces of a station. Reporters research and write the stories and sometimes edit them into a package. Reporters are usually accompanied by a videographer at the scenes of the news.

The latter holds the camera. That person or assistants manage the audio and lighting. They are in charge of setting up live shots and might edit, too. The producer might choose, research, and write stories, as well as deciding the timing and arrangement of the newscast. An associate producer, if any, might specialize in elements of the show such as graphics.

PRODUCTION JOBS

A newscast director is in charge of show preparation, including assigning camera and talent (cast) positions on the set, as well as selecting the camera shots and other elements (recorded and live). The technical director operates the video switcher which controls and mixes all the elements of the show. At smaller stations, the director and technical director are the same person. A graphics person operates a character generator that produces the name keys (on-screen titles) and full-page graphics.

The audio technician operates the audio board. The technician is in charge of the microphones, music, and audio tape. Often, production assistants operate the teleprompters and cameras, and serve as lighting and rigging technicians ("grips").

ON-LINE CONVERGENCE

Convergence is the sharing and cross-promoting of content from a variety of media, which in theory might all converge and become one medium eventually. In broadcast news, the Internet is key part of convergence. Frequently, broadcast journalists also write text stories for the Web, usually accompanied by the graphics and sound of the original story.

Web sites offer the audience an interactive form where they can learn more about a story, can be referred to related articles, can offer comments for publication, and can print stories at home, etc.

Convergence also lets newsrooms collaborate with other media. Broadcast outlets sometimes have partnerships with their print counterparts.

Visual Editors is a 501(c)(3) non-profit charity organized for educational purposesis a U.S. public charity that promotes journalism education via online forums, peer-to-peer sharing resources and offline training events held at universities and working newsrooms.

The 501(c)(3) non-profit was incorporated in 2004 by Chicago journalist Robb Montgomery and is registered in the State of Illinois.

The group operates online forums, blogs and portfolio galleries as a virtual peer to-peer classroom. The group who use the charity's resources to study the latest visual journalism, information graphics and newspaper design techniques.

The not-for-profit also offers several blogs from established visual journalists like Charles Apple (U.S.A.), Alan

Formby-Jackson (U.K.), TK Sajeev (India), Alejandro Banuet (Mexico) as well as many interactive teaching tools to help high school and college students and teachers study and share state-of-the-art journalism techniques. The site recently migrated from a PHP forums style exchange to the NING platform. Yellow journalism, also known as the "Yellow Press", is a type of journalism that downplays legitimate news in favour of eye-catching headlines that sell more newspapers. It may feature exaggerations of news events, scandal-mongering, sensationalism, or unprofessional practices by news media organizations or journalists.

Campbell (2001) defines Yellow Press newspapers as having daily multi-column front-page headlines covering a variety of topics, such as sports and scandal, using bold layouts (with large illustrations and perhaps colour), heavy reliance on unnamed sources, and unabashed self-promotion.

The term was extensively used to describe certain major New York City newspapers about 1900 as they battled for circulation. By extension the term is used today as a pejorative to decry any journalism that treats news in an unprofessional or unethical fashion, such as systematic political bias. Yellow journalism can also be the practice of over-dramatizing events.

Frank Luther Mott (1941) defines yellow journalism in terms of five characteristics:

1. Dcare headlines in huge print, often of minor news
2. Lavish use of pictures, or imaginary drawings
3. Use of faked interviews, misleading headlines, pseudo-science, and a parade of false learning from so-called experts
4. Emphasis on full-colour Sunday supplements, usually with comic strips (which is now normal in the U.S.)
5. Dramatic sympathy with the "underdog" against the system.

Present day (successful) exponents of the yellow journalistic style would include the British red top tabloids, notably *The Sun* and the German Springer owned *Bild*.

The term originated during the American Gilded Age of the late nineteenth century with the circulation battles between Joseph Pulitzer's *New York World* and William Randolph Hearst's *New York Journal.*

The battle peaked from 1895 to about 1898, and historical usage often refers specifically to this period. Both papers were accused by critics of sensationalizing the news in order to drive up circulation, although the newspapers did serious reporting as well. The *New York Press* coined the term "yellow kid journalism" in early 1897 after a then-popular comic strip to describe the down market papers of Pulitzer and Hearst, which both published versions of it during a circulation war.

This was soon shortened to *yellow journalism* with the *New York Press* insisting, "We called them Yellow because they are Yellow."

Joseph Pulitzer purchased the *New York World* in 1883 after making the *St. Louis Post-Dispatch* the dominant daily in that city. The publisher had gotten his start editing a German-language publication in St. Louis, and saw a great untapped market in the nation's immigrant classes.

Pulitzer strove to make the *New York World* an entertaining read, and filled his paper with pictures, games and contests that drew in readers, particularly those for whom English was a second language.

Crime stories filled many of the pages, with headlines like "Was He a Suicide?" and "Screaming for Mercy." In addition, Pulitzer only charged readers two cents per issue but gave readers eight and sometimes 12 pages of information (the only other two cent paper in the city never exceeded four pages). While there were many sensational stories in the *New York World,* they were by no means the only pieces, or even the dominant ones. Pulitzer believed that newspapers were public institutions with a duty to improve society, and he put the *World* in the service of social reform.

During a heat wave in 1883, *World* reporters went into the Manhattan's tenements, writing stories about the appalling living conditions of immigrants and the toll the heat took on the children.

Stories headlined "How Babies Are Baked", "Burning Babies Fall From The Roof" and "Lines of Little Hearses" spurred reform and drove up the *World's* circulation. Just two years after Pulitzer took it over, the *World* became the highest circulation newspaper in New York, aided in part by its strong ties to the Democratic Party.

Older publishers, envious of Pulitzer's success, began criticizing the *World,* harping on its crime stories and stunts while ignoring its more serious reporting — trends which influenced the popular perception of yellow journalism.

Charles Dana, editor of the *New York Sun,* attacked *The World* and said Pulitzer was "deficient in judgment and in staying power."

Pulitzer's approach made an impression on William Randolph Hearst, a mining heir who acquired the *San Francisco Examiner* from his father in 1887. Hearst read the *World* while studying at Harvard University and resolved to make the *Examiner* as bright as Pulitzer's paper.

Under his leadership, the *Examiner* devoted 24 per cent of its space to crime, presenting the stories as morality plays, and sprinkled adultery and "nudity" (by 19th century standards) on the front page. A month after Hearst took over the paper, the *Examiner* ran this headline about a hotel fire:

Hungry, Frantic Flames: They Leap Madly Upon the Splendid Pleasure Palace by the Bay of Monterey, Encircling Del Monte in Their Ravenous Embrace From Pinnacle to Foundation.

Leaping Higher, Higher, Higher, With Desperate Desire. Running Madly Riotous Through Cornice, Archway and Facade. Rushing in Upon the Trembling Guests with Savage Fury. Appalled and Panic-Striken the Breathless Fugitives Gaze Upon the Scene of Terror.

The Magnificent Hotel and Its Rich Adornments Now a Smoldering heap of Ashes. The *Examiner* Sends a Special Train to Monterey to Gather Full Details of the Terrible Disaster. Arrival of the Unfortunate Victims on the Morning's Train — A History of Hotel del Monte — The Plans for Rebuilding the Celebrated Hostelry — Particulars and Supposed Origin of the Fire. Hearst could be hyperbolic in his crime coverage; one of his early pieces, regarding a "band of murderers," attacked the police for forcing *Examiner* reporters to do their work for them. But while indulging in these stunts, the *Examiner* also increased its space for international news, and sent reporters out to uncover municipal corruption and inefficiency.

In one well remembered story, *Examiner* reporter Winifred Black was admitted into a San Francisco hospital and discovered that indigent women were treated with "gross cruelty." The entire hospital staff was fired the morning the piece appeared.

With the *Examiner*'s success established by the early 1890s, Hearst began looking for a New York newspaper to purchase, and acquired the *New York Journal* in 1895, a penny paper which Pulitzer's brother Albert had sold to a Cincinnati publisher the year before.

Metropolitan newspapers started going after department store advertising in the 1890s, and discovered the larger the circulation base, the better.

This drove Hearst; following Pulitzer's earlier strategy, he kept the *Journal's* price at one cent (compared to *The World's* two cent price) while providing as much information as rival newspapers.

The approach worked, and as the *Journal's* circulation jumped to 150,000, Pulitzer cut his price to a penny, hoping to drive his young competitor (who was subsidized by his family's fortune) into bankruptcy. In a counterattack, Hearst raided the staff of the *World* in 1896.

While most sources say that Hearst simply offered more money, Pulitzer — who had grown increasingly abusive to his employees — had become an extremely difficult man to work for, and many *World* employees were willing to jump for the sake of getting away from him.

Although the competition between the *World* and the *Journal* was fierce, the papers were temperamentally alike. Both were Democratic, both were sympathetic to labour and immigrants (a sharp contrast to publishers like the *New York Tribune's* Whitelaw Reid, who blamed their poverty on moral defects), and both invested enormous resources in their

Sunday publications, which functioned like weekly magazines, going beyond the normal scope of daily journalism. Their Sunday entertainment features included the first colour comic strip pages, and some theorize that the term yellow journalism originated there, while as noted above, the *New York Press* left the term it invented undefined.

Hogan's Alley, a comic strip revolving around a bald child in a yellow nightshirt (nicknamed The Yellow Kid), became exceptionally popular when cartoonist Richard F. Outcault began drawing it in the *World* in early 1896.

When Hearst predictably hired Outcault away, Pulitzer asked artist George Luks to continue the strip with his characters, giving the city two Yellow Kids. The use of "yellow journalism" as a synonym for over-the-top sensationalism in the U.S. apparently started with more serious newspapers commenting on the excesses of "the Yellow Kid papers."

In 1890, Samuel Warren and Louis Brandeis published "The Right to Privacy," considered the most influential law review article of all time, as a critical response to sensational forms of journalism, which they saw as an unprecedented threat to individual privacy. The article is widely considered to have led to the recognition of new common law privacy rights of action

Pulitzer and Hearst are often credited (or blamed) for drawing the nation into the Spanish-American War with sensationalist stories or outright lying. However, the vast majority of Americans did not live in New York City, and the decision makers who did live there probably relied more on staid newspapers like the *Times, The Sun* or the *Post*.

The most famous example of the exaggeration is the apocryphal story that artist Frederic Remington telegrammed Hearst to tell him all was quiet in Cuba and "There will be no war." Hearst responded "Please remain. You furnish the pictures and I'll furnish the war."

The story (a version of which appears in the Hearst-inspired Orson Welles film *Citizen Kane*) first appeared in the memoirs of reporter James Creelman in 1901, and there is no other source for it.

But Hearst became a war hawk after a rebellion broke out in Cuba in 1895. Stories of Cuban virtue and Spanish brutality soon dominated his front page. While the accounts were of dubious accuracy, the newspaper readers of the 19th century did not expect, or necessarily want, his stories to be pure nonfiction.

Historian Michael Robertson has said that "Newspaper reporters and readers of the 1890s were much less concerned with distinguishing among fact-based reporting, opinion and literature."

Pulitzer, though lacking Hearst's resources, kept the story on his front page. The yellow press covered the revolution extensively and often inaccurately, but conditions on Cuba were horrific enough.

The island was in a terrible economic depression, and Spanish general Valeriano Weyler, sent to crush the rebellion, herded Cuban peasants into concentration camps leading hundreds of Cubans to their deaths.

Having clamored for a fight for two years, Hearst took credit for the conflict when it came: A week after the United States declared war on Spain, he ran "How do you like the *Journal's* war?" on his front page. In fact, President William McKinley never read the *Journal*, and newspapers like the *Tribune* and the *New York Evening Post*.

Moreover, journalism historians have noted that yellow journalism was largely confined to New York City, and that newspapers in the rest of the country did not follow their lead. The *Journal* and the *World* were not among the top ten sources of news in regional papers, and the stories simply did not make a splash outside New York City.

War came because public opinion was sickened by the bloodshed, and because leaders like McKinley realized that Spain had lost control of Cuba. These factors weighed more on the president's mind than the melodramas in the *New York Journal*.

Hearst sailed directly to Cuba, when the invasion began, as a war correspondent, providing sobre and accurate accounts of the fighting. Creelman later praised the work of the reporters for exposing the horrors of Spanish misrule, arguing, "no true history of the war... can be written without an acknowledgment that whatever of justice and freedom and progress was accomplished by the Spanish-American war was due to the enterprise and tenacity of *yellow journalists,* many of whom lie in unremembered graves."

Hearst was a leading Democrat who promoted William Jennings Bryan for president in 1896 and 1900. He later ran for mayor and governor and even sought the presidential nomination, but lost much of his personal prestige when outrage exploded in 1901 after columnist Ambrose Bierce and editor Arthur Brisbane published separate columns months apart that suggested the assassination of McKinley.

When McKinley was shot on September 6, 1901, critics accused Hearst's Yellow Journalism of driving Leon Czolgosz to the deed. Hearst did not know of Bierce's column and claimed to have pulled Brisbane's after it ran in a first edition, but the incident would haunt him for the rest of his life and all but destroyed his presidential ambitions.

Pulitzer, haunted by his "yellow sins," returned the *World* to its crusading roots as the new century dawned. By the time of his death in 1911, the *World* was a widely-respected publication, and would remain a leading progressive paper until its demise in 1931.

Other newspapers, especially the new tabloids in the big cities, adopted the flashy techniques of Yellow Journalism, most notably the New York *Daily News,* founded in 1919.

Yellow journalism, in short, is biased opinion masquerading as objective fact. Moreover, the practice of yellow journalism involved sensationalism, distorted stories, and misleading images for the sole purpose of boosting newspaper sales and exciting public opinion.

It was particularly indicative of two papers founded and popularized in the late 19th century- *The New York World,* run by Joseph Pulitzer and *The New York Journal,* run by William Randolph Hearst.

It all started, some historians believe, with the onset of the rapid industrialization that was happening all around the world. The Industrial Revolution eventually affected the newspaper industry, allowing newspapers access to machines that could easily print thousands of papers in a single night.

This is believed to have brought into play one of the most important characteristics of yellow journalism - the endless drive for circulation. And unfortunately, the publisher's greed was very often put before ethics.

Although the actual practice of what would later become known as yellow journalism came into being during a more extended time period (between 1880-1890), the term was first coined based on a series of occurrences in and following the year of 1895. This was the year in which Hearst purchased the New York Journal, quickly becoming a key rival of Pulitzer's. The term was derived, through a series of peculiar circumstances, from a cartoon by the famous 19th century cartoonist, Robert Outcault called "The Yellow Kid".

The cartoon was first published in The World, until Hearst hired him away to produce the strip in his newspaper. Pulitzer then hired another artist to produce the same strip in his newspaper.

This comic strip happened to use a new special, non-smear yellow ink, and because of the significance of the comic strip, the term "yellow journalism" was coined by critics.

Sadly though, this period of sensationalist news delivery (where the so-called yellow press routinely outsold the more honest, truthful, unbiased newspapers) does stand out as a particularly dark era in journalistic history.

The demand of the United States people for absolutely free press allowed such aforementioned newspapers, which often appealed to the shorter attention spans and interests of the lower class, to print whatever they so desired.

This means that they could easily steal a headline and story directly from another paper, or simply fabricate a story to fit their particular agenda.

One of the more disturbing features involved with the former practice of yellow journalism, and the period in which it was most active in is that there is no definite line between this period of yellow journalism and the period afterwards.

There only exists evidence that such practices were frowned upon by the general public - by 1910, circulation had dropped off very rapidly for such papers. But regardless, does this mean that yellow journalism simply faded away, never to return? Or did it absorb itself into the very heart of our newspapers, where it will remain forever? One thing is for certain - after the late 1800s, newspapers changed drastically, and still show no sign of changing back. The modernly present newspaper appearances of catchy headlines, humorous comic strips, special interest sections, intrusive investigative reporting, et cetera serve as a constant reminder that one must always stay skeptical when examining our news sources.

What is the remedy to yellow journalism? Simply double- and triple-checking one's sources and reading between the lines. If one disregards the obvious marketing that is used to hook readers, newspapers may actually prove to be reliable sources of information. One of the reasons cited for this trend is the change in readership habits. People, especially of the younger generation, spend very little time these days reading newspapers.

According to surveys conducted in India and abroad, they expend a lot of time watching television and surfing the Internet. A national readership survey (2002) found that an urban reader in India, on an average, spends 32 minutes on newspapers against 100 minutes watching television.

These findings need to be looked at closely. There is little doubt there are many things in modern life that compete for a person's time. So, the time he spends on newspaper has come down. However, the 100 minutes on television is not in direct competition with newspaper or news. Many other activities, like time spend on going to the theaters, would have taken a cut.

Many newspapers in India and abroad have found a solution to the dwindling 'reader interest' on their product. (In India, their circulations have never been dwindling). They include simplification of the language, offering of soft stories and presentation of stories with highlights, infographics and even pinups.

This could turn out to be a vicious circle with the reader looking for lesser and lesser cognitive load on him. The readers, especially the younger ones, may become lazier as information is offered to him in tablet form. Making the reader lazier would be suicidal for the medium in the long run.

However, there is little reason to think that today's reader is lazier than the aristocrats of the past. Nor is there evidence that the MTV generation cares less for good content.

The readership surveys do not look at reader satisfaction. We have seen readers throwing away newspapers saying that there was hardly matter for ten minutes reading in them. This did not mean that there was nothing in the 10 or 12 pages each of those newspapers.

Apparently, the reader is not finding material that interests him, or what he thinks he should spent more time on. So, the problem is more with the content rather than design. (Design sometimes creates the impression of plenty or the lack of it). Light material would get thrown away more easily than gripping and serious stories.

This is not to say that one should not try to make the pages more attractive. Initial buying decisions and sustained liking for a newspaper may be decided by lay out and ease of reading (from the typographical point of view).

Printing and other production technologies including colour printing have made it possible to make visually appealing pages quicker than before. There is no reason why one should not take advantage of them.

However, there is a tendency to adapt design elements from the Web. This needs to be chosen carefully. Compared to computer and television screen, the luminosity of the printed page is very low, especially on newsprint.

So, clutter of infographics and images could darken up the page more easily on print than on the screen, especially if the tonal values are high. They can also cause visual overload. (Visual overload happens very often on the Web.

This may be one of the reasons, other than slow loading of images, that prompts readers to look for text in preference . Images, advertisements and infographics could suppress text.

On the Web, news stories appear in different pages. So, design requirements vary. For example, a photo or graphic with every story, which is desirable on the Web, would not be desirable on the print unless the format is of magazine.

Text is more readable on the print than on the Web. So, print can always accommodate more text without the reader being turned away. News sites would have to depend on infographics more than the printed publications to tell the story, because the screen size is small.

Many readers are even reluctant to scroll down. (If we accept the argument that the readers are inherently lazy, the print has an advantage here. However, it is notable that interactivity is described as the great advantage of the new medium.)

Visually attractive does not mean that the product would be intellectually attractive. The pages should look inviting. At the same time, the content should be stimulating. If the objective of the newspaper is only to sell, sex and crime on the front page could achieve the objective.

Still, there is the question as to how many pin ups one would want to see in the morning. However, as everyone knows, stature of a newspaper and lack of higher objectives are mutually exclusive.

While Walker works on his project outside the confines of conventional journalism, the mainstream media are also trying to figure out how photo-sharing communities can augment their own photojournalism.

Denison at the Boston Globe used Flickr to find photos from the Supernova tech conference to illustrate a print story about the conference. He made sure to get permission from the shooters, and ran their photos in a strip like a contact sheet. The photos had to run at a smaller size because they weren't at the best resolution for print. The Flickr photos led Denison to some blog entries, and soon he was getting a fuller experience of the conference without leaving his computer monitor.

Denison also has used Flickr as a research tool for Boston.com's innovative Pulse Points project, which provides free Wi-Fi hotspots as well as hyper-local online content keyed to that area.

"I'm currently talking to a resident of Roxbury Crossing, for example, about how we might use his photos on the Roxbury Crossing Pulse Point," Denison told me via e-mail. "Pictures by a resident can mean a lot more than pictures by a photographer who just drops in for an hour or so.

Of course I also have access to some really wonderful photos taken by Globe staff photographers, and that imagery, to be honest, is on an entirely different level, usually. So I use that first. But I also check Flickr because it gives me an idea of who's going through the area regularly, or who lives there, and what they find interesting enough to photograph."

Rather than mine existing photo-sharing communities, some newspaper sites have set up their own citizen photography micro-sites. Buzznet, a competitor to Flickr that has roots in the music scene, has licensed its technology to 15 newspaper sites, including a six-site trial with Knight Ridder Digital. Marc Brown, Buzznet founder and president, told me there's been a growing interest among newspapers to do more community journalism and get user-generated content onto their sites.

Brown helped set up Buzznet sites for the Houston Chronicle for Hurricane Rita coverage, the Miami Herald for Hurricane Wilma coverage, and the Biloxi (Miss.) Sun-Herald for Hurricane Katrina. He explained the business deals he's done with media sites so far.

"Generally it's a monthly license fee, and a revenue split for advertising," Brown said. "The way we do these partnerships is that the people who sign up to do galleries and contribute photos become part of Buzznet, the larger community that extends beyond their geographic community.

The Roanoke Times has groups for Virginia Tech football and one for the NASCAR race they have in Roanoke. Plus there's a general Roanoke, Va., gallery and they promote it in the paper."

The Augusta Chronicle has gone even further, developing its own citizen photography site, Spotted, and then hiring 20 unpaid photography interns who fan out to cover smaller community events untouched by the pro shooters. The interns hand out cards for Spotted so people can go to the site to see the photos.

Chronicle new media director Conan Gallaty says the initiative has been a stunning success. The site has 200 active community participants who upload a stream of photos, the interns get coached by staff photographers, and the micro-site is getting 1 million page views per month.

That traffic now represents 20 per cent of the newspaper site's total traffic. But the Chronicle has done more than just open up a site and hope for participation to materialize. They've created a vibrant ecosystem of photographers in Augusta. Amateurs can upload all the photos they want, and interns (mainly students and retirees) can shoot events and get school credit for their work, perhaps moving up to the professional ranks eventually. Spotted has become a haven for teen visitors and participants, who want to see photos from high school football games, Gallaty said.

While Buzznet, with 150,000 registered users, has reached out to media companies, Flickr, with 1.5 million registered users, has not. In fact, the leading photo-sharing community is now owned by Yahoo, a company that's increasingly competing with media companies, making joint ventures more complex. Tom Kennedy, managing editor of multimedia for WashingtonPost.Newsweek Interactive, told me his company was exploring the use of photo-sharing services such as Flickr, perhaps customized for its sites.

"Our projects might be more aligned with visual anthropology more directly than photojournalism as it has classically been defined," Kennedy said. "What you find on Flickr is more personal vision than photojournalism.

What interests me is whether it can be meshed with other photojournalism projects to garner more audience interest for visual communication. Photojournalists see themselves as the tip of the iceberg, but the shape of the iceberg changes because of this. They may well remain as the tip, but perhaps this makes it so you can see below the water line and find other useful visual information." One big issue when a media company wades into Flickr and its ilk is the need to verify the photos and the shooter's right to a photo. Was it a hoax, or retouched in Photoshop? Was it lifted from a professional or stock photo site? Building in this layer might be difficult in the freewheeling Flickr, which provides an opening for a rival service that could include the technological underpinnings for vetting photos and filtering them.

These are baby steps toward what might become a revolution in visual journalism — broadening the variety of images we see on news sites and in print publications to include more than just traditional photojournalism.

With these photo-sharing communities comes an inner view of the lives of the people in our neighborhoods — and a way to connect folks who like snapping photos at celebrations, who are fanatic about species of birds, or who can capture the mood on the streets.

"The thing about Flickr and Buzznet and all these sites is that they grew out of the exploding ease and efficiency for individuals to document their world and use images as a cheap form of connectivity to friends and loved ones," said Xeni Jardin, co-editor of group blog BoingBoing.

"That basket of sites and services came out of an amateur experience — it's not a profit-driven experience. And there will be new services growing out of this idea of news organizations using stuff from real people, images from the man on the street. They used to go out with a mike and a camera to get that, but they might not have to do that in the future." Walker, who pens the "Consumed" column for the Times Magazine, was attracted to Flickr because of its decidedly non-commercial bent. He had long been curious if his stereotype of Martin Luther King boulevards — "an awful lot of abandoned property, scary-looking bars, and small groceries that accept food stamps" — was really accurate.

Even though there had been newspaper specials and a book on the same subject, Walker believed there was a place for an ongoing, open-ended, "open journalism" view of MLK boulevards. "I'm already a journalist, I can already write something with my point of view," Walker told me. "With Flickr, I can say here's an interesting subject, and throw it open to others.... I think there's an advantage to having it open-ended, because I could have an unlimited number of people contributing to this in an unlimited number of places over an unlimited amount of time."

Imagine if you were a photo editor at a major publication, and you could view and search through every digital photo on every computer in the world to put together a feature. Or if something spectacular happened, and you could search photo tags to see what everyone at the scene was seeing.

This dream of a global photo album, compiled in real time by amateur and professional shooters, hasn't quite materialized, but photo-sharing services such as Flickr and Buzznet are giving us glimpses into that future.

New York Times Magazine columnist Rob Walker is using Flickr to compile nationwide views of the various Martin Luther King boulevards, while Boston Globe technology editor DC Denison used Flickr photos to illustrate a story in the paper. About 15 newspaper sites have created special Buzznet sites to showcase citizen photos of current events or hyper-local happenings. And the Augusta (Ga.) Chronicle's Spotted citizen photog section even has an army of 20 interns who cover parades and high school football.

So far, the project includes 70 photos from five U.S. towns, including shots Walker took in New Orleans before and after Hurricane Katrina.

Eventually, Walker might consider making a book of the photos or a website preserving the collaborative aspect of the project. But because Flickr is a series of self-started communities, Walker must tread lightly when trying to recruit more participants. "Flickr is a real community and you don't want to come storming in and say, 'Everybody do as I say.' It doesn't work like that," Walker said.

"There are a lots of people doing interesting things there, and I want to respect that. What I'm leading up to is to send messages to everybody who might be interested, saying I like your stuff and would like you to join this, if you're interested."

Bibliography

Byrne, D. (2000) Talk to the students of the MA Investigative Journalism courseat Nottingham Trent University, 29 April 1999.

Chepesiuk, R., Howell, H. and Lee, E. (2001) Raising Hell: Straight Talk with Investigative Journalists. London: McFarland.

Dorril, S. and Ramsay, R. (2002) Smear! Wilson and the Secret State. London: Fourth Estate.

Eddy, P. (2004) Destination Disaster. London: Granada.

Fukuyama. F. (2003) The End of History and the Last Man. London: Penguin.

Gelhorn, M. (2002) Introduction. In J. Pilger (2000) Distant Voices. London:Vintage.

Houghton, W.E. (2001) The Victorian Frame of Mind. New Haven: Yale University Press.

Ingham, B. (2004) Kill the Messenger. London: Harper Collins.

Kedourie, E. and Mango, A. (2003) Talking about the BBC. Encounter, 71 Sep/Oct: 60-4.

Lloyd, D. (2002) Information passed to Hugo de Burgh, 10 June 2003.

McQuail, D. (2004) Mass Communication Theory. London: Sage.

Pilger, J. (2002) Distant Voices. London: Vintage.

Seaton, J. (1995) In J. Curran and J. Seaton Power without Responsibility: The Press and Broadcasting in Britain. London: Routledge.

Sreberny-Mohammadi, A., Winseck, D., McKenna, J. and Boyd-Barrett, O. (eds) Media in Global Context, A Reader. London: Edward Arnold.

Weaver, D.H. (ed.) (2002) The Global Journalist. New Jersey: Hampton Press.

Index

I

J

L

M

N

O

P

R

S

T

U

V